Quantitative Methods in Educational Research

Quantitative Methods in Educational Research

The Role of Numbers Made Easy

Stephen Gorard

Continuum
London and New York

Continuum

The Tower Building
11 York Road
London SE1 7NX

80 Maiden Lane
Suite 704
New York
NY 10038

www.continuumbooks.com

First published 2001

Reprinted 2006

British Library Cataloguing-in-Publication Data
A catalogue record for this book is available from the British Library.

ISBN 10: 0-8264-5307-4 (paperback)
ISBN 10: 0-8264-5306-6 (hardback)
ISBN 13: 978-0-8264-5307-5 (paperback)
ISBN 13: 978-0-8264-5306-8 (hardback)

Typeset by Paston PrePress Ltd, Beccles, Suffolk
Printed and bound by MPG Books Ltd, Bodmin, Cornwall

FOR SEE BENG HUAT

Contents

List of figures

List of tables

Abbreviations

BERA   British Educational Research Association – the main professional organization of educational researchers in the UK

BERJ   *British Educational Research Journal* – the five-yearly research journal of BERA

BPS   British Psychological Society – the main professional organization of psychologists in the UK

BSA   British Sociological Association – the main professional organization of sociologists in the UK

CASS   Centre for Applied Social Surveys – resource centre of the UK Economic and Social Research Council. It aims to strengthen skills in survey design and analysis within the social science research community

CERI   Centre for Educational Research and Innovation – a dedicated research centre of the OECD

DfEE   Department for Education and Employment – the main UK government department for education, with chief responsibility for schools and colleges in England (rather than Scotland, Northern Ireland or Wales)

ESRC   Economic and Social Research Council – major public funding body for social science research in the UK

ETAG   Education and Training Action Group – a temporary body formed in Wales after devolution to create an education and training policy for the new National Assembly

EU   European Union

FSM   free school meal (eligibility for) – an indicator of a child from a family in poverty, counted on the annual census return by schools in the UK

GCSE   General Certificate of Secondary Education – the main

	academic qualification taken in England and Wales at age 16 which is the end of compulsory schooling
ICT	information and communications technology
KS	Key Stage – one of four periods of statutory assessment in schools in the UK, from KS1 at age 7 in primary school, to KS4 at age 16 in secondary school
LEA	Local Education Authority (or Unitary Authority) – local government-appointed body responsible for running most schools and colleges in their area
LFS	Labour Force Survey – quarterly survey of the employment and training of a rolling sample of 150,000 people in the UK
NACETT	National Council for Education and Training Targets – a body created to set up and monitor targets for participation and achievement in lifelong learning in the UK. Replaced in 2001 by the Learning Skills Council
NERPP	National Educational Research Policy and Priorities Board of the USA
NHS	National Health Service – the free to all, at point of delivery, health service in the UK
NHST	null hypothesis significance testing – calculating the probability that two or more sets of scores are actually from the same population
NRC	National Research Council of the USA
OECD	Organization for Economic and Commercial Development
OFSTED	Office for Standards in Education – the name of the school inspection system in England
OHMCI	Office of Her Majesty's Chief Inspector for Schools – the name for the school inspection system in Wales
RG	Registrar General
SEN	Special Educational Needs (or Additional Educational Needs)
SPSS	Statistical Package for Social Sciences – a set of related computer programs for storing, analysing and reporting on statistical results
TTA	Teacher Training Agency – government-appointed body in UK responsible for teacher training, recruitment, curriculum and qualification

Preface

The idea for this book arose from my teaching on research methods courses at the Cardiff University School of Social Sciences, and my work as examiner for similar courses in other institutions. Part of my teaching role involves holding 'surgeries' for students and staff on research design and analysis. In these, novice researchers come to me for advice and solutions to problems, particularly relating to quantitative approaches in educational research. Year on year, and despite the best efforts of lecturers including myself, the same problems arise again and again. Such problems include collecting data with no clear idea how to analyse it, over-use of statistical tests, inappropriate use of statistical tests, confusion between levels of measurement, confusion between design error and random variation, over-use of frankly shoddy questionnaires, attempts to measure the unmeasurable, and several more. I hope that this book deals with all of these problems, and many more, and will therefore reduce their occurrence (please!).

Educational research as a field faces several problems. It is being questioned in terms of its quality and its relevance. There appears to be a growing schism between those who use measurement (who are prepared to try 'quantitative' techniques), and those who do not and perhaps cannot. There is therefore a danger of quantitative researchers becoming a band apart, refereeing each other's work, beholden to no one, and divorced from the majority of work in their field. This book attempts to deal with these problems, by arguing that all researchers need a working knowledge of the techniques explained herein, if only to enable them to make informed criticism of the work of others. The book does not set out to argue that quantitative techniques are better than the more usual interview, ethnography, or case study approaches. In fact, I hope to make quite clear that all approaches should be seen as complementary, and that a researcher who can't do numbers is as dangerous as a researcher who only does numbers.

I am engaged professionally in capability-building within the educational research community. I see this book as an important part of that process. There is a mystique about statistics that can often create a climate of fear for some, and sometimes a climate of complacency and even arrogance for others. I hope to show that, for the most part, quantitative methods in educational research are easy – common sense with arithmetic perhaps. Did you know that 'statistics' as you probably envisage it now (probabilities and significance testing and so on) is actually redundant in most quantitative research designs? Their sole purpose is to separate out the random error in your results due to the nature of your sample. If you do not use a sample (which is what I recommend in this book), or do not use a probability sample, or if your design error dwarfs the variation due to your sample (as it does in most educational research designs), then statistics of that kind cannot help you. Nevertheless, people might still use null hypothesis significance tests out of habit, ignorance, for a rhetorical flourish, or to prevent you from criticizing their work perhaps. Therefore, this is not a traditional textbook, not a book on statistics, nor a technical cookbook. It is, in essence, a plea to use your common sense with simple arithmetic. Numbers *are* easy.

In addition to descriptions of standard techniques for research design and analysis, and discussion of wider issues relating to social science research, this book also contains genuine examples of research which I believe contain simple mistakes in the design, analysis or reporting of results. Where this research has been published in peer-reviewed journals by well-established researchers, I have identified the authors. However, it should be noted that the examples are only selected because they relate to the fields in which I do the most reading. From the reports of others and my own wider reading I have no reason to believe that the areas in which I work are any different in terms of analytical errors from any other areas of educational research or even social or natural science in general. In fact, I have collected equivalent examples from medicine, dentistry, criminology, housing, astronomy and many others. Where I have used examples of problems from the work of students, I make no individual identification. All of us make mistakes. They are a valuable component of learning. In fact, someone who claims not to make mistakes is probably not doing enough work. I hope that the reader will learn from the mistakes, mine and others, illustrated in this book.

THE STRUCTURE OF THIS BOOK

This book can be envisaged in several ways. It can be split into five main sections. Chapter 2 looks at sampling issues, Chapters 3 and 4 describe uses of secondary data, Chapters 5 and 6 deal with questionnaire design and analysis, Chapters 7 and 8 consider the conduct and analysis of experiments, and Chapter 9 provides a brief introduction to multivariate analytical techniques. On the other hand, the book can also be divided into a section on the design of research and the collection of data (Chapters 3, 5 and 7) and a section on the analysis of results (Chapters 4, 6, 8 and 9). The first half of the book tends to deal with non-parametric approaches (using data in categories) and the second with parametric approaches (using real numbers). However, the connecting passages in each chapter have been written for someone wishing to read the book in its entirety from beginning to end.

Chapter 2 illustrates, through real-life examples, the importance of having a large sample, offers simple techniques for estimating the sample size needed, and describes common methods of selecting cases for the sample.

Chapters 3 and 4 concern the growing use of data already collected for another purpose, such as official statistics. This is discussed from the point of view of a researcher wanting to provide context for a small-scale study, a researcher wanting to judge the quality of an achieved sample, and a researcher intending to use only secondary data. A variety of simple techniques for analysis are presented.

Chapters 5 and 6 present guidelines for designing and conducting a survey, with illustrations of both good and poor techniques. The illustrations continue with elementary analyses of categorical data, introducing the chi-square test of significance.

Chapters 7 and 8 present guidelines for conducting laboratory experiments and field trials. The illustrations continue with elementary analyses using real numbers, by introducing t-tests and analysis of variance.

Chapter 9 introduces measures of correlation, and the associated techniques of linear and logistic regression. Again, these techniques are illustrated with real examples.

—1

A changing climate for educational research

WHY WE ALL NEED NUMBERS

I have encountered books on all forms of educational research, some on statistical analysis, and some on specialist topics such as survey design, or sampling. There is not, to my knowledge, another practical book of advice for students on carrying out an educational research project using quantitative techniques which links the three main methods of data derivation (secondary, survey and controlled trials) with their common methods of analysis. This is an important point, since the somewhat artificial separation of design and analysis leads to many of the common problems actually faced by students and those who deal with them (such as 'I have collected all this data, now please tell me what to do with it'). These issues are becoming more important as the climate in educational research changes in favour of evidence-based policy and practice, with a growing interest in large-scale experimental trials and the more general use of official data already collected for another purpose. This use of secondary data allows all students, perhaps for the first time, to carry out significant projects within a realistic time scale.

Above all, there is no book which steers a middle path of suggesting that *all* researchers should use numbers routinely in their research (even if only as 'consumers' of the quantitative research of others), while also cautioning against the potential artificiality of quantitative approaches and other associated perils. As well as laying out specific designs for large-scale educational research, the book therefore seeks to combat two idealized 'villains' – the student who does not 'do numbers' and is therefore forced to ignore all numeric results, and the student who is only prepared to 'do numbers', and accepts all numeric results at face value. Both extremes are common, in my experience, and dangerous. The emphasis throughout this book is therefore on selecting and using appropriate techniques, while emphasizing the limitations inherent in any one approach.

There are many reasons why all researchers should learn something about quantitative techniques. These reasons are outlined here and then presented in more detail throughout the book.

- *So we won't get fooled again.* The first and most obvious point is that the process of research involves some consideration of previous work in the same field. All researchers read and use the research of others. Therefore they need to develop what Brown and Dowling (1998) refer to as a 'mode of interrogation' for reading and using research results. If they do not have any understanding of research techniques involving numbers, then they must either accept all such results without question, a very dangerous decision, or ignore all such results, a very foolish decision. In practice, many commentators attempt to create a middle way of accepting some results and rejecting others even though they do not understand how the results were derived. This usually means that results are accepted on the basis of ideology, or of whether they agree with what the commentator wants to believe. This is both dangerous *and* foolish.
- *Some techniques are common to all research.* The choice of a sample, for example, is a common phenomenon in all kinds of research using many different approaches to data collection and analysis. This book describes the process of sampling as it applies to all research involving samples, and is not specific to what have traditionally been considered as quantitative designs.
- *We need an ideal.* It is made clear in this book that experimental approaches have severe limitations in social science research. Nevertheless the ideal experiment, by isolating cause and effect, can provide us with a universal template for the perfect piece of research which leads to safe knowledge. We can then judge our more limited studies against that ideal, and so understand and explain the ways in which our own findings are less than secure (for sadly such is the fate of all real-world research). True experiments may be rare in educational research, but for the above reasons all researchers should still be able to design one (at least as a thought experiment).
- *Context is everything.* Whatever your choice of primary method, there is a good chance that your research involves numbers, at least at the outset. You may wish to discover why women are less likely than men to be primary school heads, or to document the educational experiences of the growing number of homeless people from

ethnic minority backgrounds. In both cases, whatever approach you use (participant observation, action research, focus groups, anthropology, and so on), you must start from a quantitative basis. In order to direct your search you should use as much information as is available to you from the outset. In the first example, you need to establish not only that women *are* under-represented in school management but also perhaps what the trend is over time, and where the problem is greatest in geographical terms. Such figures, termed 'secondary data', already exist, and therefore a preliminary analysis of them is the best place to start any study. In the second example, you need to establish not only how many homeless people there are, but also where they are, how the socio-economic and ethnic patterns of these groups change over time and space, and so on. Only then can you sensibly select a smaller group (a sample) for more detailed study. Existing statistics, whatever their limitations, provide a context for any new study which is as important as the 'literature review' and the 'theoretical background'.

- *Because it is easy*. Above all, it is important to realize that quantitative research is generally very easy. Much analysis in social science involves nothing more complex than addition or multiplication – primary school arithmetic, in fact. Even this, along with any more complex calculations, is conducted for you by a computer. You have no need for a paper and pencil. There is no need to practise any sums, or memorize anything. Not only does this book *not* generally explain how to derive the formulae we use, generally it does not even state what those formulae are. These formulae are finished and complete. Therefore no mathematics is involved in basic quantitative work. You can use statistics perfectly safely, just as you would drive a car, without knowing or even caring how it works. There are always other books, software and expert advisers available to help if you 'break down'. The purpose of this book is to help explain when and how to use statistical techniques, and how to report their results. The difficult bit lies in explaining your results and transforming them into practical reports for the users of research. This stage is, of course, common to all forms of research.

INTRODUCING TWO VILLAINS

I have written this book as a general introduction to social scientific research design and statistical analysis for all students of education. However, in doing so I have been particularly concerned to hinder the creation of two 'villainous' identities, both of which I meet regularly among students and even among more established researchers. They represent, if you like, two extreme viewpoints about numeric data – 'numbers are fab' and 'numbers are rubbish'.

Numbers are Fab

This villain is perhaps most common in relatively established disciplines such as psychology, where there has been a tradition that only numeric data is of relevance. Students are therefore encouraged to count or measure everything, even where this is not necessarily appropriate (as with some attitude scales, for example). One outcome is that statistical analysis is done badly and so gets a bad press. Allied to this approach is a cultural phenomenon I have observed particularly with some international students and their sponsors which again approves only research involving numbers. A corollary for both groups appears to be that forms of evidence not based on numbers are despised, while evidence based on numbers is accepted somewhat uncritically. This latter is clearly a particular problem, as I quite regularly come across findings which when reanalysed show the opposite to what is being claimed (e.g. Gorard, 1997a, 1999a, 2000a, 2000b; Gorard and Fitz, 1998a; White and Gorard, 1999). In fact, I suspect that some social science journals, books and edited chapters are full of quite basic arithmetic errors.

As you will see throughout this book, I am a great fan of using computer software packages for statistical analysis, but the increasing quality and availability of these have exacerbated the problems outlined above in two ways. Software allows more and more complex statistical models to be built and used, so that in the end most consumers of educational research simply cannot, or would not wish to, comprehend them. Even those who work on such high level models have trouble transforming their findings into a package that does their analysis justice but also makes any sense to practitioners and policy-makers (see Goldstein *et al.*, 2000). This means that the 'average' consumer of research has to either implicitly accept the findings, or reject them as incomprehensible. Linked to the greater use of computers is the shotgun or dredging approach to analysis in which multiple exploratory analyses are run with the same set of data (see Chapter 8). As well as liberating us from the drudgery of multiple calculations the computer has therefore increased the frequency of the 'blind or mindless application of methods without regard to their suitability for the solution of the problem at hand, or even in the complete absence of a clearly formulated problem' (Pedhazur, 1982, p. 3).

Normal statistical textbooks describe ideal procedures to follow, but several studies of actual behaviour have observed different common practices among researchers. 'Producing a statistic is a social enterprise' (Gephart, 1988 p. 15), and the stages of selecting variables, making observations, and coding the results, take place in everyday settings where practical influences arise. The divergence between the ideal and actual is probably growing because of the increased accessibility to statistical software packages, and a tendency to see these as 'expert systems' rather than convenient calculators. Statistical packages are making decisions for us that we may not even be aware of (through default settings). The possible dangers of this are increased because statistics have an under-stated rhetoric of their own, able to persuade specific audiences of their objectivity (Firestone, 1987). Perhaps this helps to explain why so few academic disputes over figures, and subsequent corrections by authors, appear in the educational literature.

Numbers are Rubbish
The other villain is perhaps more common in the sociological tradition. Having realized that numbers can be used erroneously, sometimes even unscrupulously, some researchers simply reject all numeric evidence. This is as ludicrous a position as its opposite. As Clegg (1990) points out, we know that people sometimes lie to us but we do not therefore reject all future conversation. Why should lying with numbers be any different? I suspect, through my contact with students, that the key issue with numbers is a kind of fear, or lack of confidence. But lack of confidence *can* be seen as a reasonably helpful characteristic for a researcher. It is surely better than the unjustifiable over-certainty represented by the 'numbers are fab' villain.

If we reject numeric evidence and its associated concerns about validity, generalizability, and so on as the basis for research, then we are left with primarily subjective judgements. The danger therefore for 'qualitative' research conducted in isolation from numeric approaches is that it could be used simply as a rhetorical basis for retaining an existing prejudice. Without a combination of approaches we are often left with no clear way of deciding between competing conclusions. My argument is therefore not just that numeric evidence forms the basis of good qualitative studies, and can be used to test its findings (the middle way, see Gorard, 1998a). I am not even convinced that the very distinction between the two forms of evidence is a useful one.

Qualitative and Quantitative Evidence

The supposed distinction between qualitative and quantitative evidence is essentially a distinction between the traditional methods for analysis rather than between underlying philosophies, paradigms, or methods of data collection. As Heraclitus wrote, 'logic is universal even if most people behave differently' (for if logic were not universal we could not debate with each other, so making research pointless). To some extent all methods of educational research deal with qualities, even when the observed qualities are counted. Similarly, all methods of analysis use some form of number, such as 'tend, most, some, all, none, few', and so on. This is what the patterns in qualitative analysis are based on (even where the claim is made that a case is 'unique' since uniqueness is, of course, a numeric description). Words can be counted, and numbers can be descriptive. Patterns are, by definition, numbers, and the things that are numbered are qualities (Popkewitz, 1984). In fact, I sometimes wonder whether some writers use qualitative analysis precisely to avoid the criticism that would be aimed at a more formal analysis. Examples of numeric analyses disguised as qualitative research appear later in this book. For now, please at least consider the possibility that 'qualitative and quantitative evidence' refers to a false dualism (Frazer, 1995; Pring, 2000), and one that as researchers we would be better off without (despite the title of this book). One practical reason would be that we could cease wasting time and energy in pointless debates about the virtues of one approach over the other.

THE PENDULUM SWINGS

During the last decade, the value and effectiveness of research as a contribution to the improvement of education have been increasingly called into question (e.g. Hargreaves, 1997; Hillage *et al.*, 1998; Tooley and Darby, 1998). In the UK, educational research has been accused of being both 'second rate' and irrelevant to the needs and interests of practitioners. The Chief Executive of the Teacher Training Agency argued that 'despite the expenditure of over £65 million of public funding on educational research each year, there are surprisingly few studies which individually, or collectively, contribute systematically to the development of a comprehensive body of high quality evidence about pedagogy' (Millett, 1997, p. 2). Her Majesty's Chief Inspector for Schools claimed to have given up reading research because:

life is too short. There is too much to do in the real world with real teachers in real schools to worry about methodological quarrels or to waste time decoding unintelligible, jargon-ridden prose to reach (if one is lucky) a conclusion that is often so transparently partisan as to be worthless. (Woodhead, 1998, p. 51)

This 'epistemological crisis of confidence' (Furlong, 1996), is not confined to the UK having already happened in the USA, see for example (NRC, 1999; NERPP, 1999, 2000; Resnick 2000).

At heart, these criticisms address two main issues. The first, the claimed lack of real-world relevance of much research, need not concern us here (although you may be interested to know that I reject this criticism). The second is a system-wide gap in expertise in conducting large-scale studies, especially field trials derived from laboratory experimental designs. Much educational research in the UK is small-scale, non-replicable, or interpretative, leading to insecure conclusions (clearly, I have more sympathy with the second criticism). Most researchers are now avowedly qualitative in approach, but politicians and funders want to see the pendulum swing back towards a more balanced portfolio of skills. This does not mean that we all need to adopt very complex techniques. Our approach could start from a consideration of the importance of 'truth' (Bridges, 1999), and a return to a political arithmetic tradition (Mortimore, 2000).

COMMON PROBLEMS IN RESEARCH

In each section of the book I illustrate some of the points being made through a consideration of problems I have encountered in my own research, the research of others, and my work with novice researchers. To start with, here are two classic situations that you may find yourself in once you start to research.

- Now ... how do I analyse all this?
- Deciding on a method before a topic.

Now ... How Do I Analyse All This?
Anyone who has dealt with student/novice researchers will have encountered this problem. In my institution this is not as frequent as it was, but I still see a reasonable number of people per year (perhaps sent by their supervisors for advice) who say 'I have conducted a survey. Now can you tell me what to do with the answers?'. This is

usually clear evidence of poor design. The reason that this book has alternate chapters on design and analysis is to try and help you see the two phases of research as concurrent. You cannot possibly design a sensible research instrument without considering in some detail how you will analyse the data you set out to collect. Otherwise you will not know if you have asked the right questions, or collected data in the right format. The apparently separate phases of reading, formulating research questions, design, collection of data, analysis, and reporting are really concurrent and iterative.

Deciding on a Method before a Topic
Students have been heard to exclaim before deciding on a topic and research questions that they intend to use 'qualitative' methods of data collection or analysis, or that they are committed to the idea of a questionnaire. Perhaps 'it comes as no particular surprise to discover that a scientist formulates problems in a way which requires for their solution just those techniques in which he himself is especially skilled' (Pedhazur, 1982, p. 28), but to understand this temptation is not to condone it. You must decide on your research topic and the questions you are curious about first, and only then consider how best to answer them. Don't fit your proposed study to your favourite approach (a case of the cart pulling the horse), and then try to disguise this as a philosophical, rather than a methodological, decision. This is another reason why all researchers need some knowledge of all methods.

As outlined above, this book combines a consideration of the design and analysis of educational research involving numeric data. There is very little epistemology here. For those interested, my principles of research, such as they are, are very similar to the five norms described by Hammersley (1995, p. 76). I particularly like the first which is that 'the overriding concern of researchers is the truth of claims, not their political implications or practical consequences'. For more on the ethical issues involved in research see Chapter 7. For a simple, sometimes amusing, discussion of issues to put you in the 'right' frame of mind to grapple with research see Fairbairn and Winch (1996), Huff (1991), and Thouless (1974). If you feel the need for some reminders about simple calculations see Solomon and Winch (1994). For a good introduction to social science research read Gilbert (1997), to statistics Clegg (1990) or Fielding and Gilbert (2000), and for help on writing a dissertation see Preece (1994).

Sampling: the basis of all research

In *How to Lie with Statistics* Huff (1991) quotes a report from one of the early Hispano-American wars. During this conflict the casualty rate in the US navy was approximately 10 in every 1000. During the same period the number of deaths among inhabitants of New York was approximately 20 in every 1000. A newspaper reporter might therefore conclude that it is generally safer to fight in a war than it is to live in New York. If you can see why such a conclusion is invalid, then you are well on the way to understanding the significance of the material in this chapter. In many cases the apparent conclusions of our research are determined less by the social reality under investigation and more by the nature of the samples we use to collect data from. Sampling is therefore the basis of all research.

WHY DO WE USE SAMPLES?

I may have exaggerated slightly in calling sampling the basis of all research but not by much (see Gilbert, 1993). It is true that a high quality sample alone does not guarantee a successful piece of research and that many 'famous' pieces of work have not used particularly impressive samples. Piaget and Freud are widely used examples, but whether their contributions are empirically meritorious would have to be the subject of another book. In order for your work to have the widest appeal, it is important to pass through several stages, at least informally. It is also important that you subsequently refer to the decisions you make at each of these stages when you publish the work.

The first, and perhaps most commonly omitted, stage in sampling is deciding why you need to use a sample at all. Not all research is based on samples. Even discounting solely theoretical work, it is not clear that all empirical research should involve a sample. Much of my own work has not involved sampling in a strict sense, using instead data relating to whole populations. In many respects, and wherever possible, it is preferable to use such complete datasets rather than to introduce the additional bias and error involved in selecting a sample (although a good sample can be better than an inaccurate set of figures for a population). This approach is considered further in Chapters 3 and 4.

The main reason that samples are used is to save time and money for the researcher. Sampling is a useful short cut, leading to results that can be almost as accurate as those for a full census of the population being studied but for a fraction of the cost. Most studies are subject to a law of diminishing returns, in that after a certain number of cases/individuals have been involved each successive case is likely to add little to our understanding and do little to change any emerging patterns.

A second reason is that nearly all methods of formal data analysis are based explicitly on sampling theory. Most notably, for example, all the statistical tests of significance described in later chapters of this book assume that the data were collected from a sample drawn independently and randomly from a previously defined population. In the absence of secondary data relating to the entire population, a high quality sample is a necessary precondition for the pursuit of high quality, and therefore safe, research findings.

When conducting research, bear in mind throughout the sampling procedure that you are using a sample because you are unable to use the entire population for a range of pragmatic reasons. Choosing to use a sample is the first in a series of compromises that you are bound to make as part of the research process. Keep a log of your reasons for using a sample and rehearse them whenever you publish your work. As with all such decisions you will not be able to persuade all readers that they would have done the same as you, but you can at least make them aware that you have considered the alternatives and rejected them for substantial reasons.

DEFINING THE POPULATION

The purpose of sampling is to use a relatively small number of cases to find out about a much larger number. The group you wish to study is termed the 'population', and the group you actually involve in your research is the 'sample'. When you have collected results from the sample you will want to generalize (or apply) your results to the population. Since the population is the group to whom the results can be generalized it should always be defined in advance as the target of your research (e.g. primary school teachers in the UK, or third-year university students in Scotland, or anyone with a nationally recognized qualification working in the US steel industry). It is perfectly possible to have a population consisting of institutions, examination papers, or training companies, for example. Whatever your unit of population, the same logic described below applies, but your respondents would be training companies and so on rather than individuals. For simplicity it is assumed in most of this chapter that your population and sample consist of individual people.

It is only from your previously defined population that the sample will be drawn, and of which the sample will be representative. Therefore if, for example, you only have the resources to carry out research in the immediate area of your home or institution, you cannot have a national or regional population. Anything you discover in your research will apply only to your immediate area. A sample drawn from the primary school teachers in one Local Education Authority (LEA) has primary school teachers in that LEA as its population. This may sound obvious, but is easily overlooked in practice. Teachers of other age groups, or in other LEAs, may note your findings with interest but logically there is no contradiction if they deny that the results are relevant to them. The researcher only sets out to generalize to the population from which the sample was drawn.

In an ideal study you will be selecting cases from the population at random (by chance) to form your sample. Thus, you need to start with a list of all cases in the population and give each of them a non-zero chance of being selected. Any case that, in reality, has zero chance of being included in your study is not in fact in the population. This is another way of defining the population to which your results generalize. It is the list of all the cases which could be, or could have been, picked as part of your sample.

The list of all cases is called a 'sampling frame'. One reason why it is given a special name (not population list) is that in real life (not an ideal study) your sampling frame will be an incomplete list of the population. You may know or suspect that the best list you can achieve has gaps, but you may not know how to rectify these gaps. For example, a household survey based on the electoral register will lead to several discrepancies and omissions. The register will be out-of-date for, however recent it is, at least some people will have moved since, and it will always be incomplete since some people simply do not return the form for the register. Similarly, a survey of pupils drawn from those present in school on the day of the study will lead to notable omissions, such as the long-term sick, those excluded or suspended from school, and those with a pattern of unauthorized absences. The first survey is likely to under-represent the most mobile elements of society, whether 'transients', travellers, or professionals who tend to work in national organizations and structures. The second survey is likely to under-represent those least committed to attending school. In both cases, these limitations to the sample should be published with the results and their likely impacts taken into account. This may be the first sign of 'slippage' between the ideal and the actual.

As your sample design progresses, these slippages will increase, and each one weakens the force of your findings, and this is only for the sample, not counting the compromises you will also be forced to make in collecting and analysing the data. Some researchers appear to behave as though the existence of these compromises means that rigour is impossible and they can therefore do pretty much as they like. On the contrary, I am advocating being realistic about slippages from the ideal, documenting them, publicizing them, and above all worrying about their effects. Anxiety is therefore a very natural and healthy (for the research at least) state of mind for a good researcher.

In a, possibly apocryphal, PhD viva in my department a candidate studying truancy from school was asked whether they thought in retrospect that only talking to the pupils at school on the day of the fieldwork had been a mistake. The candidate did not get a PhD and their supervisor did not get any more candidates. This type of problem is frighteningly common for very practical, but rather lazy, reasons. Captive audiences make convenient pseudo-samples. For example, almost the whole field of participation studies in adult and continuing education has been based on data gathered from participants in adult education (often from the same institutions as the researcher). The resulting notions of widening access to participation in adult learning via breaking down barriers such as cost and travel are therefore based solely on the views of those who are already participants. Rarer, and more expensive, studies of non-participants who can only be contacted via door-to-door work reveal a somewhat different picture (see Gorard *et al.*, 1999b).

In some approaches to sampling it is not necessary to have an actual list of the entire population, which might be too long or too expensive to obtain (but note that some companies maintain commercial databases of addresses). The important thing is that such a list is at least possible. If obtaining a full sampling-frame is too difficult, an acceptable compromise alternative is to characterize the population in terms of theoretically important variables. In this approach, rather than simple random selection of cases the researcher is working towards a clustered or a stratified sample (see below). These are both weaker alternatives, flouting the cardinal principle of statistical analysis which is computed on the basis of random sampling (see Chapter 6). Nevertheless, properly done, both clustering and stratification can lead to effective results.

THE SIZE OF THE SAMPLE

The third major issue of sampling concerns size. The sample must be large enough to accomplish what is intended by the analysis, and perhaps of the order of five or ten times the number of variables used. Small samples can lead to the loss of potentially valuable results, and are equivalent to a loss of power in the test used for analysis (Stevens, 1992). Cases in the sample will be lost at several stages of a study, and so redundancy needs to be built in. Surveys will have forms not returned, some questions not answered, some answered unintelligibly, and some transcription errors, for example. Therefore data will be lost before the analysis is even started. As soon as data is cross-tabulated, to look at the responses by gender, for example, the number of cases drops again, often at an alarming rate. All these issues are considered in this section.

How large should a sample be? There are several methods to help decide on an appropriate sample size, but my general advice is to have as large a sample as possible. There are many reasons for saying this, but consider first my astonishment and appreciation when I started my research career at how easy it is to find people and organizations willing to take part in research. I once had a, very brief, job selling fire extinguishers door-to-door and it produced in me a terrible fear, or terminal embarrassment, of approaching people in a 'cold' situation. Yet, I have learnt that approaching someone as a researcher, while still scary, is a lot easier and a lot more successful. So be ambitious in your sample size.

It is also the case that the actual number in your sample is not always a great determinant of your time or cost. You will naturally have to code and transcribe all cases, but this stage is a very small part of the research. Talking to ten people in one institution does not take ten times as long as talking to one person, because of the time taken to negotiate access and travel. Using a computer to add up a list of 1,000 figures takes no longer than using a list of ten cases. Posting

100 envelopes does not take appreciably longer than posting ten, and so on. In fact, once you have written an access letter, designed your research instrument and planned your analysis, then the actual process of collecting data can take very little time in comparison.

If you are looking for a difference or pattern among the data you have collected from a well-designed study, then your success or failure is determined mainly by four things. First, there is the effect size of the phenomenon you are studying (or, of course, its rarity). In social science research, including education, effect sizes are often very small. For example, studies of the impact of schools on student examination results suggest that around 85–95 per cent of the variation in results is due to the prior attainment and characteristics of the individual students. Only 5–15 per cent at maximum is due to the impact of teachers, departments and schools, and any error component. Therefore looking at differences *between* schools in terms of curricular development or management style involves examining small differences within what is already a fairly small difference between schools.

Second, there is the variability of the phenomenon you are studying. For example, if you are interested in comparing the examination results by sex in two schools, the results may be quite similar in many respects. The difference between the highest and lowest achievers in either school is likely to be much larger than the differences between the schools or between the sexes. If boys and girls are gaining fairly similar results in both schools, then the effect size you are looking for (difference between sexes) is small in comparison to the overall variability of your chief variable (examination results).

Third, there is the 'power' of the statistical test that you use to discern the pattern (power is explained more fully in Chapter 8). In summary, power is an estimate of the ability of the test to separate the effect size from random variation.

Fourth, there is the sample size. Successful identification of effects is assisted by a strong effect, by using measures of low variability, a powerful test and by having a large sample. A change in any one of these factors is equivalent to a change in any others. Increasing the sample size therefore has the same effect as using a more powerful test, or decreasing the variability of the measure. However, of these four aspects only the sample size is clearly under the control of the researcher. Research questions are driven by importance, relevance, curiosity and sometimes autobiography. Researchers do not decide what to research because of its variability or its effect size. Similarly they will generally use the most powerful test that their design allows. Selecting a large sample is therefore the only chance you have to influence directly your chances of success. Note that even if you were to find *no* pattern this lack of pattern will only be convincing to your audience if the sample was large enough to have found one if it did exist.

In addition to these considerations, cases will be lost to attrition at every stage of the design. If you set out to get 100 respondents, maybe only 50 will respond. Many of these will have missing variables (questions not answered, official records not found, etc.), and others may be lost at coding or transcription (researcher error or unreadable responses). You may actually achieve only around 30 fully completed responses for analysis. This emphasizes the same point about sample size. Whatever size you choose is simply the maximum you could achieve. From that point on your sample can only get smaller. So again, be ambitious.

Another important factor in choice of a sample size is the number of sub-groups needed for your analysis. Most social science research is not particularly directed at measuring the frequency of variables in a population. Rather, it is concerned with the distributions of those variables among identifiable groups in the population – examination results by sex, patterns of participation by age, absenteeism by socio-economic status. Once the population is broken into two or more groups, then all the comments made so far about sample size also apply to the size of the sub-sample for each group. Therefore, the more sub-groups used for the analysis, the larger the overall sample needs to be, and this is one of many reasons why the researcher must design the analysis at the start of the project.

In my PhD work (see Gorard, 1997b), although the total number of respondents (parents and children) was 1,267, only the 543 adults were asked about their religion, and only 272 of these gave intelligible responses to one of the other questions in which responses were made on a 3-point scale. If parental religion is coded on a 7-point scale, the table cross-tabulating the two questions has 7 by 3 (21) entries known as 'cells'. Any analysis of responses to the second question in terms of religion therefore has fewer than 13 cases per cell on average, making any test of significance very weak (see Chapter 6). It is quite frightening how suddenly the number of cases for analysis can 'melt' away. Such alarming calculations highlight the need for a very large initial sample, in order to draw conclusions of a bivariate nature. In designing your sample, start from the minimum number of cases required in each cell, multiply by the number of cells, and then add 50 per cent (and then some). As long as this is equivalent to several times the number of variables in the study, it should be a good sample size.

For the simplest bivariate analysis such as a chi-square test (see Chapter 6), it is recommended that we work with at least ten cases expected per cell. Using this base, and multiplying by the number of cells in the most complex analysis required can produce a 'rule-of-thumb' guide to the size of the sample required (which assumes an even distribution of responses among categories). For example, if the most complex analysis is to be bivariate with one two-category variable (gender) and one seven-category variable (social class), then the table for analysis has 14 cells. If each cell is expected to have a minimum of ten cases (assuming nothing is yet known about the likely distribution between categories), then the sample must have at least 140 cases. This kind of estimate is part of the reason why a detailed scheme for analysis should be created at an early stage (long before data is collected). It can be imagined how quickly the number of cells grows, and therefore how large a sample is needed, if a multivariate (more than two variables) analysis is attempted (see Chapter 9).

In sampling theory the most important determinant of sample size is the required 'confidence interval' for the findings. The intention of the sampler is to generalize the results to the population of interest, and the confidence interval gives an indication of the accuracy of the findings as estimates for the population. The larger the sample, the more accurate the results are likely to be as an estimate for the population, and the smaller the corresponding confidence interval will be. This interval is defined in terms of a 'standard error'. The standard error is equal to the standard deviation (a measure of the variability of the ages in our sample, see Chapter 3) divided by the square root of the number of cases in the sample.

To make this clearer with an example, imagine we are looking at a numeric variable such as the age of the respondents. If we were to create lots of different high quality samples taken from the same population, then each sample is likely to have a slightly different average age. The average age of each sample would be an estimate of the actual average of the population we are studying. Sampling theory suggests that the distribution of these sample averages will follow a well-known pattern known as the 'normal distribution' (the famous bell-curve, see Fielding and Gilbert, 2000, for more on this). The characteristics of this distribution are known, and one of the things we know about it is that 68 per cent of its area is within one 'standard error' of the population mean, 95 per cent is within two standard errors, and so on. Thus, if we take only one sample for our research (as we would usually do), this means that we can be 95 per cent confident that the actual population average is within two standard errors of the average age for our sample.

So, finally, this is the point of the last two paragraphs. When taking a sample we can never be totally sure that what we find is actually very representative of the population, but we can control how *confident* we are about it. Since the quality of our result (e.g. the sample mean) depends on the variability of the item we are measuring (over which we have no control) and the size of the sample, it is clear that we can only control the quality of our results by varying the sample size. Suppose a sample produces a mean of 3 and a standard deviation of 2 on a particular variable, then the standard error is two divided by $\sqrt{N}$ (where N is the sample size). In this case, 95 per cent of any sample means we could collect would lie between $3 - 1.96 \times 2\sqrt{N}$ and $3 + 1.96 \times 2\sqrt{N}$. If N is 9, then the sample mean of 3 tells you that the population mean probably lies between 1.7 and 4.3 (so we should not very confident about our result). If N is 100, the sample mean of 3 tells you that the population mean probably lies between 2.6 and 3.4. But if you want to be within 5 per cent of the likely population mean (i.e. from 2.85 and 3.15), then you need nearly 700 cases. See Hinton (1995) for further details of using the standard error to produce confidence intervals.

When the standard error is plotted against the size of a sample (in this example for a variable with a standard deviation of one), it is immediately clear that increasing the size of your sample leads to a lower standard error and so to more accurate estimates of values (parameters) for the population (see Figure 2.1). For samples less than 20, the standard error is very large, while for samples of 60 or more, the standard error is very much smaller. After 80 or so cases, each addition to the sample size makes relatively little difference to the accuracy of your sample. So this visual representation helps to clarify the distinction between large- and small-scale research. Small-scale research could be defined as having a sample so small that the reliability of any results are too small for orthodox analysis, and where the addition or subtraction of one or two cases makes a considerable difference to the results (less than 30 cases perhaps). Large-scale research could be defined as having a sample of at least 60 cases for each group in the main analyses (i.e. 120 for a comparison of mean age between two groups, 180 for a comparison between three, and so on).

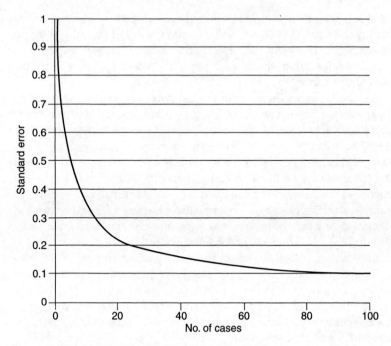

Figure 2.1: Standard error decreases with size of sample

As noted above, your resources for the research, including time and money, are probably a strong influence on your chosen sample size but do try not to exaggerate their importance. On the other hand, if your consideration of other factors suggest that you need to use a sample size that simply cannot be achieved with the resources available to you, then the study must be modified. Do not go ahead in the knowledge that your sample size is totally unsatisfactory for the work you are doing. Incidentally, one of the factors you do not need to consider is the size of the population. The quality of a sample bears little relationship to its size proportionate to the population. A sample does not have to be a certain proportion of the population. If a sample of 100 cases was appropriate for a particular study, it would be appropriate whether the population was 1,000 or 1,000,000. Note, however, that if the sample to population ratio is high, then an equally effective sample can be designed with fewer cases (see Henry, 1990 for details of this 'finite population correction').

An increase in the size of your sample is equivalent to an increase in the power of any statistical test or model that you use. Power, remember, is a measure of the test's ability to separate out genuine effects from random variation. If a statistician devised a new and more powerful test whose use with existing data was able to settle debates that social scientists had been having for decades, or conversely to throw doubt on other more established explanations, they would be rightly famous. Improvements in method are thus often the precursor to an improvement in knowledge. Yet you could achieve exactly the same effect as this by using a larger sample than you anticipated or than is normal in your field. Be ambitious. In practice, you may find that tradition, your hunches, the number of sub-groups, your desire for accuracy, and your resources will all point to a similar size of sample.

SELECTING THE SAMPLE

If you followed the steps above you now have a reason for using a sample, a population, a description of the population either as a list of cases or a summary of characteristics, and a target sample size. You are now ready to select cases from the population.

Random Selection

In theory, sampling theory that is, there is only one way to go about selection of a sample. A random number generator (computer, table, die, top hat with pieces of paper in it, etc.) should be used to select cases one after another from the sampling frame. In using a random number table or generator you number the cases in the population, start anywhere in the table or list, and take the numbers and therefore the appropriate cases in sequence (ignoring any numbers out-of-range). This means, of course, that the sample could be very strange and non-representative of the population. However, the probability of this is small (by definition, since extreme distributions are less likely than representative ones). The larger the sample is, the less likely such a 'freak' selection is.

Random sampling has two key advantages. It is free of the systematic bias that might stem from choices made by the researcher, and it enables the analyst to estimate the probability of any finding actually occurring solely by chance. Also, as discussed above, the sampling error can only be used to estimate confidence intervals where random sampling is used. Apart from the practical problems of obtaining an accurate list to work from, and maintaining the sub-list of selected cases (which task can in any case be delegated to a computer), the technique of random sampling is also very easy – perhaps the easiest method available.

Probably the chief reason that simple random sampling is used so infrequently in educational research is that it produces a scattered sample (such as a few cases in every town). Where travel is involved in the fieldwork, clustered sampling is therefore often preferred (see below). Another slight problem emerges with the issue of replacement. Researchers generally do not want the same case to appear more than once in the sample, yet this is the possible outcome of true random sampling. A case is selected at random from the sampling frame and copied to the sampling list. When a second case is selected there is nothing to stop the randomizer from picking the same case again (equivalent to rolling two sixes in succession with a die). Generally, the researcher prevents this by deleting selected cases from the sampling frame (equivalent to pulling raffle tickets from a hat) or rejecting any cases already selected. This solution could be seen to bias the true random sample, and so lose us some of the statistical 'high ground' that such samples occupy. However, if the sample is small compared to the population (i.e. the sampling fraction is low), then the probability of repeated selection is very low and the issue of replacement makes little practical difference.

Alternatively, either systematic or stratified selection can produce a sample very similar to a good random one. Systematic sampling is the simpler of the two, and more convenient. It involves selecting a random starting place on the list of potential cases, and the sample cases are then chosen at equidistant points on the sampling frame (e.g. every seventeenth case from the list of cases in the population). Beware of periodicity (choosing the sixth apartment on every floor in a block with a multiple of six apartments per floor for example). As long as the list is in no particular order, through having been shuffled for example, the process is equivalent to random sampling without replacement. This approach is even more convenient if used hierarchically, with the researcher making systematic selections at progressively lower levels of aggregation. For example, you may select wards in a city, then streets in a ward, then households in each street (as long as the chances of each ward and street being selected are proportional to their size).

Stratified samples are somewhat more complicated. Cases are selected in proportion to one or more characteristics in the population. For example, if gender is considered relevant to the study and the population is 58 per cent female, then the sample must be 58 per cent female. Within each stratum such as gender the cases still need to be selected randomly or systematically else the sample merely becomes a quota one (see below). The number and type of characteristics (or strata) are chosen by the researcher on theoretical grounds of relevance to the study. The researcher must use or find expert knowledge to decide which characteristics of the population could be significant for the study findings, and then work out the pattern of distribution of these characteristics. This is not always an easy task, as the characteristics need to be considered in interaction, and the researcher may need to carry out a census anyway to uncover the nature of the population. So this approach to sampling is generally harder than simple random selection. The researcher needs a good reason not to use random sampling.

The stratified approach can lead to a high quality sample by reducing the risk of a 'freaky' result, in terms of the strata characteristics at least. Its problems include the fact that it can require decisions about complex categories (race, occupation) or on sensitive issues (income, age). If several background characteristics are used, then the selection process becomes complex as each variable 'interacts' with the other. If both gender and occupational class are used, then not only must the proportions for gender and class be correct, but so must the proportions for gender in each class (if 23 per cent of the population are female and professional, this must be reflected in the sample).

For example, a study of motivation to become a teacher may be unable to obtain a list of all entrants to teaching training in a particular year (the population for the study). Many colleges will not release personal details to you perhaps, so you might decide to use as many cases as you can find which match, in aggregate, the characteristics of the population. Suppose that your knowledge of the field led you to believe that sex of trainee was an important variable, you would need to know the sex breakdown of all trainees (and such information is easier to obtain than a list of all trainees). If 40 per cent of trainees were male, you would then set out to obtain a sample containing 40 per cent men. Again, if you believe *a priori* that there will be different motivations for teaching different age groups, then you need to know the breakdown of trainees between the post-compulsory, secondary, junior, infants and nursery sectors. If 30 per cent of trainees were secondary school specialists, then 30 per cent of your achieved sample should be also. If 66 per cent of secondary trainees in the population were male, you would also need to find this out (how?) and reflect this in your sample so that 20 per cent (66 per cent of 30 per cent) of your sampled trainees were male secondary specialists, while the overall sample remained 40 per cent male. If you also, quite reasonably, considered ethnicity, socio-economic status, prior qualifications or subject specialisms as important factors, then the calculations quickly become complex. You would need both to know the proportion of the population who were white, male, with a professional background, secondary mathematics specialists with a first degree in a subject other than mathematics, and you would need also to reflect this in your sample. Such an example emphasizes two things. First, despite its lack of popularity judging from its rarity in the literature, random sampling is actually a lot easier than stratified sampling. Second, even where the purpose of the study is to collect new data (on the motivation of trainee teachers, for example), it is often important to conduct a fairly detailed secondary analysis first in order to identify the characteristics of the population being studied (see Chapters 3 and 4).

Clustering
Using a clustered sample implies not so much a difference in selection procedures as a difference in defining population units. The cases we are interested in often occur in natural clusters such as schools. So we can redefine our population of interest to be the clusters (schools) themselves and then select our sample from them using one of the above procedures. The schools become the cases, rather than the individuals within them. This has several practical advantages. It is generally easier to obtain a list of clusters (schools, employers, voluntary organizations, hospitals, etc.) than it is to get a complete list of the people in them. If we use many of the individuals from each cluster in our selected sample, we can obtain results from many individuals with little time and travel involved, since they will be concentrated in fewer places.

For example, in a survey of teachers we might select a random sample of 100 of the 25,000 schools in England and Wales, and then use the whole staff of teachers in each of these selected schools. As with systematic sampling, it is important that the odds of a cluster being selected are in proportion to the number of individuals they represent (i.e. schools with more teachers should be more likely to be picked). Despite this complication in the calculation (and the need to have at least some information about each cluster), this approach is growing in popularity (see Chapter 7). Its chief drawback is the potential bias introduced if the cases in the cluster are too similar to each other. People in the same house tend to be more similar to each other than to those in other houses, and the same thing applies to a lesser extent to the hamlets where the houses are (people in each post-code area may tend to be similar), and to the regions, and nations where they live (and so on). This suggests that we should try to sample more clusters, and use appropriately fewer in each cluster. As usual, the precise compromise between resource limitations and the ideal is down to the judgement of the researcher. Being aware of, and recording, this judgement are probably the most important safe-guards against the undue influence of bias.

Other Sources of Bias

As we shall see, statistical analysis usually proceeds as though the cases in a study are independent of each other with an equal probability of selection, and that random sampling has been used. Alternatively, clustering and stratification techniques can be used to select cases as outlined above, and produce a sample that is similar to a good random sample, in which all population elements have a known non-zero probability of selection. If any other method of selecting a sample is used, standard techniques of statistical analysis are inappropriate (Lee *et al.*, 1989).

One apparent deviation from this principle of equal/proportionate probability of selection is where a boosted sample is used. In this design, the probability of selection is boosted for some rare sub-groups to ensure that sufficient are obtained for a comparison to be made (black ethnic groups in northern Scotland might be a current example of a rare sub-group, usually insufficiently represented in a regional poll for any serious analysis to proceed). This approach is valuable and perfectly valid as long as the, then, over-represented cases are re-weighted.

A classic problem in sampling comes from bias through the use of 'volunteers'. Whether you provide an incentive for participants, or use captive subjects, it is quite clear that those willing to devote an afternoon to taking part in your study could be very different from those who are not. Captive subjects are those forced to take part. On many university psychology courses, for example, undergraduates are required to sign a contract agreeing to take part in a certain number of studies as a condition of their acceptance. This can understandably lead to many problems such as sullenness, and even the outright sabotage of experiments. At best, it means that much of what psychology tells us only applies to the population of captive psychology undergraduates, and therefore does not have much external validity beyond this specific group. Nineteenth-century psychology was often based on what a researcher found out about themselves (introspection), while later twentieth-century psychology was chiefly based on what psychologists found out about each other. There are some signs in the twenty-first century that psychology is now becoming more concerned with people at large.

NON-PROBABILITY SAMPLES

An implicit assumption has been made in this chapter so far that our sample will be what is termed a 'probability' sample, where cases will be selected either randomly or systematically. There are two good reasons for this focus. First, this kind of sampling is generally more technical than its alternatives, thus requiring more explanation for a new researcher. Second, this kind of sampling is preferable in almost every way to any of its alternatives in all research situations. Thus, a simple guideline would be that probability samples should be used in all circumstances in which they are possible. A high quality sample is crucial for safe generalization to take place (for high 'external validity'). Non-probability samples should therefore be reserved only for those projects in which there is no other choice.

The most common, and over-used, form of non-probability sampling is the convenience sample, composed of those cases chosen only because they are easily available. A researcher standing in a railway station, or shopping centre, or outside a student union and stopping people in an *ad hoc* manner would lead to a convenience sample. This approach is often justified by the comment that a range of people use such places, so the sample will be mixed in composition. The approach is sometimes strengthened, for example, in market 'research', by determining quotas for groups of cases (such as men and women) and then deselecting people (e.g. by not stopping them) once the quota for each group is filled. Note that this is different to stratification where a probability sample is used within each strata. I hope that by the time you have finished this chapter you will be clear how threatening a quota design can be for the security of your findings. Large numbers of people rarely travel by rail, shop in city centres or use a student bar. These people would tend to be excluded from your sample. The time of day could make a difference. Those in paid employment may be less likely to be in shopping centres during the day, while older people may be less likely to go out at night. The researcher may also make (perhaps unconscious) selections, by avoiding those who are drunk, or who appear unconventionally attired or coiffured. Even with a quota system therefore, convenience sampling introduces a very real danger of biasing the sample, and it does so unnecessarily in far too many studies.

Non-probability samples are more properly used for pilot studies (see Chapter 5), where the intention is to trial a research design rather than collect usable data. Even here, however, a first-class pilot study will trial the actual sampling method to be used along with the other components of the design. Sampling is so important as a stage in research that it is not clear why it is so often omitted from the pilot.

Non-probability samples are also more properly used when the intention is not to collect data on a general population but to use 'cultural experts' to help explain an educational or social process. We might want to ask Directors of Local Education Authorities how they allocate their annual budget, or headteachers how they allocate the places in their school. We may want to ask politicians about the background to a new policy. In each example we are approaching informants as experts. In some studies the number of experts is so limited that we must use whoever is available to us, since there are not enough to select cases at random from a list. In these cases, we must accept that probability sampling is not possible, and so record our reasons, and try to estimate the possible bias that will result from using our judgement concerning who it is appropriate to select. *If there is no other way.* In the example of headteachers, of course, it may well be possible to produce a random sample even when our intention is to consult them as experts. The key issue is not what our sample is for, but how small the population of experts is.

Perhaps the clearest example of the appropriate use of a non-probability sample is where a snowball technique is necessary. In some studies, of drug use, truancy, or under-age sex for example, we are unable to produce a sampling frame even where the population of interest may be imagined as quite large. Indeed, one of our key research objectives may be to estimate the size of an unknown population. In such a project we might quite properly approach a convenience sample to get us started, and once we have gained their trust ask each individual to suggest other informants for successive stages. In this way, we hope that our sample will 'snowball'. As with small populations, difficult-to-reach populations can also make probability sampling impossible. We simply accept this, and do the best we can with what is available. This approach is very different from using a convenience sample simply because it is ... convenient.

There are advanced techniques available to help estimate the size of unknown populations. For example, an approach developed from ecological studies involves using the intersection between successive samples to gauge the size of the group from which they come (known as 'mark-recapture'). In ecology, a sample of a species of birds may be selected and tagged. Later, a second sample is selected. The proportion of already tagged birds in the second sample will be related to the total number of birds. If a high proportion are already tagged, it means that the population will be not much larger than the sample size. If a low proportion are tagged, the population will probably be much larger than the sample size. Similar techniques (hopefully using more subtle tags!) can be used with homeless people, or housebreakers, for example, to estimate the prevalence of these phenomena in society. However, we are then faced with several further problems, including the fact that the probability of any homeless person being in the second sample may be affected by having been involved in the first, or that re-offending housebreakers may be simply less competent than those never caught. These practical difficulties reinforce the message above. A probability sample is to be preferred not only because it is superior in quality, but also because it is generally easier to work with.

It is interesting that despite their patent disadvantages non-probability samples are by far the most common type found in UK educational research, mostly used without any apparent justification at all. By way of example the first four issues of the prestigious *British Educational Research Journal* (BERJ) in the year 2000 contained 28 articles. In my opinion, 14 of these were non-empirical or else non-systematic summaries of previous research (i.e. not research syntheses), 10 used small non-probability samples without any attempt at explanation or justification, and only 4 used probability-type samples of any kind. The reports for these 4 contained substantially more about the nature of the samples, and about their research design in general. BERJ is probably the most widely circulated journal in the UK, and one which insists on a substantial research content for all of its articles.

NON-RESPONSE

In an ideal world you, as a researcher, would select a high quality sample, and all of those people selected to participate in the study would agree to do so. In reality this will not happen. Cases will be lost to non-response in at least two ways. Some cases will provide no data at all. People selected by you will refuse to participate in your experiment, or will not return your questionnaire. Part-cases will also be lost where only incomplete data is collected. You may face people dropping out during an experiment yielding a pre-test score but not a post-test score (see Chapter 7). People may return a questionnaire but omit some questions through lack of motivation, incompetence, or ignorance of the answer (see Chapter 3). All these examples will cause problems through bias, equivalent to using an inferior sample and similar to the problem of volunteer bias. There are proven systematic differences (some apparently trivial) between those who tend to respond and others. Some respondents may be more highly educated and have higher incomes, for example.

Once you have selected your ideal sample, one of your main priorities for the rest of your research design should therefore be to minimize any non-response. Relevant issues discussed in later chapters therefore include methods of delivering surveys, simplifying experimental designs, asking non-threatening questions, negotiating access, the use of incentives, following up missing cases, and even the colour of the paper you use. If you have designed a good sample you want the sample you achieve to be as close to the ideal as possible. Therefore, make it as easy as possible for people to take part in the study. Incidentally what you should not do is decide that as some non-response is inevitable you do not need a good sample design in the first place because 'it will only go wrong after all'. As we will see, each further stage in your design requires compromises, and, as we have already seen, each stage within sampling, such as listing the population, may require compromises. If we also introduce unnecessary weaknesses, we are well on the way to arguing that as accuracy is not possible, we may as well make the results up (and I have heard a distinguished sociologist of education state in public that accuracy was less important to them than producing shocking 'results', in Gorard, 2000c).

Whatever you do, there is likely to be some non-response in your sample (and there have been suggestions that average rates of response to surveys are declining over time – through societal research fatigue perhaps). This means that you should record (and report) the rate at which this non-response occurs, try to estimate the bias introduced as a result, and consider methods of ameliorating it. This is not easy, but you as the researcher are in the best position to consider the likely impacts and decide how to improve the situation.

Recording and reporting response rates are relatively simple tasks. You should record the different response rates to each item, or each component of a design. You may like to distinguish, where possible, between refusal to take part in the study (by saying no to an interview, for example) and non-response (by not returning a postal questionnaire, for example). This could be useful in helping you form an estimate of bias. For in the same way that those who do not respond may differ systematically from those who do, those who refuse to take part may tend to differ in key characteristics from those who do not respond. Those not responding to postal requests are more likely to be transient and therefore to come from the extremes of any classification of socio-economic status (by being either homeless or employed in a national-based profession involving travel or more regular moving house perhaps). Those returning a questionnaire uncompleted may be busier or less literate, for example.

Reporting non-response is important, but commonly ignored. Even where it has been reported, commentators do not seem to consider the possible bias that this has introduced. For example, Gleeson *et al.* (1996) selected a sample of 800 cases but received replies from only 254 of these (32 per cent response rate). In their otherwise excellent report of the findings from this study they make no mention of the very great caution therefore needed in attempting to generalize to the 800, instead implying that the results may even be generalizable to a population beyond the 800. As I have said, many research reports have even lower responses than this and the majority probably do not report the figures at all.

While 100 per cent is an ideal rate of response, even figures close to this may lead to significant bias since the small group excluded by a high response rate could consist of the most extreme cases with the characteristics of non-responders (the 'distilled essence' of non-responders, if you like). It should also be recalled that the sampling frame may have already inadvertently excluded some of the more extreme cases, such as those not on the electoral roll, or without a telephone, or without access to the Internet. Nevertheless, it is almost certainly true that the nearer you are to 100 per cent response the better. Some textbooks have published very low expected rates of response, to surveys, for example, and novices may find these very reassuring. But these figures often include the rates for long-winded market research, 'cold calling' on the telephone, and other poorly constructed designs. Using the approaches described in later chapters of this book it should be possible for an academic researcher to obtain much higher rates such as 70 per cent or above as a minimum. If non-response is small and apparently random in nature, then we can ignore it, but there is already clear evidence from previous studies that non-response is non-random.

Not all institutions and individuals asked to take part in a piece of research will agree, often because they are too busy. By necessarily using only those prepared to take part, a study is therefore open to the charge of bias. Questionnaires may be more readily completed by those who are more literate, opinionated, confident, or who have greater leisure time. If a popular newspaper published a finding that 95 per cent of the population were in favour of the restoration of capital punishment for a particular crime, because that was the supporting proportion of their sample on a phone-in poll, we would be doubtful of the external validity of their sample. Aside from the issue of the self-selected readership, and the fact that people may call twice and be double-counted, there is also the question whether those in favour of capital punishment are more motivated to call because they wish to change the status quo.

In the same way, but to a lesser extent I hope, academic samples are open to bias. David *et al.* (1994) provided a clear example of the importance of this issue. They questioned pupils and parents about the process of choosing a new school, but only 50 per cent of the parents responded, giving them two notional groups of pupils – those whose parents were interviewed, and those who were not. There was a clear difference in the results obtained from the two groups, with the first group of pupils putting more emphasis on educational reasons for picking a school, while the second, whose parents refused interviews, gave primarily convenience reasons. This is indirect evidence that the responses of the two groups of parents would also be different, if they could only be compared. David *et al.* subsequently managed to interview some non-volunteer parents, and found that they were indeed different from the volunteers, being more concerned with the child's wishes, but otherwise being less active in making the choice. This is valuable evidence of the dangers of non-response bias.

One approach to estimating the bias involves looking at the order in which people respond. An argument can be constructed that those who reply later to a postal survey, for example, are more like those who do not respond at all than are those who reply early. Thus, we can estimate the character of non-respondents by looking at the difference between early and late responders. This is certainly worth a try, and there is no harm in recording when and how a response appears, and how much cajoling/reminding was necessary. However, other studies have suggested that the empirical basis for this approach is weak (Giacquinta and Shaw, 2000). Using late returners to estimate the sample bias induced by non-returners may not be very effective, and may even lead to a poorer estimate than the original.

Another common approach to dealing with non-response is to find suitable replacements for the missing cases. If you are conducting a postal survey of 100 people, and 30 do not respond even after a reminder, then you can preserve your sample size by adding another 30 cases. Unfortunately even if your sample is stratified and you try to replace like-with-like in terms of your strata you will still be left with the possibility that those who do respond are more alike in some way than those who do not (see below for an example of this from my own work). Replacement is a useful approach, but should always be accompanied by scrupulous records showing the response rate of the initial sweep (the first 100 in our example) as well as for the final achieved sample. Otherwise you could continue the process of replacement indefinitely and always get a perfect 100 per cent 'response' rate.

Perhaps the most effective, but rarely used, method of controlling for non-response is to use weights. Weights are adjustments made to the perceived bias in your achieved results by using post-stratification corrections. If you know that the achieved sample differs from the population in some crucial respect you can use corrective weights to produce a better estimate of your result. In fact, many sample designs implicitly require such weighting, which are therefore not optional extras and can have a fundamental effect on the outcomes (Lehtonen and Pahkinen, 1995).

For example, imagine that you have collected a stratified sample of 1,000 respondents, of whom 600 (60 per cent) lived in urban/ suburban areas and 400 (40 per cent) lived in rural areas. However, you had set out to achieve a proportion of 80:20 urban:rural respondents because the census of population for the region tells you that this is the actual proportion in the population. Your sample therefore over-represents rural respondents. One of the substantive questions you asked this sample was whether they had considered using any school other than the current one their child attends. The overall result was that 440 (44 per cent) had considered another school, and therefore the modal average (most frequent) response for your sample is 'no' (56 per cent).

You then separate these responses by area of residence, and discover that 60 per cent of the urban inhabitants but only 20 per cent of the rural ones had considered another school for their child. This is a very large systematic difference. What difference might have been made if your sample had fully represented urban respondents, and these extra urban cases had answered the question about schools in the same proportions as we actually found? This is what weighting tells us. If we had achieved a sample of 800 urban and 200 rural cases, and both groups had answered the school question in the proportions we found, then we would expect 60 per cent of the 800 urban cases (480) and 20 per cent of the 200 rural ones (40) to answer 'yes'. On this calculation, since area of residence makes such a difference and our sample over-represents the views of rural residents, our best estimate of the population figure considering another school would be 520 per 1000. Therefore the modal average response is actually 'yes', even though our achieved sample suggested 'no'.

Although this seems rather fiddly, most researchers could cope with it since the actual calculations would be performed by a computer package. The key role of the researcher is to decide, on theoretical or prior knowledge, which of the background variables form important strata. This is another reason why the use of secondary contextual data (see Chapter 3) is an important skill for all researchers. As with the original stratification of a sample, the complexity of weighting arises in the interaction of the strata. If, in the example above, you decide that sex of respondent is another important factor then you will need to consider the four groups consisting of male and urban; female and urban; male and rural; and female and rural separately. If you add ethnicity, first language, level of education or social class, then the calculations become mind-boggling, and these are only some of the 'standard' contextual variables. Therefore, as with stratifying, you need to select a few really crucial background variables for your specific study, and work with those only.

AN EXAMPLE OF SAMPLING

A genuine fully random sample is rare for many of the reasons given above. I have tended to work with clustered random samples, perhaps using schools as the unit of sampling (see, for example, Gorard, 1996, 1997b, 1998b), or with systematic stratified samples (see, for example, Gorard *et al.*, 1998a, 1998b, 1999a, 1999c). In the second of these studies I was trying to collect 1,100 retrospective learning histories from the populations of three contrasting local authorities in industrial South Wales.

As in previous studies of this type, the decision as to which geographical areas to use for the sample was made partly on strategic grounds (Banks *et al.*, 1992) and partly on the basis of the population characteristics in each area. Although it is normal for a study of this size to select a diverse and well-spread sample which can then be divided into gender or class categories, since the differences in local economic effects are so varied in the UK, a more focused study was required to make these local effects explicit. Three sites were chosen to represent the range of experiences in industrial South Wales. Bridgend could be briefly characterized as an expanding town, Neath Port Talbot as an established manufacturing conurbation, and Blaenau Gwent as a depressed coalfield valley. Three electoral divisions (wards) were selected within each site to reflect the range and diversity of their social and educational conditions as evidenced by 1991 population census data. Secondary analysis was used to characterize the nine wards, the three sites, and South Wales in terms of a range of social and educational measures capable of disaggregation at each level. This data provided the sampling frame for the survey and part of the context for the primary analysis (Gorard, 1997c). Households in each division were identified from the electoral registers, which were the most accurate and up-to-date available listings of addresses. These lists were considered appropriate since the target population for the first wave was only those adults aged 35 to 64.

Systematic sampling was an appropriate method to use, but to avoid problems of periodicity and special methods of variance estimation, repeated systematic sampling was used. The sample was also stratified in an attempt to reduce the sampling variance and to ensure sufficient cases in certain categories, and this stratification was proportionate (i.e. the sampling fraction for each strata was uniform within wards). Stratification was appropriate as the sample to population ratio was large, and the population was well characterized (Lehtonen and Pahkinen, 1995). Four points were chosen at random in each electoral division and every *n*th household after those points was selected for inclusion in the survey as a primary respondent with the 10 subsequent addresses set aside as potential reserve respondents. The sampling fraction $1/n$ was similar for each division but was determined by the precise number of electors. A quota was devised such that half of the respondents in each electoral division were male and half female, while one-third were aged 35 to 44, one-third were 45 to 54 and the remainder 55 to 64.

The primary address was visited three times at different times of the day in successive weeks (to allow for holidays and shift working) until contact was made with one of the householders. In a house with two or more householders, either was interviewed, according to quota and as convenient. If the house was clearly empty (having been 'gutted' by builders, for example) or all of the householders were out-of-strata, the first house on the reserve list became a new primary and the process started again. If the primary householder refused to take part or was not contacted after three calls, the first house on the reserve list was used instead, followed, if necessary, by the second reserve and so on. In the latter cases the response was recorded as a reserve for accounting purposes. This procedure of repeated systematic sampling produced a set of respondents stratified by age and gender within electoral divisions chosen to represent the educational and socio-economic diversity of the three research sites, which were themselves selected as representatives of the range of socio-economic experiences in industrial South Wales over the past 50 years (Gorard, 1997c).

A second wave of the survey was based in the same areas as the first and was also stratified by gender and age. Half of the respondents in the second wave were aged 15–24 and half were 25–34. These became the two younger cohorts, so that the sample as a whole represented education and training experiences throughout working life from just before finishing compulsory education to retirement. However, in order that the study could also examine family influences more fully, the two younger cohorts were selected by repeated systematic sampling from the children of those respondents in the first wave. Several of the respondents in the second wave therefore no longer lived in South Wales or even the UK. This second stage was similar in many ways to the method of boosting a sample in order to obtain a higher proportion of respondents with certain characteristics (SCELI, 1991; Gershuny and Marsh, 1994; Park and Tremlett, 1995). The survey was designed to include at least 800 respondents in the first wave and at least 200 in the second. From this grand total of over 1,000, around 150 were selected strategically for in-depth interviews. In this way, the study involved a large-scale survey comparable in size to those of Deloitte Haskins and Sells (1989), Davies (1994), or Park (1994), or to one research site in larger studies (e.g. SCELI, 1991; Banks *et al.*, 1992), as well as a more qualitative segment comparable to previous studies of training providers, such as Pettigrew *et al.* (1989), and considerably larger than many studies of participants in training (e.g. FEU, 1993; Hand *et al.*, 1994; Taylor and Spencer, 1994).

In using sites and wards as administrative units to select the sample, the survey can be described as 'complex', so that some standard statistical procedures might not be appropriate without weighting (Lee *et al.*, 1989). Weighting was possible since the entire sampling frame for the survey at each stage of this multi-stage design was known, at least in principle, and each element had a known non-zero chance of being included in the sample since a record was kept of the probabilities of inclusion at each stage of the design. However, the sample was automatically self-weighting at the ward level since the probability of selection within a ward was proportionate to the size of the ward. Similarly, within each ward, although each household of whatever size had an equal chance of selection, the sample was of householders only and stratified by gender, therefore it was not necessary to correct for the probability of selection in terms of the number of people in the house, as has been done elsewhere (SCELI, 1991; Gershuny and Marsh, 1994).

Weights were used in this survey for two main reasons: to attempt a correction for missing values and to form a more reliable estimate of the population characteristics for industrial South Wales, since even a self-weighting sample can have non-response and design errors. Where a questionnaire was incomplete or had other missing values, a simple method of imputing the missing value was devised if possible, such as using the mean of all other cases. To attempt a correction for bias in the sample through self-selection, where this was related to demographic composition, and at the same time expand the data to fit the background characteristics of industrial South Wales better, the responses were reweighted via a post-stratification adjustment factor. This factor adjusted for the different response rates within categories and adjusted demographic variables to those of the known population. The adjustment factor is the population distribution divided by the sample distribution for each demographic sub-group. For example, if the proportion of men aged 35–44 in South Wales is 12 per cent, and the proportion in the sample was 10 per cent, the factor is 1.2. Weighting and imputing were only used for the production of descriptive statistics and the estimation of current population parameters. The analysis of the determinants of participation in learning covers 50 years from 1945 to 1996, therefore no one set of population characteristics from a snapshot date would be appropriate to use as the basis of weights for that whole period.

I have described my sampling procedure in this project in some detail as an example of how samples can be reported, and to show that, whatever its peculiarities, considerable care was taken to draw it, and to record what happened in doing so. I and my colleagues achieved 1,104 responses with a primary response rate of over 75 per cent, and a sample almost perfectly stratified by age, sex, and geography. In retrospect, however, I am fairly sure that the techniques used combined to over-represent the long-term sick and disabled since these would be more likely to be at home when we called. I can only guess from evidence of the subsequent interview details, since disability was not recorded in the survey (as in retrospect it is clear that it should have been) and could not therefore be stratified or weighted. Since the sample was so large, the work was partially contracted out to a professional company. It is therefore possible that some interviewers (paid on piece-work rate) would have been tempted to use the reserve households more often than the design allowed (differences between sub-contracted researchers in large studies is another important source of bias). If so, this would have the effect of further increasing the proportion of relatively housebound respondents. The battle against bias is never won.

COMMON ERRORS IN WORKING WITH A SAMPLE

This bullet list summarizes some of the common problems relating to sampling encountered in the educational research literature, and in the work of research students. I have not repeated here what I consider to be the worst example (see above) of omitting from the sample the very people under study, by carrying out a study of truancy within a school setting for example.

- not using the sample size;
- not specifying the population;
- ignoring drop-out;
- using an unjustified non-probability sample;
- not using weights;
- obscuring the response rate.

Not Using the Sample Size

A report on the quality of educational research commissioned by OFSTED (Tooley and Darby, 1998) found that only around one-third of the empirical articles they considered from four of the most prestigious journals in the UK described the size of their sample. Indeed, around one-third made no mention of their sample or sampling procedure at all. Of 399 papers reported in four UK journals, only 57 (or 14 per cent) were clearly quantitative in method, and a maximum of five (1 per cent) were mixed in methodological approach. Of the rest, 30 per cent were qualitative but the majority (54 per cent) were non-empirical. One of the three themes to the criticism in the report was 'problems of methodology' and the most startling of these involved sampling. In the *Oxford*

Review of Education, for example, around one-third of the empirical articles did not report their sample size (i.e. there is no mention of it and therefore no way of telling how large or small the sample is), another third reported size but gave no information at all about the method of selection, and the final third gave some generally inadequate information about size and selection. Very few researchers discussed the possible limitations of their approach. I suspect that this practice is at least as common elsewhere (in less prestigious journals, for example). Any afternoon spent examining the contents of current journal issues in your local library will confirm that the report was hardly exaggerating the scale of these defects. It means, of course, that when a researcher claims that a certain proportion or percentage of individuals responded in a particular way we can have no idea of the significance of their finding, and should, in all probability, ignore it as unsafe.

A further specific example is provided by the writing of Cheung and Lewis (1998). Their study of the expectations of employers of school leavers was reported in 14 pages, including a reference list of two pages. They include seven pages of background/introductory material but only a paragraph on the methods used. It is therefore very difficult to judge how important or valid their reported findings might be. Most crucially they do not report their sample size, while all of their frequencies are presented as percentages (implying that the sample was in hundreds). It is important to realize that putting the number of cases at the bottom of each table would have taken no extra space in the report, therefore suspicion should immediately be aroused that the sample size, if reported, would be inadequate for its purpose (i.e. not in hundreds). The benefit of the doubt here should rest with tentative scepticism.

Cheung and Lewis contacted an equal number of employers from each category of a 'Standard Industrial Classification', even though the relative frequency of each type is not equal in the population of Hong Kong where the work was done (and some categories such as agriculture are likely to have no cases). We are not told how the sample was selected, nor what the response rate was. The study was carried out in three phases, each separated by two years, but the authors do not state whether the findings presented are for one phase only, or all aggregated (and then there is a problem of employers' views changing over six years, especially in light of the intervening handover of political control to China). In the light of these points, we can have little confidence in the sample as it has been reported.

Not Specifying the Population

Even more common is the absence in research reports of any reference to the population involved. The work of Reay and Lucey (2000) is typical, and far from the weakest, of a whole genre of research that appears to evade critical reading by claiming to eschew quantitative analysis (while still basing their conclusions on arithmetic logic using terms such as 'majority', 'few', etc.). While their work describes a sample size, this is not drawn from a clear population. In their own words

> It focused on 90 Year 6 children (aged 10–11) in two primary schools in one inner-London borough, chosen because of its demographic diversity. Forty-four children were involved in focus group interviews and a further 20 children, 15 of their parents and three teachers were interviewed individually. (ibid., p. 85)

Only a subset of these are cited in their paper, including 'five with parents' (ibid.). There is clearly an approach to the notion of sampling here in the mention of numbers, types and demographic diversity. But is the sample meant to represent the Year 6 in the two primary schools, or in all primary schools in the LEA, or inner-London LEAs, or all LEAs? How much can the authors generalize from this study? If the study focuses on 90 children, why are there only 64 children involved (44 in the focus groups and 20 separately)? Are the 90 the total Year 6 population of these schools? Either way, how were the 64 selected for inclusion (we have seen above the potential bias in a non-systematic selection method)?

Perhaps we could argue that these questions do not really matter. The authors have used a non-probability sample (although without explaining why), and are only interested in the individual accounts they collect. They will therefore not seek patterns within, nor generalizations from, this dataset. Unfortunately, this is precisely what they do attempt. Their abstract includes the following phrases – 'a strong pattern of class-related orientations to class', the 'vast majority of children' involved in choice, and 'less choice for black and white working-class boys than for other groups of children' (ibid., p. 83). The full text makes it clear both that the authors have divided their already small sample into sub-groups for occupational class (of family), gender, ability level, and ethnic group, and that they are keen to draw general conclusions about the differences between these groups. They conclude that 'despite the idiosyncrasies and cross-cutting inflections of personal characteristics and ability levels, a majority of the children operate within class-differentiated horizons of choice' (ibid., p. 98). We are given no indication of the relative size of the sub-groups, but given that the total sample is only 66 cases, dividing these by class, gender, ethnicity and so on means that the actual number of cases in any comparison must be very small.

This is most obvious in the discussion about parents, where the authors state that 'in the parental interviews, a majority of the working-class parents concurred with their child' (ibid., p. 90), and 'a significant deviation from this class trend was mothers of mainly black working-class boys' (ibid., p. 90). So, from their 15 interviews with parents, the authors have apparently been able to analyse responses separately by class, ethnic group and gender of child. If we make a charitable assumption (and note that this should not be necessary since it would take little effort for the authors to have provided all the relevant details) that the parents were roughly half of girls and half boys, then there would be seven or eight parents in each gender group. Again, if we assume that half of each of these groups were middle-class and half working-class (and assuming that only two categories were used), then there would be three or four cases in each gender/class cell for comparison. Finally, if we assume that half of each of these groups were black and half non-black (again making the favourable assumption of only two categories), then there would be one to two cases in each cell for comparison. When Reay and Lucey state that a majority of working-class parents agreed with their child they may be talking about as few as four parents from a sub-group of seven. There is no way that such a 'finding' is significant (see Chapter 6). When Reay and Lucey state that mothers of mainly black working-class boys differed from this pattern, they could be talking about as few as one or two mothers.

For social science purposes this scale is clearly insufficient for any generalization, and as with some other examples cited in this book it is rather surprising that the peer-review process for the journal in which the paper was published did not pick some of these problems up. The reason could be the continuing and over-used dichotomy between quantitative research and other research. The referees involved may have been in sympathy with the methodological style (and perhaps the conclusions) of the paper, and not looked too carefully at the figures on which the authors base their case. The net effect is to allow authors to make unsafe 'generalizations' from one or two cases in a way that may propagate through the research literature, leading to an increasingly defective cumulation of knowledge.

Ignoring Drop-out

We have already considered the potential damage caused by non-response, since non-responders may differ significantly from those individuals taking part in a study. The same problem arises during sampling designs based on repeated use of the same cases (see also Chapter 7 on subject 'mortality' in experiments). Some studies use longitudinal approaches (tracking people over time), including some of the famous large surveys mentioned in Chapter 3 (the Youth Cohort Study, for example). Each time the researchers return to their sample, sometimes after a number of years, some of the cases will drop out. Some may be out of contact, some have died, emigrated or simply be unwilling to continue. The percentage dropping out is nearly always reported, but less often are the full implications of this thought through. A good example is presented by Huff (1991) where a university follows the careers of its graduates into later life and advertises their average annual income. If they can only trace 75 per cent of the cohort from a particular year, although 75 per cent is a high 'response rate', do you think this could lead to an over-estimate of the average income? How many of the missing cases are likely to be national politicians, consultant heart surgeons, or sporting or cultural superstars, for example?

Using an Unjustified Non-probability Sample

Aside from a very few studies, for example, where the snowball technique is necessary, all researchers are faced with an early decision to use or not to use a probability sample. This applies to those interviewing cultural experts as much as those doing large-scale trials. There is no obvious reason, other than necessity, why any researcher would choose to use a non-probability sample. Whatever the sample size and purpose, a random or systematic or stratified sample is better than a convenience, purposive or quota one. Yet the majority of the educational research literature reports the use of non-probability samples and no good reason is given for their use. The questions of representational bias and whether to use corrective weights generally do not arise in the literature. I have a feeling that many authors are using the technical term 'sample' to mean simply 'the cases I involved in my research'. By using the term sample they gain some of the associated prestige, and an apparent ability to generalize from their findings without any of the difficulties of actually using a properly selected sample from a previously defined population. This is not leading the educational research community to the safe and cumulative knowledge that it requires (in so far as this may be possible).

Not Using Weights

As shown above, the existence of post-stratification weights is very good news for the researcher. They mean that even if your sample deviates radically from an ideal and is clearly biased in some respect, you can estimate corrections even after collecting your data. As long as the number of variables used for weighting is kept to a minimum of the really crucial ones for your study, and you use a computer for all of the hard work, then corrective weights are fairly simple to operate. It is therefore quite surprising how seldom they appear in use in the educational research literature. Not using weights can lead to significant misrepresentation of your findings, and if further, more complex analyses are performed using the same data, then the representation errors will propagate, sometimes alarmingly (see Chapter 9 for a discussion of error propagation).

Obscuring the Response Rate

It is important to keep a close eye on the number of cases in your (and others) research. This number (often reported as 'N') can have several meanings. Is it intended to be the number of responses, the number of usable responses, or the number of responses used in a specific table of results? Does it include those people contacted who were ineligible (too old, for example), who terminated the interview, or were not at home when you called? Decisions such as these can affect your apparent response rate.

A large-scale survey called 'Future Skills' was carried out in Wales in 1998 to coincide with the creation of the new National Assembly when Wales was given a limited form of self-governance. It was carried out by MORI for a group of public sector clients including the Welsh Office, the Training and Enterprise Councils, the Welsh Development Agency and the Further and Higher Education Funding Councils. The results attempted to match available workforce skills and future employer demands to determine a national strategy for training and reskilling. These results have been extremely influential in the setting of National Targets for Lifelong Education and Training, and in the policies formed by the post-16 education committee. It is the only empirical evidence used in the Education and Training Action Plan for Wales (ETAG, 1999). The sample was carefully constructed, stratified, and corrective weights were used. The summary of the main report (the document likely to be used by politicians and other policy-makers) does not include the response rate, however, although the figure in general use is 45 per cent for the survey of employers, for example. While less than impressive, this 45 per cent is sufficient to demand some respect for the results. This response rate is calculated as the number of achieved interviews (5,790) divided by the total of the number of achieved interviews (5,790) plus the number of refusals (6,528) and the number of interviews terminated (607). The appendix to the technical report describes this as the 'valid response rate' (Future Skills Wales, 1998). In the terms used in this chapter this is not really a response rate at all, but a non-refusal rate.

The survey actually drew a sample of 29,952 employers to contact. The researchers did not contact 6,207 of these because they were not needed to fill quotas. Therefore the survey contacted 23,745 employers and held successful interviews with 5,790 of them. This is a response rate of 24 per cent (or 19 per cent of the initial sample drawn). The reasons given for not including the remaining 10,820 employers include finding a telephone number engaged, not recognized, or unobtainable (1,866), having too few employees or not carrying out recruitment themselves (2,330), and appointments made and not kept (1,222). Each of these reasons, and others like them, could clearly lead to bias in the achieved sample. Small businesses, for example, may be more likely to fail and therefore no longer have the advertised telephone number. Therefore, excluding any cases who cannot be contacted by telephone may overestimate the views of medium and large employers. There may be little that the researchers could have done about this, and in a sense they have given sufficient information for the reader prepared to wade through the technical appendices. This example is used to show the importance of reading 'between the lines'. The actual response rate to this influential survey is around half of that advertised. This may affect our impression of the significance of the findings, or it may not. But we, as consumers of research, should have this information and be able to make the decision ourselves.

SUMMARY: THE STAGES IN SAMPLING

- Decide whether to use a sample, and why.
- Define the population of interest (be as precise as possible).
- List the inhabitants of the population (create a sampling frame), or characterize the population.

- Estimate the size of sample you need (consider sub-groups, stability, effect sizes and resources). Make it large.
- Choose a method of selecting population elements (consider random, systematic, stratified, clustered, or non-probability).
- Decide on methods of correction (consider response rate, refusal rate, weighting).
- Characterize the achieved sample and compare with the ideal (or the population).
- Apply corrections if necessary.

This chapter described the key stage of deciding who participates in our research. In summary, a good sample is representative of a wider population, and large, with a high participation rate. It is risky to accept the generalizations made in previous work, without first considering their sampling strategy and the potential biases this introduces. If, after reading this chapter, you would like to know more about sampling, some useful starting points would be Henry (1990), Bernard (2000), or Cohen and Manion (2000). The next chapter looks at ways of finding or collecting information for analysis by looking at sources of secondary data.

Collecting secondary data: the 'idle' researcher

USING SECONDARY DATA

Consider this. I am not involved in running our university library, have never been to Newcastle, and do not work for the Department of Education and Employment. Nevertheless, without leaving the desk in my office, I could assemble within thirty minutes:

- a breakdown of the number and type of books borrowed in Cardiff by the country of origin of all students (and therefore decide, for example, whether students from the western Pacific Rim read more books on statistics per year than those from the USA);
- an analysis of the educational qualifications of the population of Newcastle broken down by the floor level of their permanent residence (and decide, for example, whether those living above first floor level tend to have lower formal qualifications);
- a consideration of the rates of unauthorized absence from school in each region of England in relation to the local population density (and decide, for example, whether 'truancy' in secondary schools is higher in towns and cities than in rural areas).

Now, of course, these findings may be of little interest to you, and I have certainly never done any research on these topics (although see Gorard *et al.*, 1998c). They are simply examples of using what is termed in this chapter 'secondary data', which are data used by a researcher who did not also collect them. Most researchers, especially new researchers carrying out small-scale studies on a limited budget, tend to go out and collect their own new (primary) data. It takes a little experience to appreciate the value of secondary (second-hand) information, and to know what to do with it when you get it. This chapter and the next will provide that experience. My prediction is that once you have experienced the power and economy of secondary analysis you will not want to design any further studies without incorporating at least an element of it. It can transform a post-graduate dissertation from something that gathers dust on a library shelf to a project worthy of further dissemination through publication, and worthy of further attention by other researchers in your field. Yet it can take less time to complete and cost less to produce than a small questionnaire survey or a handful of interviews.

WHY USE SECONDARY DATA?

The call to make better use of existing records in social science dates back at least to the writing of Bulmer (1980) and, in a loose sense of the term, all academics already use secondary results in constructing their review of literature (Hakim, 1982). The background to a primary study, the relevance of the research questions and the importance of the findings are usually presented in relation to previous and existing work on related topics (often under the unappealing title of a 'literature review'). More recently, the drive towards creating research results with more impact has led to a demand for evidence-based practice in education (see Chapter 1). The evidence in question has generally been seen as a precise and measured type of review of existing work, using a model derived from similar 'what works' approaches in medical research. These are known as research 'syntheses' (see Cooper, 1998).

A step beyond a synthesis is a meta-analysis in which the actual results of many studies on the same topic are arithmetically combined to provide an overall answer (Glass *et al.*, 1981, see also Chapter 4). The fundamental difference between all of these and a full secondary analysis as the basis for a project lies in the notion of originality. Most academic institutions lay stress on 'originality' for their students' dissertation work, and many students therefore assume that their data must be original as well. But in the same way as it is possible for a researcher to review previous work in any field and still go on to carry out original work, it is possible for a researcher to carry out a secondary data analysis and still go on to carry out original work, but without necessarily collecting any further data.

There are many reasons why you might decide to use secondary data in a project, and these are described briefly below (and illustrated in the remainder of the chapter).

Speed and Cost
These are probably the most obvious advantages of using secondary

data. Since the data already exist they are by definition, quicker to 'collect', involving less travel and minimal cost. This means that the researcher can make a lot more progress in any given time period (such as the one year of a full-time Masters course). Some existing datasets do involve a financial charge for access, and some of these charges sound quite large when they are presented as a total. However, it is likely that even these datasets will end up cheaper to use than incurring the costs of travel, telephone, printing, postage, and subsistence involved in carrying out primary data collection. In addition, there are very many valuable datasets available free of charge or with nominal administrative costs (see below).

Sometimes the distinction between primary and secondary appears a little blurred. In assembling the data for my earlier work on the socio-economic composition of schools (Gorard and Fitz, 1998b), I needed the annual census returns from schools for six Local Education Authorities (LEAs) for as many previous years as available. These records were only held centrally (by the Welsh Office in this case) for the past two years. To get any earlier records I had to negotiate access to the six LEAs, and in most cases travel to their offices and spend half a day in a dusty cupboard full of the school census archives (for which opportunity I am still very grateful). Since this stage was the unfunded pilot for what became a much larger study, I used LEAs close to home wherever possible and arranged my visits to minimize wasted mileage. The end result was that I completed the study for a total sum of less than £100 for travel, postage and telephone. If I had ignored the existing archive material, not only would the ensuing result have taken longer and been more expensive, it would inevitably have been of significantly lower quality. As it is, this £100 project, while still the subject of considerable debate, has changed the field of school choice research and attracted both media and political interest on an international scale.

Contextualization

Although I have been involved in several small studies using only secondary data (see below for a further example), in most studies the power of secondary data is allied to the flexibility of primary data techniques. One way in which all studies can gain from integrating secondary data is to set the context for the primary data. Even relatively large-scale data collection cannot compete in size and quality with existing records, so re-analysis of these records can be helpful in a variety of ways. It can provide the figures for each strata in a stratified sample (how else do you know what proportions to use?). It can be used to assess the quality of an achieved sample by providing some background figures for the population. These figures can then be used to weight the sample if there is clear bias in its composition.

Contextual secondary data can also be used to show that a problem exists that needs to be addressed using other techniques, and to begin to describe the nature of that problem. If you intend investigating the causes of shortages in secondary Maths teachers, or the reasons for boys' under-achievement at school, for example, you need to show via secondary data that these problems actually exist (and many such media panics are based on misreading of the existing data). You can also show via secondary data something about the nature of the problem you are investigating. Are insufficient Maths teachers being trained, or are the trained teachers leaving the profession early? Are boys achieving lower school outcomes than girls at all ages and levels or only at the highest grades? Only then, once you have created your sample, justified your study and begun your examination – all via secondary data – would you sensibly move on to the primary phase of your investigation in an attempt to create a plausible explanation. I really cannot see how any researcher can avoid the necessity to use secondary data for at least the early part of an empirical investigation.

Authority, Quality, and Scale
Extremely large-scale, long-term and official datasets carry a certain authority, and this can be reflected in any further work involving the same data. A dataset like the Labour Force Survey (LFS) covers hundreds of variables relating to 150,000 people collected every three months and with the results from the last decade available in spreadsheet format. Whatever its faults (see below), it is clearly of a much higher quality than anything most of us could ever hope to achieve in a small project. Therefore, analysis of these figures can lead us to higher quality findings than we could achieve on our own, and we would be crazy to try and collect any of the variables covered in this survey ourselves. Obviously, there may be biases built into any secondary figures we use (which are discussed below), and as with our own research we need to be aware of them and work around them. Nevertheless, if you claim, for example, that job-related training for over-35s has declined in Northern Ireland in the past ten years you are more likely to be believed (and quite rightly so) if your source is a re-analysis of the LFS than if it is a survey of 100 people. Yet it will be both quicker and easier for you to use the LFS data than to collect 100 survey responses.

Cumulation

If there is a purpose to discovering new knowledge it surely involves that knowledge being used as the basis for further work, as well as for its immediate implications for policy and practice. So, apart from the need for replication which is rarely met in educational research, it may become less and less necessary to do *some* forms of primary research since these have already been completed, and more important to build on previous work. Why 'reinvent the wheel'? It is also, at least in theory, becoming harder to carry out primary research to collect data that already exist. Funding bodies allocating publicly funded grants or commissioning research, such as the UK Economic and Social Research Council, require applicants to show that they have looked to see if the data they require already exist, and to present evidence that they do not. In addition, once a publicly funded project is completed, the datasets generated must be lodged with a public data archive (see below), therefore increasing the chance for each new proposal that something similar already exists in the archive.

Cross-pollination and Originality

It may seem odd to suggest that using 'old' data can lead to more original research than getting new data, yet I believe this to be precisely the case where what I have termed 'cross-pollination' of datasets is involved. I have lost count of the number of times I have spoken to research students carrying out small-scale surveys of teachers' attitudes, or interviewing headteachers' about the management of change. While they always manage to claim originality by changing the institutional or national setting, I am afraid that I generally no longer expect the results to be definitive or even very interesting (and am therefore pleased when I am proved wrong).

Contrast this kind of small project to one that I carried out in one afternoon in my 'spare time' while a research student (see Gorard, 1998c, 1998d). As background, it is important to realize that it has been a 'given' of educational policy in Wales for a long time that schools in Wales do not perform as well as those in neighbouring England. Children have, it is argued, been 'schooled for failure', and models of improvement in Wales have therefore been predicated on policy borrowing from more successful schools elsewhere (Reynolds, 1990). It is certainly the case that in raw-score terms, schools in Wales have had lower average public examination benchmarks (such as the percentage of pupils with five GCSEs grades A*–C) than England. I set out to test whether the results for education authorities in Wales are actually worse than those of equivalent authorities in England. The key word here is 'equivalent', as Wales is a generally poorer and more sparsely populated region than England, with lower economic activity rates.

I needed, for the basic study, the examination results for each LEA in England and Wales for the past year (published annually in the series represented by DfEE, 1994a and Welsh Office, 1995a). From these I formed my outcome measures (GCSE benchmark, GCSE failure rate, and so on). I also needed estimates of the proportion of children from families in poverty (those eligible for free school meals). These formed one of my input measures, and I obtained them from the same series as the results for Wales, and from DfEE (1994b) for England. All of these booklets were in my local library. Among other input measures I used the population density, percentage of householders in each social class, and the percentage of school-age children in fee-paying (private) schools for each LEA. All of these were obtained from the 1991 population census, available on-line at any level of geographical aggregation (see below). These figures suggested (and the conclusion has now been confirmed by more complex analyses at school level) that the schools in LEAs in Wales were producing results that were as least as good as those of LEAs in England which matched them in terms of the input measures.

The findings of this simple value-added analysis ran contrary to the schooled for failure thesis. They defended children, teachers and schools in Wales, and met with considerable local media and some political interest. The study is clearly very far from perfect but it made a key contribution to an important regional debate, and like many studies has led to further research (for example, of the validity of international comparisons of educational systems). I therefore repeat what I said above. The complete study including data collection, transcription, and analysis took me one afternoon at an additional cost of less than £10 for photocopying and access to census figures. I would have been very happy to have done this study for my Masters dissertation instead of traipsing around schools conducting yet another survey (which is what I actually did). I would have saved time, money and produced more interesting results for my discussion section (something to get my teeth into). All that was involved was an idea, and the cross-pollination formed by bringing together three existing datasets in a way that had not been thought of before.

LIKELY SOURCES

Once you have opened your eyes to secondary data, the difficulty is not so much whether what you want exists but where to find it. Suggestions of likely sources are made here for illustration but the specific details, especially of Internet resources, are likely to date very rapidly. It is also the case that sources of interest will vary between countries. Obviously the search engines and databases available in your library are a good place to start (librarians themselves can be very useful), along with the search engines available on the Internet (see Peters, 1998 for an introduction to finding research material on the web, the structure of URLs, and how to guess the address you want). The Teacher Training Agency (TTA) has a website at <http://www.teach-tta.gov.uk/itt/funding/alloc.htm>. This has its own search routines and a 'quick navigation menu' leading to figures on initial teacher training targets, funding and applications, for example. The Department for Education and Employment (DfEE) has a website at <http://www.dfee.gov.uk/index.htm>. This has an index, search routine, and news flashes as well as sections on the Office for Standards in Education (OFSTED), the National Grid for Learning (NGfL), and Statistics. The Statistics section provides monthly figures back to October 1998 (at time of writing) on policies such as the New Deal, nursery provision, admission appeals against school placements, the destinations of leavers from higher education, work-based training, special educational needs, student numbers in colleges, teacher sickness absence, exclusions from school, National Curriculum assessments, teacher vacancies, pupil:teacher ratios, and class sizes (among others). It is almost a one-stop shop for the beginning secondary analyst, containing everything that appears in 'league tables' of school examination results and much more.

A further useful source is the Economic and Social Research Council Data Archive (see Useful Addresses section), which keeps a copy of the 'quantitative' datasets collected by all past ESRC-funded projects. Other Research Councils have equivalent archives. The data in these archives are available to researchers on request (and usually a fee). Whatever aspect of education you are interested in, the chances are that something similar has been done before. It is almost as important not to ignore this previous data as it is not to ignore the findings of previous relevant research in your own review of the literature. Some recent acquisitions include large-scale surveys on adult literacy, patterns of lifelong learning, and the new British Household Panel Survey. The archive retains older datasets such as the Social Change and Economic Life Initiative (SCELI) and the 16–19 Project. It also holds, or has access to, international datasets including such diverse sources as Bulgarian microdata, US marital instability over the lifecourse, the Dutch Panel Survey, and even the physical stature of Georgia convicts from 1770–1860, for example. Perhaps of more interest to most readers is the UNESCO Education Database. The related website of the Teaching Resources and Materials for Social Scientists is at http://tramss.data-archive.ac.uk/, where data from large and complex social science datasets can be downloaded along with free analytical software for multi-level modelling.

A key starting point when looking for existing data is the UK government's Central Statistical Office (see Useful Addresses section). The CSO hold a large and rapidly growing range of datasets. They produce a large number of annual publications based on these figures and, perhaps most usefully at this stage, they produce catalogues of their data and publications. These catalogues are free on request, and they include a brief guide to sources of government statistics with a list of relevant offices, publishers, and contact details. Their public enquiry services will give you, by fax or email, the latest macro-economic statistics including tables and graphs within minutes of their official release time of 9:30 a.m. There is no room here for an exhaustive list of the other publications handled by CSO, but these include the following.

The Social Focus on Children (1994) report is a summary of national statistics relating to children, such as what they read, how they spend their money, and what their leisure interests are. *Social Trends* is an annual production in book and CD-ROM format giving figures on education, health, employment, leisure, transport and housing. As it is an annual produced since 1970, an examination of past figures allows the creation of trends over time. *Regional Trends* produces similar figures on policy and life in the UK broken down by regions. *Family Spending* reports the findings of the regular *Family Expenditure Survey* (again allowing the creation of trends over time) showing how households distribute their incomes between food, travel, housing and other demands. *The New Earnings Survey* is another annual report, allowing trends over time and regional analysis, and showing ages, occupation, sex, work hours and earnings of the UK workforce by occupation or industry. *Retail Prices 1914–1990* uses the retail price index and the earlier cost of living index to present monthly figures for the price inflation (and deflation) affecting UK consumers. *Statistics of Education UK* shows the annual figures for many education-related topics (with past years to 1972 for comparison) including the number of teachers and students by school and sector, and participation and qualification rates for each age group of students. The CSO also publish descriptions of the national education systems in other countries, and annual reports of the first destinations of UK graduates, and trends and predictions for the supply of graduates to industry.

Several of these publications involve a cost. The researcher might have to pay from around £5 to around £100 for a particular survey (past years often come free). However, these costs are small in relation to the real and opportunity costs of carrying out fieldwork. Many publications should anyway be available in a local library. The data from several of these surveys, including the ten-yearly census of population, and others is available from the National On-Line Manpower Information System (see Useful Addresses section). Using this system, for which there is a registration charge, researchers have access to datasets such as the Labour Force Survey and 40 years of census returns to generate reports for chosen geographical areas. The available geographical areas include enumeration districts, electoral divisions, travel-to-work areas, and education authorities. Census data disaggregated to a local level is also available free of charge from the Manchester Information and Associated Services (MIMAS at <http://www.mimas.ac.uk/>). Using this system it is possible to calculate the Townsend Deprivation Index for enumeration districts and transfer the results to local digitized maps, for example.

The Office for the National Assembly for Wales (formerly the Welsh Office) produces the annual *Wales in Figures*, a summary of figures for population, economy, education and health. The Welsh Office Statistical Directorate, like the CSO, publishes a catalogue of their statistical publications. These include the *Digest of Welsh Statistics* which contains figures on educational issues back over several years, the *Digest of Welsh Local Area Statistics* (with figures broken down for each of the 22 local authorities), the *Child Protection Register*, two annual volumes of the *Statistics of Education and Training in Wales* – one for schools and one for post-compulsory education and training – another on schools (including their finance, number, size, type, meals service, and record of SEN statements), and an equivalent for Further and Higher Education and Training. The Welsh Office also produce their own survey data, such as the *1992 Welsh Social Survey: Report on Education and Training* (Welsh Office, 1994), the *1994/95 Welsh Education and Training Survey* (Welsh Office 1995b), the *Welsh Training and Education Survey 1995/96* (Education and Training Statistics, 1997), and the *1996 Welsh Employers Survey* (Welsh Office,

1996). The Welsh Office produces a large number of statistical briefing papers, such as those measuring progress towards the national targets for education and training (Welsh Office, 1999). The latter, along with several of the publications listed here, are free on request. Equivalent publications are available for England, Scotland, and Northern Ireland.

The DfEE 'Skills and Enterprise Network' is free to join, and provides regular reports and statistics on lifelong education and training in England. These include a quarterly Labour Market Report, with figures for training disaggregated by age, industry, gender, and so on, and with trends over time. There are also reports on graduate employment, and comparative figures for basic skills. All are currently available from DfEE Publications in Nottingham, or e-mail dfee@prologistics.co.uk, and the Datasphere website is a gateway to data and commentary on labour market, learning and skills (see www.dfee.gov.uk/datasphere). Also available from the DfEE and elsewhere are reports of large-scale educational surveys. See, for example, NACETT (1995) and later versions for trends over time in progress towards national targets for education, or the Basic Skills Agency (1997) for an analysis of patterns of literacy and numeracy skills and their lack, or Beinart and Smith (1998) for a full report of the National Adult Learning Survey 1997.

Most developed countries have equivalent sources of national data about education and training. Some have longitudinal studies, such as the US High School and Beyond Survey, and the US Cohort Study similar to the UK National Child Development Study which could make a very interesting comparison for a small project. The European Union produces a variety of statistical summaries allowing comparisons of most European education systems, and the socio-economic systems from which they emerge. It is sometimes necessary to examine two or more of these publications to get a useful set of indicators, one on education and one on wider social policy for example (CERI, 1997 and CERI, 1998, or Eurostat, 1995 and Eurostat, 1998). The Organization for Economic Co-operation and Development (OECD) also produces a range of figures on education for developing and less developed nations, often in the form of trends over time (e.g. OECD, 1993). OECD (2000) *Education at a Glance* is the latest (at time of writing) annual report of statistical information relating to the education and training systems of the members (plus 16 non-members). Some indicators therefore apply to over two-thirds of the world population. It is both a yearbook showing trends over time and an encyclopaedia showing how things stand today in terms of: the national context of education in each country; the financial and human resources invested in education; access to education, participation and progression; the learning environment and organization of schools; individual, social and labour market outcomes of education, and student achievement. Like all secondary data, especially at this high level of aggregation, the figures must be used with all the accompanying footnoted caveats in mind, and it is useful that the book includes three annexes showing how the indicators are defined, collapsed and compared over time. Nevertheless this is precisely the type of book that all of us should refer to more often for contextual figures. To whet your appetite I describe some very simple conclusions that could be drawn from such figures.

The book (OECD, 2000) starts with four pages of 'Highlights' and a three-side pull-out summary chart. These highlights generally show two patterns running across all member countries. The first pattern is one of general improvement. Indicators of real expenditure on education, and therefore on students and on teacher salaries, are rising. The average length of formal education is increasing, the prevalence of qualifications is improving, and participation throughout the lifecourse is widening. The second pattern is one of divergence. Despite (some economists might say because of) these general improvements, the differences in educational take-up within and between countries remain substantial. For example, it is recorded that between 1990 and 1998 the average time a 5-year-old can expect to spend in initial education rose from 15.1 years to 16.4 years – but the figure still varies from 12 to 20 years across OECD countries. Similarly, as part of the 'information revolution' nearly all lower secondary students in Canada, Finland and Iceland have access to the Internet. Yet despite improvements in Belgium, the Czech Republic and Hungary 60 per cent of students in these countries are in schools with no Internet access.

In the UK a higher proportion of those aged 16–25 years gained IALS literacy level 3 (56 per cent) than the same age group in the USA (45 per cent) or those aged 46–55 years in the UK (47 per cent). However, in the USA the older cohort had a higher proportion (51 per cent) than the equivalent in the UK. There are at least two possible interpretations of these, and related, figures. They could suggest that in the UK literacy skills are more a product of the initial education system, whereas in the USA they are more a product of post-school experiences. Or, they could suggest that literacy skills are improving in the UK and declining in the USA.

The UK has a relatively high ratio of students to staff in early childhood education (21.5) compared to the USA (18.0) or New Zealand (5.6). The UK has relatively high 'survival' rates for tertiary level education with 81 per cent of students completing their course compared to 62 per cent in the USA and 55 per cent in France (in a comparison of courses of similar length). Around 4.5 per cent of OECD students in their eighth grade are absent from school on a 'typical' day. However, in Scotland the figure is 8 per cent while in Japan it is 2 per cent. In the UK the unemployment rate for men aged 25–64 years without post-compulsory education (13.7 per cent) is almost twice that for women (7.3 per cent) and over twice that for UK men in general (5.6 per cent). In Spain, on the other hand, women with no post-compulsory education are more than twice as likely to be unemployed (25.6 per cent) as men (12.6 per cent). The unemployment rate of men with no post-compulsory education is hardly different from that of Spanish men in general (11.3 per cent). Why does this difference exist? Investigating this kind of question, derived from secondary data, can form the basis for a small project.

WATCH OUT FOR LIMITATIONS

Despite the obvious advantages of using data that someone else has already collected, there are potential problems with this approach to research. Such problems do not, in my view, mean that we should spurn other people's work but that we should be aware of the limitations of what we are using. We should publish these limitations, and take them into account in our findings. Even official statistics are not simple 'facts' but have been socially constructed (May, 1997), so using them may involve an unconscious acceptance of their social values.

The availability of figures can determine what is considered researchable, rather than the other way around. In choosing to use secondary figures we are giving up access to the field notes and other incidental observations we might have made during the process of primary collection. Perhaps most importantly, prolonged 'desk-based research' might lead to an unhelpful isolation from the subject of study, and therefore to a lack of practical realism in the research findings. It is also the case that the very speed and cheapness of secondary data may be seen by some as a disadvantage. Sponsors and supervisors who believe that a project should take a certain amount of time may be reluctant to accept that a quicker and superior method is available. Ironically, researchers in need of grant-funding might prefer primary analysis not because it is necessary, but because it takes longer and therefore requires the services of more research employees whose salary brings in overhead expenses to the university or research institution (although of course this is not a reason to waste public money).

Examples of the difficulties of using official statistics are endless. If the figures from the National Crime Survey depend upon the level of crime reported to the police, then changes in frequency over time could be due to changes in the level of crime or the level of reporting or both. Using secondary data we have no way of knowing which interpretation is correct (and there appears to be no simple way of deciding this point even with primary data). We need to treat secondary figures as we would any other research findings, with tentative scepticism. We would therefore need to know how the definition of unemployment has changed over time before accepting apparent changes in official figures. In international comparisons of educational test results, we need to consider the conditions under which the tests were administered in each country. When looking at improvement in scores for Key Stage assessments since their inception, we need to recall the early disruption caused by teachers' lack of cooperation in the UK. When using examination figures in any way we need to recall the difficulties of ensuring comparability of standards between subjects, syllabuses, examination boards, years, modes of assessment, and regions. A secondary analysis, done well, therefore requires a thorough examination of the pedigree of its raw materials.

AN EXAMPLE OF USING SECONDARY DATA

A recent example of a project involving only secondary data was my study with colleagues of the impact of National Targets for Education and Training (represented by Gorard *et al.*, 1999d, 2000b). As a consequence of a report by the Education and Training Action Group (ETAG, 1999) to the new National Assembly for Wales, we were asked to predict progress towards the National Targets, and make recommendations for modifying them where necessary. Although there was also an element of user consultation, the bulk of the project involved learning how progress towards targets was usually calculated, and using secondary data from a variety of sources to model future rates of progress. I shall describe two findings here, one from each of these parts of the project. Both relate to the caution above to check carefully what is actually being measured by official statistics.

One finding was that, as far as we could tell, the setting of targets for lifelong learning has had no impact at all. There has been growth towards the target figures, but only because the targets are set for those of working age. Young people leaving education today and joining the workforce generally have higher qualifications than the older people leaving the workforce at retirement. So the 'workforce' becomes more qualified without anyone of working age gaining any qualifications. If these changes are discounted, fewer people have actually been qualified as adults than was the case before the setting of targets. This is not 'lifelong' learning.

Another finding was that our estimates of the qualifications of the workforce gained from the Labour Force Survey (LFS) were considerably lower than the figures published as official indicators of progress towards the targets. This difference was mainly accounted for by official assumptions about missing answers to the survey question about people's highest qualification. The DfEE and Welsh Office assumed that cases giving no response and responding 'don't know' could be allocated a qualification level in proportion to those cases giving a valid answer. Therefore, in their analysis, an equivalent proportion of those people not responding were 'awarded' a PhD as were reported as having no qualifications at all. Attempts such as these to rectify non-response appeared to be seriously inflating the actual reported levels of qualification.

Although both of these points are clearly methodological, they are also significant findings that should have been fed back to the post-16 committee of Assembly Members as affecting the then national debate about targets. In fact, none of the members felt able to attend the dissemination organized for them by the Statistics Division of the Welsh Office. It was almost as though they did not want to hear what we had to say!

This chapter has looked at some of the advantages, and potential problems, in using secondary data. For further discussion of these points try reading Dale *et al.* (1988) or May (1997). The next chapter continues by examining some simple methods for analysing secondary data, as an introduction to the world of descriptive statistics.

4

Simple analysis: the index wars and other battles

This chapter introduces some basic approaches to working with the kinds of data discussed in Chapter 3. It should not be treated as a complete guide to calculation, or to the use of a statistical package on a computer. There are already many of these (see below). Rather, it considers some of the key issues in analysis. Chief among these is the relationship between the methods of analysis used and the substantive conclusions reported, for 'the conclusion drawn by the investigator ... is often only vaguely related to the actual results' (Rosenthal, 1991, p. 13). I would go further, and say that different methods *can* produce contradictory results using the same data. In such examples the research findings are totally dependent on the method chosen and therefore not at all dependent on the data actually collected. This chapter begins to explain how and why this can be so.

THE PRELIMINARIES

Analysis usually proceeds via the essential, but mostly trivial, stages of coding, transcription and cleaning of the dataset generated by your study. Coding of data, converting observations and responses into scales or measurements, should be relatively simple since the actual coding scheme is usually inherent in the design of your data collection (see Chapter 5). Designing the coding scheme is a complex and important issue, but not one to be faced after data have been collected (except where a reappraisal is required in light of experience). In using secondary data, of course, coding has usually already been completed for you and, as you may imagine, this is both a benefit and a source of frustration.

The key virtue in coding is consistency. Some 'authorities' argue that coding should be made into an entirely separate stage, by writing coded responses onto individual completed questionnaires for example. However, for an individual researcher (rather than a large team) I can see no great disadvantage in typing these codes directly into a computer spreadsheet or statistical package. In fact, there is considerable potential advantage in this approach since the data are then transcribed only once, rather than twice (once to the questionnaire and once from the questionnaire to the computer). As you will recall if you have ever played the game that I learnt as 'Chinese whispers', the more times a piece of data is copied, the more likely it is to get garbled. So be prepared to ignore, and defend yourself against, the coding 'fundamentalists' who will try to insist that you code and transcribe separately.

The key virtue when copying your results onto another medium is accuracy. So keep going back and carrying out spot checks on the figures entered as a form of quality control. My advice would be to carry out the transcription yourself, in a systematic way, in concentrated batches, with no one else in the room, and no distractions like background music (however much you might believe that music helps you to concentrate!). Note that even if you want to use a package like SPSS but do not have it at home, you can still do the lengthy entering of data at home into a spreadsheet file which can then be opened by a more sophisticated package at work, college or library. When using secondary data this stage has usually already been completed so your alternative task is to learn as much as you can about a coding and transcription process that has already taken place.

Cleaning your data is a slightly more complex task than coding, but less so perhaps that it would usually appear from reading research textbooks. The essential point in cleaning is to ensure that the data you eventually use in your analysis are the correctly coded version of the measurements that you took in your fieldwork. It is a long and probably never completed process. Long but not difficult. The spot checks carried out during transcription are part of cleaning. If you find that the figures on one form or questionnaire response do not match what you have entered into a spreadsheet at that point, then stop. Now trace back and find the mistake. It could be a simple typing error in that one case, but very often the mistake is a symptom of a bigger problem (your sheets are in the wrong order, you have turned over two pages at once, etc.).

Much of the rest of the cleaning process, other than simply reading or looking at your completed dataset, takes place during simple analysis using many of the procedures described in the remainder of this chapter. Techniques such as drawing graphs, and producing frequency counts, means and standard deviations can be useful when presenting data but they can also highlight further mistakes in the data coding and data entry procedures. These are easiest to spot when extreme or otherwise unrealistic scores are reported in your analysis. If the oldest person in your (alive) sample is 768 years old, then you need to go back to the original source and correct the error. Again, note that you cannot simply assume that the problem is isolated. You may have entered the respondent's monthly income as their age which probably means that you entered their age as their highest qualification, and so on. Anxiety and pedantry on your part can be accounted virtues at this stage.

The reason that some writers make cleaning appear more difficult is that they conflate this simple but arduous error-checking with the decision to remove inconvenient data from their dataset. This issue is discussed in Chapter 8. The point I wish to make here for the beginner is that cleaning must take place, and it involves the rigorous checking for the accuracy and consistency of coding and transcription. Once this is done, there may be responses that you do not believe (a 12-year-old with 2 A Levels – a qualification commonly taken at age 17 or 18) but this is another issue entirely. If the most original form of the data available to you codes into what you have in your final dataset, and the figures are all at least possible, then that is as much as you can do at present. If you start deleting/amending figures because you do not believe them then you will need a good argument to convince me and other readers that you are not on a slippery slope towards falsifying your data or simply making up convenient results.

TWO TYPES OF DATA

This discussion of simple analysis continues by drawing a tentative but useful distinction between two types of numeric data. Although too much is often made of fine distinctions between numbering scales (or levels of measurement), the novice 'quantitative' analyst must learn to recognize the differences between descriptions of categorical information and real numbers. These differences relate in an important way to the organization of the rest of this book. Chapter 6 considers the analysis of two or more categorical variables, Chapter 8 considers analyses involving both real and categorical variables, and Chapter 9 describes approaches to analysing two or more real variables.

'Real' numbers are those that it makes sense to use in arithmetic. So a simple test of identification would be – does it make sense for me to add or subtract these numbers? The number of years a teacher has been employed in a school is a real number. To find the difference in experience between two teachers we could subtract two numbers of years and find how many years more one teacher had been at the school. We can do this because the scale we use to measure time with has equal intervals all the way along. The difference between 99 years and 100 years is the same as that between 1 and 2 years, for example. A year is a year wherever on the scale we look.

Categorical information relates to categories only, and individual cases therefore cannot be subject to arithmetic operations. The sex of a teacher is a category, and we cannot subtract a maleness of one teacher from the femaleness of another to find their difference in gender. This restriction applies even where the categories are expressed as numbers. Whereas the length of my foot is a real number, my shoe size is a category (shoe sizes are not equal interval as children's sizes increase in smaller stages than those of adults). We could add two lengths but not two shoe sizes. Arithmetic operations can, however, be conducted using the frequencies of categorical data. We could, for example, find a difference by subtraction between the number of male and female teachers in a school, or find the total number of people with either of two shoe sizes. In fact, most social scientific data has elements of both types expressed as the *number* of things of a certain *category*.

Other authors pay much greater attention to measurement theory and the issue of scales than I intend to do here (see, for example, Siegel, 1956). For me the first and clearest distinction is the one just introduced between numbers we can add together and numbers used to label categories or types of things. On reading a traditional statistical textbook you will be introduced early on to measuring scales called 'ratio', 'interval', 'ordinal' and 'nominal'. But both ratio and interval measures are real numbers and I promise that the difference between them will never make any practical difference to you. There are very few interval measures (the frequently cited example of a temperature scale actually being the only one in common use, although rarely used in social science anyway), and the kinds of statistical procedures you would use, at least for the beginner, are identical to those for ratio measures anyway. So why worry about the distinction? Both ordinal and nominal scales are categorical in nature, but in many practical situations analysts use ordinal data as though it were based on real numbers (see Chapter 8), and no real harm comes from treating ordinal data as nominal in nature. Let's worry about further niceties when, and if, we encounter them.

SUMMARIZING FIGURES

This section gives a brief account of standard methods of presenting summaries of your basic figures, whether real or categorical.

Frequencies and Percentages
When data are categorical in nature the standard methods for summarizing and describing them involve frequencies (how many cases in each category), or percentages (what percentage are in each category). These summaries can be represented in a bar chart, or possibly a pie chart (but these tend to be over-used and are not that easy to read in my opinion). All of these can be produced easily using either a spreadsheet or a statistical package such as SPSS. Table 4.1 shows the frequencies and equivalent percentages in an imaginary sample of mothers with or without degrees. Mother's qualification represents a categorical variable with two categories. Table 4.1 is both precise and easy to understand. The percentage shows how many cases in every hundred have a particular characteristic. There is an, at least informal, assumption that percentages therefore refer to figures collected from hundreds of cases.

Table 4.1: Frequency of mothers with degrees

Category	Number	Percentage
Mother with degree	217	29
Mother with no degree	542	71
Total	759	100

Figure 4.1 shows the same values in a bar chart. This and all subsequent figures were drawn using a spreadsheet. For more on how to do this see Solomon and Winch (1994). The bar chart has the advantage of making it slightly easier to see the proportion of responses in the two categories but with the disadvantage that it is now harder to read off the actual values for each with any precision (although the percentages could be placed at the top of each bar for example). As the number of categories grows so the usefulness of a bar chart increases.

Figure 4.2 shows the same results again but this time as a pie chart. Although there are many advocates of these graphs, I cannot really see much advantage over the bar chart and it makes reading off any

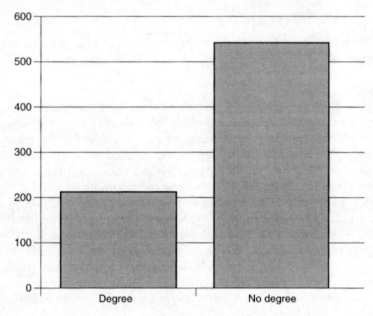

Figure 4.1: Frequency of mothers with degrees 1

figures impossible (and so necessitates the insertion of the frequency values anyway).

Simple analyses of frequencies such as these are a very useful place to start getting to know your data. In particular, they can help you identify particular features or problems in your dataset (and this applies whether you are using secondary data or have collected the information at source). If there are empty categories in your coding system, then you can delete these categories and so simplify future analyses and presentations. If, for example, there are three types of qualification that the individuals in your sample could have but no one actually has one of these types, then your analysis will proceed with only two types (and this could have important implications for the nature of your analysis, see Chapters 6 and 8). If there are entire 'variables' with no variation, then the variables themselves can be omitted from further analysis. If, for example, everyone in your sample owns a car then proceeding with any further analysis of car ownership is a waste of time.

Simple analyses of frequencies are also very useful to detect 'outliers'. An outlier is a value which is clearly out of the range expected or observed for a particular variable. You will not, for

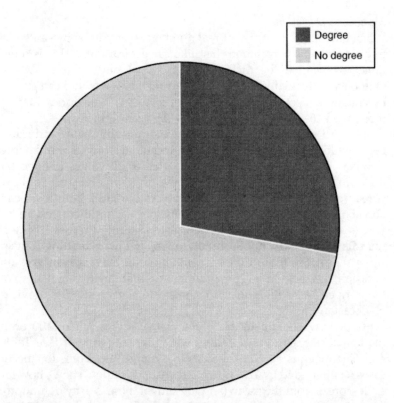

Figure 4.2: Frequency of mothers with degrees 2

example, have expected any children at school today to have been born in the nineteenth century, nor would you have expected a 73-year-old to have spent all of their life in continuous full-time education (see section on cleaning, above). What you do about such outliers is a tricky decision. You should never adjust the data without good reason and without making your changes explicit. Cleaning up data is good research practice. Falsifying data is cheating. The difference can be very slight. In the two examples here, the nine-teenth-century birth date is clearly a mistake. If you cannot correct it, then you will have to ignore it. The 73-year-old learner sounds very unlikely but this, in itself, does not allow us to ignore the finding. If we make a practice of abandoning unlikely sounding findings, then we can no longer be surprised by our research and are therefore, in my opinion, not actually doing research any more. We are seeking empirical-sounding justification for our existing prejudices.

Means and Deviations

When data are in the form of real numbers, they can be presented as frequencies and percentages just like categorical data. This is often done to examine the distribution and spot outliers (see above). Obviously this involves converting the real numbers into categories, by changing a set of individual ages into a set of categories such as those aged 16–20 years, those aged 21–25 years, and so on.

Standard arithmetic operations are also possible with real numbers (unlike categories). Standard techniques for summarizing numbers include the mean average (total of all values divided by the number of cases) and the standard deviation (a measure of how spread out from the mean the observed values are). Both the mean and standard deviation will be calculated by a computer package for you (see below). Some authorities also advocate the use of inter-quartile ranges, stem and leaf plots, or box and whisker plots to help show the distribution of data. While these do have advantages on occasion, they seldom tell you more than a high-quality tabulation of the frequencies would (and they appear to be over-used by novices on occasion).

Suppose we obtain the following set of scores out of 100 on a mathematics test from 12 individuals in an experiment (see Table 4.2). The mean is 50, computed as the total of the scores for the 12 cases (600) divided by 12. The row labelled 'deviation' shows how far each score is from the mean (and the sum of these is 0, by definition). These deviations are then squared (multiplied with themselves to eliminate negative values) and the *standard* deviation is defined as the square root of the sum of these squared values, all divided by the number of cases (or more commonly the number of cases minus one to make an arbitrary allowance for sampling error). In the example the standard deviation is $\sqrt{(2308)}/11$, or 4.37. This gives an overall idea of how spread out the actual scores are. Thus, the standard deviation (SD), by describing the amount of variation, gives an idea of how representative the mean (M) is.

Table 4.2: Scores in a mathematics test

Case	1	2	3	4	5	6	7	8	9	10	11	12	Total
score	39	45	76	34	51	51	67	46	23	49	62	57	600
deviation	−11	−5	26	−16	1	1	17	−4	−27	−1	12	7	0
squared deviation	121	25	676	256	1	1	289	16	729	1	144	49	2308

As another example, the mean of the three scores 1, 1, and 118 is 40, but 40 is not a very useful or accurate representation of that set of numbers. Their standard deviation is 47.77. So, in the first example the mean was 50 and SD was 4.37 (much smaller than the mean) suggesting that the mean is a reasonable summary. In the second example the mean was 40 and SD was 47.77 (larger than the mean) suggesting that the mean is not a reasonable summary of the figures in question. It is for this reason, above all, that whenever a mean is quoted it should be accompanied by the standard deviation. Treat the two numbers as a pair of inseparable friends.

At the time of writing there is an advertisement on UK television for Marks and Spencer clothing claiming 'if you're not average you're normal'. This peculiar sounding statement actually makes a lot of sense. The average number of bedrooms in a household may be 2.33 but no one actually has that number of bedrooms. The average earnings of UK actors in the union Equity was £15,000 in 1999, but 60 per cent of actors earned less than £4,000 and 3 per cent earned more than £100,000 (Matthews, 2000). In both cases the average is not a good guide to what is normal. It is for this reason, of course, that parents should not worry unduly if their child does not talk by the average age for such a development. If the average is a good one, then almost by definition we would expect around half of all children not to talk by that age. That is 'normal'.

THE POLITICIAN'S ERROR

The remainder of this chapter considers the slightly more complex analyses necessary when examining changes over time, or differences between things. Since the emphasis of the book so far has been on secondary analysis, an assumption is made for the rest of this chapter that we are not concerned with significance tests as such (these are introduced in Chapter 6). Rather, we shall be concerned with the apparently trivial (until examined) issue of getting our arithmetic correct. The first issue, termed here the politician's error, relates to a widespread misuse of frequencies when expressed as percentages. The importance of this misuse would be hard to over-estimate.

Imagine a country of 50 million adults, of whom 25 million are male and 25 million are female. There are 500 members of parliament (MPs or elected representatives), and all of these are male. The employed workforce is 30 million, of whom 15.125 million are male. No great analytical skill is required to see that this imaginary country has a considerable political bias towards males. Similarly, it is easy to see that the country also has a slight employment bias towards males but that the political bias is much greater than the employment bias. None of the female half of the population are MPs, while 59.5 per cent are in employment. Of the male population 0.002 per cent are MPs, and 60.5 per cent are in employment. I repeat, because of the importance of this point, that the ratio of male to female MPs is 500:0 (equivalent to an infinite amount) whereas the ratio of male to female employed is 15.125:14.875 (equivalent to 1.02). Therefore the gendered inequity among MPs is far greater than among the general employed workforce. Why am I emphasizing this point? Because the most common 'method' used to analyse such data comes to the opposite and totally wrong conclusion. This so-called method is used very widely in educational research writing, in the media, and most frighteningly of all in policy documents and policy-making. This is the method of differences between percentages.

The argument goes like this. The percentage of male MPs is 0.002 per cent and the percentage of female MPs is 0 per cent, so the difference between them is 0.002 per cent. The percentage of males in employment is 60.5 per cent and the percentage of females is 59.5 per cent, so the difference between them is 1 per cent. Since 1 per cent is much larger than 0.002 per cent, the lack of equity in general employment is greater than among MPs. This is a totally ludicrous argument making several related arithmetic mistakes, yet I would guess that all readers will have accepted this kind of 'analysis' at face value on many previous occasions. This is precisely the kind of example that leads me to argue (see Chapter 1) that all researchers, indeed all good citizens, require some knowledge of what are termed quantitative research skills. So we won't get fooled again. Perhaps you do not believe that people get away with such nonsense. Consider another imaginary example, this time written as the start of a newspaper story.

Girls leave boys in their trail!

The new GCSE results for England and Wales have just been released and they do not make pretty reading for the families of boys. While general levels of qualification continue to rise, the difference between the performance of girls and boys is growing to crisis proportions. Last year 43 per cent of girls obtained the government benchmark of five good GCSE passes while only 32 per cent of boys did. This year 58 per cent of girls got five good GCSEs and only 45 per cent of boys did. The gender gap has grown from 11 per cent last year to 13 per cent this year, reflecting the increasing problem of boys' under-achievement which faces the education system. In fact, the minister for schools was quoted last night as saying that the growing under-achievement of boys at school was one of the most serious problems faced by our society today.

Such stories, using precisely these type of figures, are commonplace in the media (see Gorard *et al.*, 1999e, 2000a for a fuller list of examples). Once you have recognized the genre, try replacing boys and girls with different ethnic groups, or regions of the UK. Try replacing GCSEs with access to health care, or car ownership. Look for an example in this week's news coverage. Can you see that the logic is the same as the example of the MPs above? In order to decide what is happening we cannot simply subtract two sets of percentages and compare the results. One of the main reasons for this is that it is not clear that the difference between two percentages is itself a *percentage*. In the newspaper example girls are not doing 13 per cent better than boys this year, they scored 13 percentage points higher than boys. The distinction is crucial. If we look at the figures as ratios as we did for the MPs we see that the proportion of girls to boys with five good GCSE passes last year was 43:32 (equivalent to 1.34). This year the proportion was 58:45 (equivalent to 1.29). What the newspaper figures actually show is that the gap between girls and boys is falling from a difference of 34 per cent in favour of girls to 29 per cent in favour of girls. So, if we are to conclude that there has been any change over time it is that boys have slightly caught up with the girls.

Of course, part of what is seductive about the percentage difference approach is that one can apparently see the gap changing over time on a graph. In Figure 4.3 the distance between the two lines is greater this year than last year. This approach is used quite widely in some respected research reports, books and journal articles (e.g. Gillborn and Youdell, 2000).

At the British Educational Research Association (BERA) annual conference in Belfast in 1998, a PhD student from my department attended a symposium on 'Education and Social Justice' in which graphs like this were used to 'demonstrate' an increase in the differences in attainment between ethnic groups in England (an important premise for the presentation). When the student asked the presenter to explain the point of the graph, the response was that the graph was obvious to all. The student continued to point to the possibility of an illusion, but the presenter defended the graph by

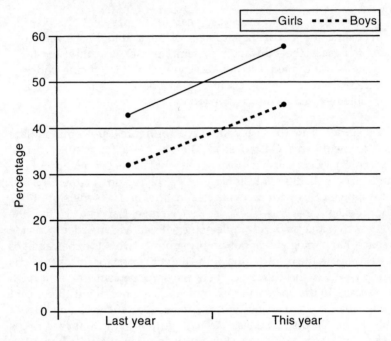

Figure 4.3: The 'growing' gap between girls and boys

accusing the student of stupidity and ridiculing him for his lack of basic arithmetic competence. To their credit, the student persisted until the chair of the session intervened and invited the audience to laugh at the student (which many did). Aside from the irony that this treatment should have been meted out in a symposium concerned with *justice*, the importance of this story is that although the senior researcher involved was wrong he could not see it even when pointed out to him. The politician's error is very seductive. In fact, despite this exchange, and the later publication of a counter-argument by the student, precisely the same graph was used for the same purpose by the same researcher in his new book two years later.

THE INDEX WARS

If we cannot use differences in percentages (or simple frequencies) to measure differences between groups, or changes over time, then what can we use? The standard reputable approach in social science is to use indices.

Consider the following example. A researcher collects secondary data from a government department about the number of students from each ethnic minority (as defined by the Registrar General for the population census) at university in England and Wales over the last five years. The researcher is also given access to the number of students attending universities over the past five years. The intention of the research is to decide whether universities have widened participation rates for students from ethnic groups other than those classified as 'White'. The researcher calculates the percentage of the total student population who are in each ethnic group for each of the five years. The researcher finds that the percentages at university in England and Wales of all ethnic groups other than 'White' have increased, and that the percentage classed as 'White' has declined in each of the five years. These findings are published as stating that participation by ethnic minorities has widened, such that the student population is now a better reflection of the total population of England and Wales. Can you see why this conclusion is unsafe? If so, you are well on the way to understanding a further reason (stemming partly from the politician's error) why we often need to use special approaches to analysing secondary data (indices).

The researcher in the example above should actually be tracking *two* trends over time. The first is the proportion of ethnic groups in universities, and the second is the proportion of the same groups in the total population. It is, of course, possible for the proportion of white students at university to decrease but for the proportion of white members of the population to decrease even faster, meaning that universities are actually increasing their over-representation of the white population. What is needed is a way of comparing the number of white students (w), the number of white members of the population (W), the total number of students (t) and the total number of people in the population (T). One formula (for the segregation ratio, see Gorard and Fitz, 2000) is: $SR = (w/t)/(W/T)$. If SR equals one, then the group in question is perfectly represented. If it is less than one, the group is under-represented, so that 0.5 means that the group has only half the expected representation, and so on. Once you have grasped this useful proportionate approach you can see that you could substitute males and females (or any categories you want) for white and non-white. You could substitute passing an examination or having a special educational need (or again any measure you want) for attendance at university. The segregation ratio is a general measure of unequal representation, which can be used to make safe comparisons over time, place and other categories because it takes into account changes in both of the proportions involved.

In our example, the segregation ratio has a problem, which is that it can only tell us about the overall figures. It might be the case that the number of white and non-white (or male/female or whatever) students was a perfect reflection of the population composition (where 80 per cent of the population and 80 per cent of students are white, for example). But there could still be considerable inequality in the system if the two groups were disproportionately represented in different universities (in the old and the post-1992 universities, for example). What is also needed is a measure of how evenly distributed the two groups are across all institutions. One formula (for the segregation index, see Gorard and Fitz, 2000) is:

$$\sum \frac{\left[\left|\frac{wi}{W} - \frac{ni}{N}\right|\right]}{2}$$

Here we are considering the pattern of distribution between the universities, rather than simply comparing the population of all universities with the total population. The value wi is the number of white students in University i, W is the total number of white students in all universities, ni is the number of students in university i, and N is the total number of students in all universities. The $|\ |$ symbols mean that we are interested only in the absolute difference between wi/W and ni/N (termed the residual), ignoring negative signs.

Using the values in Table 4.3, the segregation index is half the sum of the residuals (ignoring their signs). 80/300 minus 100/600 equals 0.1, and so on. The total of these residuals is 0.33 (one third) and half of that is 0.17. This is a measure of how segregated this imaginary university system is. Strictly speaking, it is the 'exchange proportion', which is the proportion of the white students who would have to be exchanged with others in order to achieve a perfectly balanced distribution in all universities. In this example, half of all students are white. If these were evenly distributed then University 1 would

Table 4.3: Worked example of segregation index

	White students	Total students	Residual
University 1	80	100	80/300–100/600
University 2	120	200	120/300–200/600
University 3	100	300	100/300–300/600
Total	300	600	0.33

have 50 white students (not 80), University 2 would have 100 (not 120), and University 3 would have 150 (not 100). If the 30 'extra' white students in University 1 and the 20 'extra' in University 2 were exchanged with non-white students from University 3, then there would be an even distribution of both white and non-white students. Since 50/300 is equal to 0.17, which is our calculated value for the segregation index, this tells us that the overall system is 17 per cent segregated (or that 17 per cent of white students would have to be moved to eliminate all segregation). As with the segregation ratio, this approach can be used with other categories (male/female, pass/ fail, etc.), other organizational units (schools or occupations instead of universities, for example), and any number of cases. It is a general measure of unevenness, which can be safely used for comparisons of inequality across time, place and other categories.

As can be seen, both of the indices described so far are based on a comparison between the proportion of one group and the proportion of the total population in each unit of analysis. In my experience these are the most reliable, and the closest to what we mean when we talk about segregation or inequality. However, other indices have been proposed and some of these are also in common use (such as the dissimilarity index). Since the 1930s many social scientists have been involved in 'index wars', fighting over the relative merits of each. The importance of this is, again, that the precise nature of your findings is often dependent on your selection of an appropriate index. Clearly, you cannot use differences between percentages. What you use instead requires a deeper consideration of what precisely you are trying to measure. See Gorard and Taylor (2000) or Massey and Denton (1988) for a summary of many different available indices.

META-ANALYSIS

A somewhat more advanced form of secondary analysis, and one which is likely to grow in popularity, is termed 'meta-analysis'. A traditional literature review or even a synthesis simply summarizes a set of separate research findings in a particular field, while a secondary analysis usually involves the reanalysis of figures col- lected by someone else. Meta-analysis combines these approaches by conducting a summary re-analysis of the figures from a set of separate research findings in a particular field.

One of the key current issues for education as a social science is a desire for cumulation. Much research is done, but less actual progress is made towards the creation of a body of secure and useful knowledge. For each field of investigation in education, a method is needed that can take all past studies, allot them their appropriate influence without undue bias, and so compile a clear and convincing account of the current state of knowledge in the field. Only then is it possible to see what more needs to be done. One way of achieving this aim is to use a statistical procedure for analysing a collection of findings, such as meta-analysis.

The first step for the analyst is to identify and collect all the appropriate studies to be included. These should include both published and unpublished studies (such as postgraduate theses), otherwise we could end up biasing our view of any field. It might, for example, be the case that studies leading to statistically significant results (see Chapter 6) are more likely to be published and using only these would over-estimate the effects we were analysing. There is also a danger that very original, or ideologically unpopular results are less likely to be published whatever their actual quality. Similarly, in a peer-review system where the peers used are experts in a particular field, anything which is critical of the current views of experts in that field may be less likely to be published. There is therefore, and unfortunately, a considerable amount of censorship in educational research, whereas it is vital that all available works are included in a meta-analysis. On the other hand, studies which do not report their methods or effects should be ignored, and viewed as unsafe or useless or both (even where they are published as a result of the peer-review system in prestigious journals).

In step two each study is weighted according to its size and quality. The procedure for this is clearly subjective to some extent (although panels of judges can be used) but there is little alternative. In step three the outcome measures for each study are listed. The form that these take will vary from study to study. In some cases they will be real numbers, in others they will be dichotomized measures of the presence or absence of an effect. Note that it is not necessary to have the actual data for a meta-analysis.

In step four a method of aggregation can be selected and the calculations completed, on the basis of the nature of the data collected. In fact, several models can be tried, perhaps one each based upon frequencies, rankings and correlations. Usually the analysis is constrained to work at the level of the weakest measuring scale in the various studies. One simple model would be to count those studies in which an effect appeared significant and those in which it did not – a kind of voting procedure. A more complex one would be to average the effect sizes across all studies.

For example, in the early 1990s a large number of studies looked at the reasons reported by parents for choosing a new school for their child (see Gorard, 1999c, for a literature review of this area). These studies took place in different years, regions, and even sectors of schooling. They employed differing methods, including semi-structured interviews and check-list questionnaires. It is therefore perhaps not surprising that their findings appear discordant and difficult to summarize overall. A simple meta-analysis would take the reasons reported in each study (such as 'good discipline') and the number of people reporting them, and total these across *all* studies. The result would be a good estimate of the relative importance of each school characteristic to all families faced with a choice of new school. A major problem with this approach, other than those outlined above, would be the difficulty of judging whether two choice factors which sound the same but are described using different words (such as 'good discipline' and 'firm discipline') are really identical. Only if they are identical can they be added together. Other problems with the use of extended lists in this context are described in Gorard (1997a).

There is insufficient space here to give a full description of this approach. Interested readers are advised to consult Glass *et al.* (1981) or Rosenthal (1991) for further details.

A FURTHER EXAMPLE OF SECONDARY ANALYSIS

An example of a project with significant findings using only second-ary data and taking only ten days to complete is my work with several colleagues on the differential attainment of boys and girls (represented by Gorard, 1999a, 1999b, 2000a; Gorard *et al.*, 1999e, 1999f, 2000a). The findings are still the subject of some debate, but they have clearly changed the field of research in which they appeared. Thus, as with the example in Chapter 3, they demonstrate the power and economy of working with secondary data. Having been commissioned to do the study by ACCAC (the Qualification, Curriculum and Assessment Authority for Wales), we were provided with some really powerful datasets by the Welsh Joint Education Committee and the statistics division of the Welsh Office (as it then was). These contained the public examination results for all children of the appropriate age-cohort at school in Wales from 1992–97 inclusive, and summary figures back to 1970 where possible. The figures were broken down by each Key Stage, GCSE or A Level grades, subject title, and gender. This dataset was of higher quality than those used in many previous studies for a number of reasons, most notably because it contained only the results of the 15-year-old cohort for GCSE not including the figures for adult returners for example. As with any official dataset there was still a considerable amount of cleaning and preparatory work to be done (see above). However, the stages of cleaning, analytic design, analysis and reporting took me no more than ten days of work in total (while my colleagues worked in parallel on other aspects such as the literature review and policy analysis).

The background was a 'moral panic' in the UK over the apparently growing under-achievement of boys at school, and the introduction of a plethora of suggested remedies. My conclusions were contrary to this panic. These were that in examinations at all Key Stages, GCSE and A Level there was no gender gap (i.e. no difference in overall patterns of attainment) at the lowest level of attainment. Approximately the same proportions of boys and girls of the relevant age were gaining the lowest level of each qualification (such as Level 1 at KS1 and grade E at A Level). This is good news for the assessment system, but bad news for those who were then trying to explain the gender gap in terms of boys' laddishness and poor attendance at school. The gaps, where they appeared, were greatest at the highest level of attainment mostly affecting a small proportion of the most able boys and girls.

An overall gap 'in favour' of girls existed in every year back to 1970, meaning that for as long as records exist there is no evidence that boys have ever done better than girls up to GCSE level. From 1970 to 1986 this gap was small and approximately the same every year. From 1986 to 1988 the gap grew very rapidly, so rapidly in fact that this change cannot be due to changes in society, culture or pedagogy. Again, cultures of laddishness, seating arrangements in schools, mixed or single-sex classes and so on cannot be to blame. My tentative opinion is that the rapid change arose from the flurry of policy, curriculum and assessment changes (particularly the introduction of the GCSE and associated changes) at that time. Since 1988 this gap between the achievements of boys and girls has remained relatively static but declining somewhat over time. Therefore, there appears to be no empirical justification for the recent annual panics about under-achieving boys. The gaps between other social groups, such as by first language or between rich and poor, are anyway much larger than the gender gap. This gender gap in qualification, such as it is, also declines and even reverses among adults in later life. One interpretation of these findings is that a considerable amount of government and other money is being wasted in attempting to solve a problem of boys' under-achievement at school that does not in fact exist, while much larger systematic inequalities in education are being ignored.

I repeat, these findings were controversial when first published in 1998 (and probably still are). Nevertheless, my approach to the analysis of data in this field, coupled with the quality of the data I was given, means that the findings have had some impact on a debate of national importance. Yet the work cost me very little to do, and was mostly completed using a computer in my own home. No fieldwork. No statistical analysis in the sense that we normally mean when we use the term. I did not use anything more sophisticated than multiplication in my analysis (I used a combination of the approaches outlined in this chapter). Secondary analysis has a lot going for it.

COMMON PROBLEMS IN SIMPLE ANALYSES

This section presents what I consider to be some of the most common problems in the educational research literature when presenting simple summaries of numeric data (aside from the ubiquitous politician's error discussed above). Several of these problems relate to percentages – a genuinely useful but much abused way of presenting proportions.

- using presentation to conceal numbers;
- saying the opposite to data presented;
- bogus averages;
- missing comparators.

Using Presentation to Conceal Numbers
Numbers have a rhetorical appeal all of their own, thereby giving apparent authority to a numeric presentation or article. Given this, it is very easy to allow the presentation of numbers to obscure the actual evidence supposedly being revealed. Sometimes this may be unintentional on the part of the author, while on other occasions there may be a deliberate intention to deceive. An example is the appeal to 'accuracy' stemming from the presentation of numbers to an unjustified number of decimal places. I have seen a score for an attitude scale (see Chapter 5) presented as '4.29341', representing an average for a series of integers based on a sample of 20. Is the author

really wishing to argue that their scale is accurate to five decimal places?

I recently read a report which stated that 60 per cent of the population have a computer at home, and that 40 per cent of these had access to the Internet at home. The word 'these' is used ambiguously. Later in the same piece, the figures were used in a way that made it clear that the author believed that 40 per cent of the population had access to the Internet (not the true figures of 8 per cent, or 40 per cent of 60 per cent). The first is certainly what some political observers have taken it to mean.

In another example, Swadener and Hannafin (1987) converted the responses of the 32 'subjects' in their study into percentages, so that one individual's response is reported in the paper as 3.1 per cent. Having effectively obscured the small size of their sample from the casual reader, they then proceed to divide the cases into two groups by level of attainment, and then divide these groups by sex. Eventually they have some groups with as few as five cases. When they compare the four groups in terms of their responses on the main variable for the investigation (the perceived usefulness of computers), they found no significant difference between the groups of five people. This was then reported in the abstract as their overall finding – that gender and ability make no difference to use of computers! The finding should not be seen as convincing since the numbers involved are too small, but I suspect some readers, perhaps even the referees of the paper, remained unaware of this due to the authors' use of percentages for very small numbers. I believe that 'percentage' implies 'in every hundred', so as a rule of thumb I recommend only using percentages for cases numbered in hundreds.

Another common example of disinformation appears in the labelling of graphs. In a paper by Pike and Forrester (1997) seven ostensibly similar graphs are presented. Six of these have the origin of the y axis at zero, but the seventh has the origin at 3.4. No reason is given for this, but the effect is to make the variations in the seventh graph appear much greater. Watch out for this, as it is a common problem (especially in media reporting). The seven graphs are presented as line graphs. The lines connect two points on the x axis representing, for example, 'use of stories' or 'textbooks'. These two points are categories, and the line is therefore misleading, whereas a bar chart should be preferred. Other problems in this particular paper include the lack of specification of: the population, the method of sample selection, the number of schools in the study, and the size of each of the age groups involved. These serious omissions are not due to lack of space since a large amount of apparently irrelevant information is given instead. As with the previous paper, the main conclusion was the absence of an effect between groups. Yet with six unspecified groups from a total sample of 62 perhaps little else could be expected (see Chapter 2). This paper had been peer-reviewed before publication in the journal *Educational Psychology*, and was a report of a study funded by the ESRC. It therefore represents work supposedly at the pinnacle of UK social science today.

Saying the Opposite to Data Presented
There are many examples of reported results in which the findings presented in tables are not in agreement with the accompanying description written by the researcher. These could be due to misprints, or to the inefficient working together of a team in which one person does the calculation and the other the writing, or to simple slips. Slips are common when working with notions like occupational class and socio-economic status. Where class is measured on a numbered scale it is traditional for more prestigious ('higher') classes to be denoted by lower numbers (see Chapter 5). So where a figure for class gets lower (i.e. smaller), it actually represents a move towards a higher class. This could explain what happened in Waslander and Thrupp (1997) for example. They claim in their text that certain schools have moved towards a pupil body with a more prestigious class profile, whereas their tables make it clear that the opposite happened (see Gorard, 2000c for more on this and other examples).

Bogus Averages
Perhaps because computers/calculators are so accommodating and will find the average of any column of figures we want, the use of bogus averages is frighteningly common. These arise when figures are added together and divided by the number of figures even where each figure is not of equal importance (or even where they are not real numbers). For example, if the average number of A Level points per candidate from 1995–99 was 12 and the average for 2000 was 18, it is not the case that the average for 1995–2000 is 15 calculated as half the total of 12 and 18. The average should be $(5 \times 12 + 18)/6$, or 13.

In an example of this type of error, Noden (2000) calculates the local level of socio-economic segregation in secondary schools using a specialist index of the type described above. This is fine. He then proceeds to calculate the national level of segregation by finding the average of all of the local figures. Noden adds the indices for each

Local Education Authority (LEA) and divides the total by the number of LEAs regardless of the size of LEAs (and it should be recalled that the smallest LEAs have one secondary school and the largest have hundreds of schools). Therefore, if Merthyr Tydfil LEA (4 schools) had a segregation index of 0 (no segregation at all) while Essex LEA (380 schools) had a segregation index of 1 (total segregation), then their 'average' according to Noden would be 0.5. The 'average' of these two areas should actually be close to 1 (the score for the majority 380 schools). If after a number of years, the index for Merthyr was 1 and for Essex it was 0, Noden would conclude that average segregation had not changed from 0.5, while it had actually reduced considerably from near 1 to near 0. A simple arithmetic slip such as this leads to clearly bogus 'findings', but this (and it was not the only serious error) was not picked up by the peer review system for the distinguished journal in question.

Missing Comparators
One of the most pervasive, and hard to eliminate, errors in simple data analysis is the omission of a crucial comparator. This allows writers to present one set of results as though they were in contrast to another, as yet, unspecified set. If done smoothly, many readers will never notice the error. Studies with missing comparators are widespread, almost by design, in a lot of what is termed 'qualitative' research. Social exclusion, for example, is commonly investigated through a consideration of the supposedly excluded group by itself, giving the reader no idea of how different the experience of this group actually is from the implicit 'included' group (who are often not even defined).

As an example of the power of this error in dealing with numeric data, look at the following question: 'A large survey discovered that fewer than 5 per cent of 21 year olds who had passed one or more A Levels were unemployed. Why is this not necessarily evidence that passing A Levels helps people to avoid unemployment?' When I used this as part of an examination for a cohort of 245 second and third year Social Science undergraduates I received some very imaginative replies about the difficulties of establishing comparable qualifications for A Levels, and alternative definitions of unemployment depending on whether full-time undergraduates themselves could be included in the study. All of these answers gained some credit. Only two candidates pointed out that they would, in any case, require the equivalent rate of unemployment for 21 year olds *without* A Levels. Only two. That is the power of the missing comparator (I therefore suggest no general criticism of the ability of these students). So widespread has this error become that it can almost be accounted a technique, used most prominently by politicians and by the media in reporting crises in education.

It is surprising how often commentators have a 'missing comparator' when describing changes over time. In some cases this lack is obvious, and a case in point was a recent claim that there is a growing gap in the school performance of boys and girls. This claim was backed up by the benchmark percentages for boys and girls separately but for only one year. However, figures from one year can only be used in this context to establish the existence of a gap (or not). They cannot tell us anything about growth over time. The report by Ghouri (1999) claimed 'Ministers are alarmed by a *growing* literacy gender gap. In last year's key stage 2 tests, almost two thirds of boys failed to reach the required standard in reading compared with 20 per cent of girls' (p. 9). Nowhere in the piece is there any justification given for the use of the word 'growing'. The reader is given only the figures for one year.

This chapter has considered some elementary forms of analysis, leading to descriptive statistics. As you will already have seen, there are serious debates and misunderstandings even at this simple level of analysis (and we have not even begun looking at what most people think of as 'statistics'). Please do not be scared by this statement – rather, the reverse. Be empowered. If you have followed most of the book so far, then your understanding of 'quantitative' research is already far higher than that of the majority of educational researchers. If, on the other hand, you found it difficult, then remember that you are not alone. For a reminder of simple calculation techniques and an introduction to probability, the use of spreadsheets, and simple descriptive statistics see Hinton (1995). For more on the initial use of SPSS see Solomon and Winch (1994), for example. For a simple introduction to statistical tests see Clegg (1990), and for more on SPSS see Babbie and Halley (1995), Rose and Sullivan (1993), Norusis (1993) or Bryman and Cramer (1990). The next chapter looks at collecting your own data via a survey process, and Chapter 6 introduces simple statistical tests using two categorical variables.

5

Surveying the field: questionnaire design

WHY DO A SURVEY?

Many new researchers appear to assume that their project must be based on a questionnaire survey, just as many appear to assume that it should be based on semi-structured interviews. Indeed, the practice is so widespread in educational research that some commentators appear to equate quantitative approaches only with surveys. However, the 'decision' to use a survey is often quite hard to justify – Gillham (2000b) considers the relative merits of interviews and surveys. Surveys are generally inferior as a design compared to experiments as they are less well theorized (see Chapters 7 and 8). Even good ones cannot hope to establish a causatory explanation for any observed phenomenon. Surveys are also generally less complete than official statistics, providing data of poorer quality (see Chapters 3 and 4). Their use is therefore far from automatic, and should be as reasoned as any other stage of the research design.

The use of a survey is indicated when the data required do not already exist, and the research questions are not susceptible to experimental trial for practical reasons such as lack of resources or ethical constraints. They are better at gathering relatively simple facts (such as respondent's highest qualification) or reports of behaviour (such as how often the respondent misses school) than at gathering opinions, attitudes or explanations. Viewed in this way, a survey is not a positive solution to a design problem but almost a position of last resort (and much the same comments could be made about the equally common approach of completing a couple of dozen interviews with a 'grounded theory' analysis). According to Gillham (2000a), no single method has been so abused as the questionnaire – 'the quick fix of social research methods'. Since even good ones tend to generate much poor data, when they are used it is perhaps better that they are used as part of a larger study also involving other approaches.

SAMPLING

The intricate steps involved in selecting a sample (see Chapter 2) should come before the other stages of survey design. Obviously the sample does not actually have to be selected first, but you should at least have made all of the sampling design decisions first. Most importantly, you need to make a preliminary decision about the population, sample size, and method of selecting cases. Many of the problems in survey design that follow have no best solution, but must be considered in relation to the sample required.

For example, if the population of study is 5-year-old children then a postal questionnaire is not likely to be appropriate and a face-to-face interaction may be preferable. Since face-to-face delivery is more costly in research time than postal, the sample size may therefore need to be smaller. On the other hand, if the population is all the householders in the country and the method of selection is random, then a postal delivery would seem more efficient. Face-to-face delivery would be very difficult since there would most likely be a widely scattered sample in geographical terms, necessitating arduous travel to remote areas for rather small clusters of cases. The research process is therefore iterative and messy, not linear like following the steps for an instant cake mix. Your sample depends in part on your instrument, which depends in part on how you intend to analyse the results, which depends in part on your research questions etc.

For simplicity this chapter assumes that the respondents are people, but a survey does not have to be of people. It could be of books or buildings, for example (and the comments made here would still apply).

METHOD OF DELIVERY

A key decision affecting the likely response rate, cost, speed, sample size and length of your questionnaire is how you intend to deliver it to your sample. There are many variations, but the most common choices are between face-to-face, self-administered, and technology-based. In the following discussion, these are, by implication, being compared with each other.

Face-to-face Delivery

Face-to-face delivery takes place when the researcher is present while the questionnaire is being completed, and can therefore record the responses themselves. This approach is very useful in allowing a wide response which includes those with low levels of literacy, and those with visual challenges, who would find a self-administered questionnaire very difficult. Face-to-face the researcher can read the questions aloud, explain any difficult points if necessary, and record the responses in as much detail as desired. Since they are present, the researcher can also check who is answering the questions (i.e. that it is the right person), and can stop them answering the questions in a non-standard order (i.e. by flipping ahead to see what is coming).

Conducting a door-to-door survey where you are invited into someone's home, given tea and seated on their sofa, can be a very rewarding experience. It is also possible to take a longer time, for a fuller set of questions, than you might achieve in requesting a postal response, for example. As well as being on hand to explain difficulties, you can use cue cards and visual mnemonics easily (lists of possible multiple-choice responses perhaps), and can even add an element of multi-media via a laptop computer if this is deemed helpful. In their own homes, respondents can also check the accuracy of their answers by reference to their personal records such as certificates, diaries, and so on. Maybe the single most important advantage of being present at the administration of a survey is the potential for observation, field notes and *ad hoc* interviews that other methods of delivery deny you. You can see facial expressions, type of house, age of car and a hundred other little details that might help you interpret your findings. You can talk to other people on the way in and out of the interview, and these 'staircase' meetings can be very fruitful for new ideas or contacts. Once you are on the road, everything becomes data.

The biggest single drawback for this form of delivery is the length of time it takes, and the practical consequences of this. Whereas postal surveys, for example, allow parallel mailings far afield, a visit requires travel and so constrains the nature of the sample used. Travel is more expensive than sending a questionnaire the same distance. This also creates a greater temptation to shirk on the call-back procedure for those not available at first (if you have to travel 200 miles to see someone and they are not there, will you really go back and try again next week?), and so leads to possible bias in the sample. If the research takes a long time to complete, then the nature of the phenomenon under investigation may change (due to new legislation, the natural ageing of children, etc.).

If the time problem is solved by having a team of researchers working in parallel, the design now faces the problem of ensuring consistency between them in terms of their administration of the questions. It is clear even from work with tight experimental designs (see Chapter 7) that the presence of the researcher gives unconscious cues to the other participants. This point is even more important in the more relaxed design of a survey. Respondents will react to the appearance, manner, body language and tone of a face-to-face interviewer in a way that is simply not possible using other methods of delivery. Other actors in the scene can also play a part. I once piloted a household questionnaire that asked the householder about the number of life partners they had, prior to their current relationship. It became quite clear, and seems obvious in retrospect, that the presence of their current partner making us coffee in the next room was creating a constraining influence. Finally, and quite importantly for the individual novice researcher, there is the personal safety aspect. Although unlikely, respondents might be abusive or threatening and whereas abuse by letter or telephone is unpleasant, face-to-face such a breakdown of communication is extremely alarming. All these potential advantages and disadvantages should be taken into account before a decision is made on the most appropriate compromise.

Self-administered Questionnaires

Self-administered (by the respondent) questionnaires are usually mailed. In educational research there are also considerable opportunities for dropping off and collecting forms in batches at institutions such as schools, thereby reducing the cost of postage and travel. If the respondents complete the survey form themselves, there are several key advantages. There is much less of the reactivity effect or interviewer bias which can be created by the presence of someone who has a vested interest in the results. It can be arranged that the responses are not only confidential (which is standard practice) but also anonymous (so that even the researcher does not know who completed each returned form). This can help create an atmosphere of trust and therefore lead perhaps to more truthful answers. This method of delivery is also easier if the questions come in batteries of similar types with the same scaled response (e.g. from agree to disagree) or where the list of possible multiple-choice responses is very long. Both of these designs are difficult to handle efficiently face-to-face without resorting to at least some elements of self-adminis-tration (such as show cards). Self-administered questions can also be presented in a form, such as optical marks, that are already computer readable, thus avoiding the time and potential errors involved in coding and transcription. They can be sent and returned via e-mail with many of the same advantages (see below).

There have been claims that the average response rate to postal surveys is low (20 per cent perhaps), but these claims tend to conflate figures from market 'research' which are generally lower than those from academic studies. Following the advice given in this chapter should lead you to much higher rates than those generally quoted. Aim high. Bernard (2000) suggests there is little real difference between the response rates for face-to-face surveys (80 per cent) and for well-designed mail surveys (73 per cent+).

If the researcher is not present at administration, they cannot check the identity of the respondent, or for frivolous treatment of the questions (Gillham, 2000a). They cannot preserve the order of read-ing the questions, and therefore the secrecy of later questions, and they are not available to explain the meaning of questions or to answer questions about the use to which the data will be put. Self-administration is clearly impossible for those unable to read or write effectively.

Technology-based Delivery
To a large extent, the use of ICT and technology-based delivery represents a compromise between the previous approaches. This is most obvious in the use of telephone surveys where no travel is involved and the interviewer is depersonalized to some extent (although not their accent or speech patterns), but is still available to explain questions and help motivate the interviewee. Although there is a charge for telephone calls, the cost of these is dropping relative to mail delivery and travel, and with an appropriate sample can actually lead to the cheapest form of questionnaire delivery. There are no problems of gaining access via security guards, receptionists, 'doormen' for apartment blocks, etc. The use of random digit dialling is very convenient, does not require a list of telephone numbers to start with, and can avoid the bias introduced to such lists by ex-directory and other unlisted numbers. As your research career takes off, and you find yourself running a survey with several investiga-tors, then the use of a telephone schedule with a switchboard will allow you to monitor centrally the quality and consistency of the work of each interviewer in your team.

E-mail approaches are even better in some respects, leading to cheaper use of telephone lines (or digital television), easier access to world-wide samples, and presently at least an atmosphere of camaraderie and friendly informality. Response rates to e-mail surveys may also be better than by telephone. Selwyn and Robson (1998) cite examples of between 50 and 90 per cent response rates using e-mail and they compare this to rates of between 20 and 50 per cent in conventional mail surveys (Frankfort-Nachmias and Nachmias, 1996). The times taken to respond are excellent, almost instantaneous, and the responses can be returned in an already computer-readable format.

The disadvantages of using technology to collect your data are relatively obvious. Random digit dialling cannot distinguish between the number of telephone lines for each area code, thereby over-representing those from rural areas. Not all potential respondents have a telephone, and not all who do have a telephone appear in published lists of numbers. In Wales, for example, as many as 10 per cent of people in 2000 do not even have access to a shared public payphone at home (Gorard *et al.*, 2000c). As many as 67 per cent of people in Wales in 2000 do not even have access to a computer (never mind whether it is e-mail-capable) either at work or home. In addition, and in general, those who do not have access to telephones and computers are systematically different from those who do. Any of these forms of technology are less likely to be available to those who are older, unqualified, or economically inactive. The potential bias from this is considerable when using e-mail in particular, so in order to obtain the response rates suggested above, any remotely delivered questionnaire must be brief (see the example below). In addition to all of these problems, anonymity of the sort possible in mail surveys is often just about impossible (else how do you know the telephone number or e-mail address?), but much of the tacit information available face-to-face is lost.

If I had to have an overall preference, it would be for self-administered questions delivered either by mail, or preferably by the researcher to natural groups of respondents (such as school classes, see Gorard, 1997b). This approach is generally better if the respondents are literate, well motivated, and have no clear need for individual attention. Whichever method you consider for the delivery of your questionnaire, bear in mind the issues described above, such as cost, time, geography, length, complexity, control of the question order, visual aids, the use of respondents' personal records for reference, rapport, sensitivity, sample bias, response rate, response bias, knowledge of non-responders, and so on. Perhaps a combination of methods can maximize the advantages to you as the researcher.

TYPE OF SURVEY

Another topic for brief consideration before we get to the design of the actual questionnaire instrument is the type of survey you are planning. You may find thereby that there are constraints imposed upon your design. What is the goal of the survey? Is it, for example, to describe something accurately or to test one or more hypotheses? Is it to be a one-off snapshot of a certain period, or will it collect historical information? Is it to be repeated in the future, or will it repeat questions from previous studies?

A longitudinal (repeated) survey allowing prolonged study of the lives of one group of respondents has many attractions. Data from such a study could be richer, may be more accurate and would help us to understand the process of change over time. However, it would also be expensive, time-consuming, and might entail many compromises. It can lead to complex statistical problems, so that longitudinal data are often collapsed into a format of one or more cross-sections for analysis anyway (Crouchley, 1987). Long-term studies also suffer from respondent attrition, so that even the best ones may end up with an overall response rate which clearly suggests bias through self-selection in the sample (Dolton *et al.*, 1994). For example, Banks *et al.* (1992) had response rates of between 60 and 70 per cent for the first sweep of their study, but if this response rate remained similar on each occasion that they attempted to contact the original respondents in successive years, then the overall response rate for the third sweep could easily be less than 25 per cent of the original target sample. The respondents in the Banks study became proportionately more middle class in each wave. Similarly, only 45 per cent of the respondents in the Youth Cohort Study took part in all three sweeps to 1991 (Whitfield and Bourlakis, 1991). Long-term studies also face a threat to internal validity coming from the necessity to test and re-test the same individuals (Hagenaars, 1990; see also Chapter 7).

One way around this is to use a trend design collecting data from different groups for each sweep, but this design does not allow a consideration of change in individuals, and since the second sample is not from the same population as the first, in the statistical sense, then this causes problems in looking for changes in population parameters over time. A compromise, which might have the advantages or the disadvantages of both, is to use a rolling sample whereby a proportion of the sample for each sweep remains longitudinal. For example, the Labour Force Survey (see Chapter 3) contacts 80,000 households every three months, of which 60,000 have also been used in the previous quarter.

Longitudinal studies also face problems of comparability over time (Glenn, 1977). In educational research, the modes and titles of certified public examinations change over time. Even where equivalencies between them are established, it is not clear that their value-in-exchange actually remains constant. An 'A' Level may have meant a lot more in 1970 than in 1990, not because it was any harder to attain, but simply because there were fewer of them. However, such considerations are even more problematic for a long-term study since the instrument to be used for all sweeps has to be designed before the changes that it needs to encompass take effect (a nearly impossible task), or else has to be changed between sweeps, exacerbating comparability problems and opening researchers to the charge that the study is not actually longitudinal as the questions have changed.

A retrospective study, asking respondents to recall past events, has the advantage of hindsight. A retrospective, as opposed to a simple cross-sectional, study also avoids many of the other problems noted above. Retrospective learning histories, such as the National Training Survey 1975/76 (Greenhalgh and Stewart, 1987), and employment histories, such as the 1984 Women and Employment Survey (Martin and Roberts, 1984), are much used by economists (McNabb and Whitfield, 1994). They are not, of course, immune to criticism since a wide range of life variables and events may be difficult for the respondents to recall (although the use of household records can be encouraged). Among these variables are attitudes, which are notoriously unreliable *post hoc*, and some figures such as income and health measurements (Davies, 1994).

All these factors need to be considered before designing an instrument for replication, retrospective, or longitudinal work, or a snap-shot picture (and they obviously also have implications for drawing the appropriate sample).

INSTRUMENT DESIGN

Before writing actual questions it is useful to consider the overall design of your questionnaire instrument. Perhaps the most crucial issue here is the order in which items will appear. This applies to the order of the questions in each section, and the order of each section within the whole. A good example of the importance of the first of these points is provided in the novel *Yes Prime Minister* (Lynn and Jay, 1986), where the Prime Minister's Cabinet Secretary is demonstrating to a colleague how surveys can be designed to produce whatever result a government official wants. If, for example, the government wants support for their plans to reintroduce compulsory National Service in the armed forces, they might ask their sample the following series of questions.

1. Are you worried about the rise in crime among teenagers?
2. Do you think there is a lack of discipline and vigorous training in our schools?
3. Do you think young people welcome some structure and leadership in their lives?
4. Do you think young people respond to a challenge?
5. Might you be in favour of reintroducing National Service?

Here, there is strong encouragement to answer 'yes' to question 5 to maintain consistency if you have answered 'yes' to the previous questions. Then, of course, only the responses to question 5 are published under the heading 'Majority of public support National Service'. If, on the other hand, an opponent of the government wishes to obtain a contrary view, they might ask the following series of questions.

1. Are you worried about the danger of war?
2. Are you unhappy about the growth of armaments?
3. Do you think there's a danger in giving young people guns and teaching them how to kill?
4. Do you think it is wrong to force people to take up arms against their will?
5. Would you oppose the reintroduction of National Service?

Here, there is strong encouragement to answer 'yes' to question 5 again even though it now says the opposite of the version above. Again, only the last responses might be used and published under the heading 'Majority of public oppose National Service'.

Now I am not advocating that either of these approaches is used, or that you should use leading questions at all. But this example does show how sensitive our responses can be to the precise ordering of questions in a questionnaire. Other than being aware of the problem, the best defence might be to use more than one version of your questionnaire with differing question orders. You can then allocate these versions randomly to your sample, and analyse their responses in terms of the sub-groups faced with each version. If there is no obvious difference in the response patterns between groups, then you can report with some conviction that order has been eliminated as a possible confounding variable in your results. If there *is* a difference between responses to different versions, then at least you can use these as an estimate of the size and direction of the bias.

The sections of a typical questionnaire might include an introduction (to secure the cooperation of respondents), a question or two about the respondent (as a selection, identification or quota check to make sure you are addressing the right person), the substantive questions (about the research), and background questions (concerning respondents' personal characteristics). This list is in a logical order. The introduction is first. The selection check ensures that no time is wasted answering questions unnecessarily. The substantive questions come next as they are the most interesting and are, after all, what the respondent has agreed to answer. The background questions come last because although important, they can appear intrusive. Therefore having them at the end encourages people to start the questionnaire, and once started they are more likely to complete the task. It also means that even if they drop out at this section you still have their responses to the substantive questions (and you may not need background data from everyone).

The introduction should be brief and easy to follow. It might contain the purpose of the study, who is conducting it, who is paying for it, why it is important, what will happen to the results, and why the respondent has been selected. Rather than having a complex introduction, it is preferable to use a separate covering letter. This letter could briefly explain the nature and purpose of the study, how the respondent was selected, why their help is needed, and how to return the completed form (or even if it is incomplete). If you know the respondent's name it is probably better to use it, but reassure them of the confidentiality of their answers (so if the form has any identifying marks these should be explained). Some authorities suggest using stamps on the pre-addressed return envelopes. This can be expensive, especially for an unfunded study. Alternatively, try and arrange to use FREEPOST (through your department perhaps). In this way you will only have to pay postage on those forms returned, and potential non-respondents will not be tempted to steam off your unused stamps.

If possible, do not put any questions on the front cover, but have a title and the name and address and lots of space. Similarly, on the last page you could have a simple word of thanks and lots of inviting space for any open-ended comments on the survey as a whole. Although the use of incentives for completing the form are sometimes advocated, I prefer to encourage a full response by stressing the value of each response to the study. It is also useful, and courteous, to offer to supply all respondents with a summary of your eventual findings. Curiosity about research, especially in the area of education where everyone is an 'expert', is a key motivator. Generally, the use of the words like 'University' early on in the document are useful to establish that there is no sales or advertising threat to follow. For similar reasons, words like 'study' and 'research' are more attractive to respondents than 'survey'. The use of photographs or elaborate logos on the front page is dangerous. Whatever you intend them to signify, such illustrations are easily misinterpreted.

The first substantive question in the instrument should be relevant to all respondents (since if it only applies to some, then this can be demotivating for the others), easy and interesting (so put harder or duller questions towards the end), but non-threatening and probably closed in format (see below).

I recommend a questionnaire of eight pages maximum, or preferably less for self-administered instruments. Or looked at another way, do not go much above 100 separate questions (and even this figure presupposes that most questions use the same format). Use a standard paper size (A4 in the UK), printed in black on a white background (although some authorities suggest light green is the most attractive paper colour). Questions should be grouped as far as possible into topics, with spaces between them. Each question should have no more than two sentences of instruction, and a different typeface should be used for instructions and questions. Using a different typeface to emphasize instructions is a good idea, as long as both typefaces are similar. Altering between capitals, bold, or italics, or even a different font size can be effective, with the instructions in capitals and questions in lower case, for example. Use a normal-sized reading font (12 or 14 point). Changing the font entirely (e.g. between Times and Courier) rarely works aesthetically.

Minimize, or eliminate entirely, the use of skip and filter questions or branching instructions asking respondents to move to a question other than the next in sequence. I have seen branching questions go badly wrong with even the most motivated and educated respondents (try getting undergraduates even in their final examinations to read and follow an examination rubric which is not like the one in the sample paper!). For similar reasons, although it is tempting to save paper, use only one side of each sheet. I once found that the responses to a six-side questionnaire from an entire school only covered the three sides which faced them as they flicked through the instrument. That was a very false economy for me. Again, for similar reasons do not split a question between pages.

Like many readers (I suspect) I very rarely use the grammar checker on my word processor. It just appears to continually criticize my use of the passive voice. The one occasion on which I would thoroughly recommend it is when designing a questionnaire. The grammar involved should be simple and clear, the spelling standard for your audience, and the meaning of each sentence easy to understand. Most checkers will provide you with a readability report, including measures such as a Flesch Index of readability. Make sure that the questionnaire is of an appropriate readability for the age and literacy of your entire target sample. If you are working in one language and translating your instrument into another language before completion (a common process for overseas students), then use the technique of back translation as well. In this, the translated version is translated back into the original language by a third person as a check on the preservation of the original meaning.

Finally, where possible, it is useful to have the responses pre-coded on the actual form, but also to allow space for respondents to make further comments (which are often the most interesting part of the response). Above all, do not cut corners. If, and this is a big 'if', a survey is to be your main method of data collection, then you need it to be successful. Don't be mean with photocopying, or paper, or postage. If you cannot afford to carry out a proper survey, then do not attempt it.

QUESTION DESIGN

As with the collection of secondary data (see Chapter 3), it is important to realize that you do not have to start any questionnaire from scratch. Many questions are 'old favourites' (see below). Also, many instruments are available commercially, and many are available from academic and other public archives. For example, the ESRC Data Archive (see Useful Addresses section) has the complete instruments used in much of their publicly funded social science research in the UK. The Centre for Applied Social Surveys (CASS) (see Useful Addresses section) has a large question bank formed from past studies (whose current address is http://qb.soc.surrey.ac.uk). The advantages of using such previous instruments and questions are clear. The instruments will have been piloted and used previously, probably on a far larger scale than you could envisage. They will be mature and ready to use. They may carry some extra authority for your readers. Most usefully, they will enable you to compare the responses in your study with those gained previously, to show changes over time or between locations. Looking at other questionnaires also helps you see what is good and bad about them, and this should give you confidence since even many famous instruments look terribly imperfect in retrospect.

Question design is the key to survey analysis. You do not commit yourself to any particular form of analysis just by thinking about it before designing your questions, but you do restrict the kinds of analysis available to you by the design of your instrument. Therefore, as I have already emphasized, consideration of analysis is more like the first rather than the last stage of research design. You do not want to ask any question that you cannot analyse, otherwise you will waste resources in preparing the question, waste the respondents' time in answering it (so endangering response rate), and waste more of your time coding and entering the responses. Even worse, you may need an answer to a particular question, but have asked the question in the wrong form (or even the wrong question). Each question should therefore have an explicit purpose. Once you have formed the question you need to consider whether the respondents could know the answer, can report their answer, whether they would want to, or might be tempted to lie or pretend, or would be in a rush and make a mistake?

There are many different forms of questions. They include requests for information (such as 'how many?'), tick-box categories ('yes or no'), multiple choice ('which of these?'), scales ('how strongly do you feel?'), ranking procedures ('put the following in order'), grids or tables (for multidimensional questions), and open-ended questions. Each of these is discussed below.

One of the biggest problems you will face in designing a question is likely to be that you end up using the wrong metric or level of measurement (see Chapter 4). This will affect the power and type of statistics that you can use later. You can sometimes convert from one scale to another afterwards but this introduces bias and measurement error, so it is better to ask the questions in the form that you are intending to analyse them. At best, using the wrong metric loses power and is therefore equivalent to using a smaller sample. You are effectively throwing away responses.

The best metric to use is a real number such as age, number of children, or years in school. This allows the use of all/any statistical tests including the most powerful. The weakest, but the most common metric in social science is a categorical variable, such as gender or family religion. Sometimes these categories are artificial such as occupational class (see below). If the use of categories is unavoidable, then I advise keeping the number of categories per question to a minimum. Thinking that using more categories leads to greater accuracy is a fallacy, and I have too often seen students collect answers on a seven-point scale and immediately collapse the responses to the three-point scale they intended to use all along. Why bother, and why make respondents worry about seven points?

Open-ended Questions
Perhaps the easiest types of question to design are those using an open-ended format. They are easy because they are the most natural way of expressing a question in everyday conversation. This ease does not necessarily make them the most appropriate for a questionnaire, but it may tempt researchers to over-use them. Their biggest drawback comes when they are subjected to systematic analysis. Simple scales (such that those described below) mean that the respondent is the main source of measurement error, but open-ended questions with *post hoc* classification of the results adds another layer of measurement error due to the researcher. Open-ended questions are best used in two situations: where it is clear how the responses will be analysed, or where the responses will be used not to create a statistical pattern, but to help explain it.

Such choices of question design are far from trivial. Farrall *et al.* (1997) found that the reported fear of crime was much greater in surveys using closed rather than open-ended questions. Therefore the results of your study depend on more than simply face validity (i.e. looking like the right question). People may also respond more sensitively to open-ended approaches. Since there may be so little similarity between responses to forced-choice and open-ended questions it is probably advisable to mix the types of questions in any instrument. Vocabulary and the phrasing are also more generally important in question design. In a large survey in the USA it was recorded that a much larger number of people were in favour of assistance for the poor than were in favour of welfare. The terms you use should be neutral as far as possible and familiar but not patronizing. This can lead to problems when you are dealing with very different sub-groups such as parents and their children. Should you change the wording for each group, and run the risk of asking different questions of each, or should you find a common wording and run the risk of patronizing one group?

In early studies of school choice, which tried to identify the reasons reported by families for using a particular new school, there were two main approaches. These involved giving respondents a list (or menu) of choices, or giving them a blank sheet and asking them to list their reasons. Where a list of these potential reasons is presented to respondents for them to tick or rate as appropriate, the list is usually incomplete, not containing all possible reasons for choosing a school. This can lead to serious omissions in the responses which may well bias the study (Kim and Mueller, 1978a, 1978b) by making other criteria appear more important than they truly are (Maddala, 1992). For example, a survey by Dennison (1995) used 25 choice criteria but excluded religious preference and the size of the school, which have both been shown to be important to some families in other studies. Coldron and Boulton (1991) omitted the retention rate at 16+, rate of entry to university, career prospects, and several others cited in previous studies.

Direct evidence of the importance of such omissions from a questionnaire comes from a study of choice (Gorard, 1997b). In one of my focus schools, I mistakenly issued a set of questionnaire forms with one page, containing 25 of the 73 suggested reasons, missing. The criteria accidentally left out included 'good public examination results', 'firm discipline', and 'small classes' which were all found to be very important overall. Although there was a section for respondents to write any other reasons not covered by the list, not one of the affected respondents suggested any of the 25 missing reasons, and so presumably without the prompt did not notice their lack. This would have the effect of increasing the apparent importance of other variables. Yet few researchers in any field can truly claim that they have tried to make their lists as complete as possible, and it is strange that this phenomenon is not more widely discussed in the literature. A pre-fixed list may also suggest reasons to respondents which they might, in retrospect, feel are important, but which they did not consider at the time of making a selection of schools.

On the other hand, the method of asking respondents to create their own list of reasons for choosing a school (for example) by asking an open-ended question relies more heavily on the imperfect memory of the respondents, will over-represent the views of the more literate and highly motivated (Payne, 1951), and is likely to produce as many differently worded responses as there are respondents (Oppenheim, 1992). This makes them very difficult to analyse. Some groups of respondents, those with the most education, for example, may produce more reasons each. Therefore, even if all reasons can be assumed to be simple and unrelated constructs, which they patently are not, but which should be a necessary precondition for their frequencies to be computed, they cannot all be given equal weight. It is not reasonable to assume that both of two reasons given by one respondent are each equally as important as one reason given by another. Nor can it be assumed that each is only half as important. Such considerations begin to give a clue to the complexity of the analysis of open-ended questions.

If you want to collect real number answers (in many ways the ideal), then a simple form of open-ended question is one aimed at the apparently straightforward collection of facts. Examples might be 'How many years have you worked at this school?', or the simpler 'How old are you (in years)?', or even simpler 'Which year were you born?'. In each of these examples the respondent simply writes a number. Three common problems with this type are lack of clarity, lack of knowledge, and intrusiveness. Lack of clarity can usually be sorted out at the pilot stage. One example would be lack of clarity about the units involved, such as in 'How tall are you?'. Is this in feet or metres? Another would be lack of clarity about parameters such as 'How many people are there in your school?'. Does this mean today, or on roll? Does it mean students or staff or both? Does it include service staff? If the question is 'How many schools have you been to?' does this refer to attendance as a student, or visits? Lack of knowledge arises when you ask someone about something they cannot possibly answer. Most children do not know their parents' incomes, for example, and many parents would not know the full range of subjects taken by their children at school. Some commentators believe that direct questions such as these are very intrusive anyway, and suggest that closed questions should be used instead. People may find it easier to tell you their annual income to within a certain range than to give you a figure, either because they do not know exactly or do not want to tell you.

Closed Questions
Close-ended (or closed) questions are somewhat harder to design well than open-ended questions but should then be much easier to analyse. The reasons why they are hard to design can be experienced in those semi-serious tests that appear in magazines with titles such as 'How compatible are you?' or 'Are you a thinker or a doer?'.

Whenever I attempt one of these (only at the dentists obviously), I can hardly answer any of the questions since none of the possible responses are right for me. Imagine possible answers such as 'Do you (a) whisk your partner off to Paris for the weekend; or (b) sulk for the next three weeks and then buy your partner some chocolates?'. You see my difficulty. What if it is Rome and not Paris, or only one week, or flowers not chocolates? What if my response is something completely different? Of course, these are trivial examples but even 'proper' research can lead to questions that appear to exclude the very people they are aimed at by denying them the chance to tell us what they know. Closed questions should ideally be as inclusive and flexible as open-ended ones. Herein lies their difficulty.

Make sure that each question allows for all possible responses, but without overlap. This would usually involve adding categories for 'don't know' (in my opinion a perfectly valid answer to most questions), and for 'other, please specify'. You should try and make this last option of 'other' redundant by making other categories as inclusive as possible, but still retain it as a fail-safe (at least for your pilot study). Consider the difference between these two versions of the same question:

(a) What is your highest qualification?

> A Level or equivalent (or above)
> GCSE or equivalent
> None

(b) What is your highest qualification?

> A Level or equivalent (or above)
> GCSE or equivalent
> None
> Don't know
> Other (please specify) ....

While neither version is perfect, the second is preferable to the first in allowing everyone to answer something, whereas the first will lead to some null responses.

Avoid also the use of negative statements if possible (surprisingly confusing), and double-barrelled questions (or two questions in one). Making questions easy to answer involves avoiding hypothetical situations, jargon, technical language and ambiguity. Avoid the danger of assuming a falsely shared premise. To aid recall do not ask for more information than you need (or than you are intending to analyse). If, for example, you wish to know how many GCSE grades

A*–C a respondent has, then it is not necessary to ask them to list all of their qualifications at age 16.

Now look at the following example questions that could all lead to problems. The first does not allow respondents to separate their reactions to the two parts of the question. The second (very common in style) is asking something that most people would have no evidence about and therefore should not answer. Note, however, that the added danger of asking such questions is that people may respond even when they have no knowledge. The third is ambiguous. Does it refer to the respondent or to an institution? What if they send the pupil elsewhere for punishment? Does a verbal reprimand count as punishment? And so on.

(c) How do you rate the new syllabus for ease of use and complete-
    ness?   [high/medium/low]

(d) Are people better educated today than 10 years ago?
                                    Yes/No

(e) How often do you punish a pupil?
                                    Never
                                    Monthly
                                    Weekly
                                    At least daily

Although it is also usually recommended that questions are not 'loaded', this technique can occasionally be useful to provoke responses in difficult situations. If this is what you intend, then build it into your design and your description of method. An example might be when you know that a respondent has been selected because they have a characteristic that they may wish to cover up, and you want to let them know that you know about it and that it is alright (e.g. 'How many times per week do you skip school?').

Scales
By 'scales' I refer here not just to closed questions in general, but the use of batteries of similar format questions using a standard scale aimed at the indirect measurement of an underlying concept. A very common example of such a concept would be attitude. I have already stated that, in my opinion, questionnaires are no good at gathering anything other than the most straightforward information about respondents. Therefore it should come as no surprise to realize that I am not a great fan of this particular use of scales. I will not go into

great detail here, but for those interested there is further discussion of these in Oppenheim (1992) and elsewhere.

Complex scales are multiple indicators, often used to measure things like stress, political stance, attitudes or prejudice. They should only be used when a single, and even a proxy (substitute), measure is not possible. Their use requires considerable care. Simply putting a lot of similar questions together and treating the responses to each question equally (like scoring a multiple-choice examination) does not automatically lead a social scientist to an underlying variable. There is a lot of make-believe in this technique, since multiple responses are not necessarily any more accurate than a single one. A good multiple scale requires a lot of work and much testing. Their creators often use ordinal scales such as 'strongly agree' to 'strongly disagree', with which respondents, especially less-educated ones, have a tendency towards agreement, whatever the associated statement. These responses in ordinal form are then often treated as real numbers (see Chapter 4), which has led to 'intellectual pollution' in the opinion of some writers (e.g. Mitchell, 1994). Mitchell claims that the legacy of Spearman is a pseudo-science, combining contempt for real information with a worship of false quantification, and ignoring the fact that epistemology and logic are more important than statistical technique. The users of complex scales are therefore often like the second 'villain' in Chapter 1, determined to work with numbers at any cost, and convinced of their authority regardless of their substantive meaning.

The Old Favourites

Many questionnaires you see or design will ask standard background questions about the age, sex, social class and ethnicity of the respondent. These are some of the old favourites of social researchers, because they can almost always be relied upon to point up systematic differences in the responses to the substantive questions. There are not many large-scale educational studies that do not report differences in attainment, attitude, participation, or confidence in terms of young and old, men and women, middle and working class, or white and a minority ethnic group. Questions for the first two of these are relatively simple to devise. If you feel that asking people their age is too intrusive you could ask for their date of birth instead, or year of birth if that is all you really need. Practical problems arise in forming questions about the other two, so much so in fact that I have never seen (much less devised) a satisfactory version of either question. This may be partly due to lack of clarity in the concepts and the lack of an agreed meaning for either term. On reflection, what is astonishing is that despite these flaws, the many systematic differences between these groups (however they are defined) are so great that even a poorly designed question will identify them.

Most social class schemes are actually based on occupational prestige. Until 1971, the UK Registrar General's class scheme used in the population census and other official figures was an ordinal classification of occupations according to reputed standing in community (Rose, 1996). In 1980, this notion of prestige was exchanged for levels of skill which sound more objective but are in some ways more confusing. There are other scales in common use, based on both nominal and continuous variables, but the RG scale remains the most widely used. Originally designed to relate to measures of infant mortality and adult fertility, the traditional scale looks like this (see Box 5.1).

Box 5.1: The Registrar General's class scheme

I	Professional occupations (e.g. medical doctor, lawyer)
II	Managerial and technical occupations (e.g. company director, teacher)
IIIN	Non-manual skilled occupations (e.g. clerical assistant)
IIIM	Manual skilled occupations (e.g. craftspeople, plumbers)
IV	Partly-skilled occupations (e.g. lathe operator)
V	Unskilled occupations (e.g. litter collector)

As can be seen, this list represents a mixture of both skill and occupational prestige. For many analytic purposes you may prefer to work with only three divisions – Service class (I + II), Intermediate class (IIIN + IIIM) and Working class (IV + V) – since this may lead to fewer difficult decisions in classifying cases and produces more cases per cell for analysis (see Chapter 6). The scale is primarily male in focus, not working as well with what are predominantly women's jobs. Using the scale for women tends to inflate their class since fewer are involved in manual work. It is questionable to suggest that simply working in an office makes a person middle class (Intermediate). The scale also does not recognize unpaid labour, and makes it difficult to classify those without employment.

The newer social class categories introduced in 1998 are based not on skill or prestige but employment conditions, and thus overcome some of these problems. They generally make it easier to classify the jobs of women, by giving less emphasis to the distinction between manual and non-manual jobs (see Box 5.2). Where people do not have a job, you can ask them about their usual occupation or about the occupation of their parents.

Box 5.2: The Registrar General's class scheme 1998 (used 2001)

1. Higher professional and managerial occupations
   (a) Employers and managers, company directors, health service and bank managers
   (b) higher professionals, university and college lecturers, scientists, doctors, teachers, librarians, social workers, clergy
2. Lower professional and managerial occupations, laboratory technicians, nurses and midwives, journalists, artists, actors and musicians, police
3. Intermediate professions, secretaries, dental nurses, electrical equipment installers, piano tuners
4. Small employers and own account workers, farmers, publicans, restaurateurs
5. Lower supervisory, craft and related jobs, plumbers, butchers, train drivers
6. Semi-routine occupations, shop assistants, security guards, hairdressers
7. Routine occupations, waiters, cleaners, couriers.

The other standard question that gives the researcher a great deal of trouble but which is worth persevering with relates to the ethnic background of respondents. There is perhaps even less agreement about what this constitutes than there is about social class. Again the standard question would be based on that used by the Office for the Population Census (Table 5.1).

As can be seen, this list is a peculiar mixture of skin colour, other racial characteristics, country of 'origin' and primary state religion. The situation for the 2001 census is likely to be worse. If there is a 'White UK' it is not clear why there should not be a 'Black UK', nor

Table 5.1: Ethnic groups 1991 census

Main group	Ethnic groups		
White	White		
Black groups	Black Caribbean	Black African	Black other
Indian sub-continent	Indian	Pakistani	Bangladeshi
Chinese/other groups	Chinese	Asian other	Other
Born in Ireland	Born in Ireland		

whether a respondent with white skin born in India would be 'Indian' or 'White other'. With the addition of 'Irish', 'Scottish' and possibly 'Welsh' as supposed ethnic groups, are these categories intended to be based on area of birth, residence, language or self-attribution? How many people living in Wales are Welsh? Can someone be black and Welsh? How do we classify so-called mixed respondents (my children, for example, do not fit any scheme I have ever seen, having been born in Wales to one English and one Chinese parent).

Consider the fact that as I have two parents, four grand-parents, eight great-grand-parents and so on, then 40 generations ago I had 2^{40} antecedents or over one trillion (one thousand billion) people. If each generation, for the sake of argument, reproduced on average after every 25 years, then 40 generations represents 1,000 years. Therefore, I had more ancestors 1,000 years ago than there were people alive at that time (more even than everyone who has ever been alive). Put another way, as recently as 500 years ago (the era of the Tudor monarchs and 'discovery' of the USA perhaps), everyone in the entire world must have been related to me. The notion of 'pure' ethnic groups in terms of genetics or ancestry is therefore somewhat unrealistic. If, on the other hand, ethnicity is defined by our shared local cultures and patterns of behaviour, this means that a change of lifestyle (or country) could lead to a change of ethnic group (meaning therefore that we can alter our ethnicity by altering our circumstances). Perhaps the concept of ethnicity has become so complex and delicate that it has passed its usefulness. Yet, as with social class, however poorly thought out your question, the categories you use will appear to approximate to a social process so powerful that you will still find significant differences between them.

Other Issues
A further difficult issue relates to clearly sensitive questions. Often as researchers we wish to consider emotional and controversial topics since these are also often important and interesting. The key technique here is to be clear and unemotional in wording questions. My advice is, however long you make the preamble to a difficult question, keep the question itself short. Avoid all pejorative or leading words (even commonly used terms such as 'truancy' for unauthorized absence imply something about the views of their author). I once asked a large group of students how many had been present at, or involved in, committing a crime. None had. I then asked how many had been present at, or involved in, shop-lifting,

speeding in a car or the use of illegal drugs. More than half had. Responses are horribly sensitive to the precise phrasing of the question. If you want respondents to be prepared to report danger-ous or possibly incriminating matters, a number of designs have been worked out to help. How much help they actually are is something you can decide in your pilot study (see below).

A simple example might run as follows. If you wish to ask a difficult question, use a preliminary question such as 'toss a coin, if it is heads answer the next question, if it is tails toss again and then put yes for the next question if it is heads, and no if it is tails'. In theory therefore half of the people answering the next question 'yes' or 'no' are genuine and half are talking about their second coin toss. You do not know which is which (so their anonymity is secure) but you do know that the chances of heads or tails is 50:50. So you need to subtract a quarter of your total sample from the 'yes' responses and a quarter from the 'no' to the next question to be left with the genuine answers (assuming you have a large sample). Please note that I have never tried this, and although it sounds fine in theory, there is an awful lot that can go wrong. The question just seems too complicated to work in real life.

Other notoriously tricky questions involve grids or two-dimensional tables, and those questions where respondents have to rank a set of responses, and indeed any question where the respondent can legiti-mately respond more than once. These questions are often so difficult to analyse that they are not worth including. They are also difficult to complete, and so might endanger your response rate. I suggest you keep away from these until you are more experienced. I have not managed to make one work successfully.

PILOT STUDIES

All research designs need to be piloted or pre-tested, so the comments made here about surveys could apply equally well to experiments, observation studies, interview schedules, and so on. Researchers are always working to a deadline and so the temptation to skimp on the pilot study is very strong. Resist this temptation, at least until you are more experienced. Pilots are sometimes misinter-preted as applying only to the survey instrument. Rather, a pilot study should be seen as a full 'dress rehearsal' for the whole research design. Thus, a good pilot study involves selecting a sample in the same way as intended for the final study, negotiating access in the same way, delivering the instrument in the same way, calculating response rates, and analysing the results in the same way. Problems will probably appear at every stage. This kind of pre-test does generally have two main differences from the 'real thing'. It will involve a much smaller sample, making it quicker and cheaper than the final survey, and it involves asking participants some supplementary questions about the design itself, making it slightly longer and more complex again.

I recommend a two-stage pre-testing process. First, try your questionnaire out on experts, friends, family and anybody else you can bully into helping. Ideally, try it out in a face-to-face interview or focus groups with a few people from your intended population (but not from your sample). Ask for comments and criticisms. Note where people are hesitant or do not understand the question. Note carefully any non-responses. Consider whether there are any pressures to produce socially acceptable or desirable answers. In particular, note if the respondents' first reaction is not actually an answer to the question (often a clue to a design problem). Fix any problems. And there will be problems. Anyone who tells you it is all fine is either lying or cannot be bothered to help. Then pre-test again. Remember to date each draft of your questionnaire so that you know which is up to date, but keep earlier versions in case you change your mind again.

Second, move on to the full pilot. Analysing even four responses in the way that you will in the full study forces you to design this stage early on (so that at least you will not come to my office in six months time with a pile of questionnaires saying 'So, what am I supposed to do now?'). It will also help you face up to flaws. Are the respondents really able to answer the questions, for example, do people know how many litres of petrol they used last year, or how many employees work in their company?

If the pilot leads to a few changes, you might then proceed to the main study. If, however, things go seriously wrong, then the changes you need to make are so major that you will need to pilot the whole thing again. This is the social science equivalent of your aeroplane design crashing on its first test flight.

AN EXAMPLE OF A SIMPLE QUESTIONNAIRE

The example questionnaire in Figure 5.1 comes from a pilot project investigating the relationship between use of digital technology and patterns of participation in lifelong learning (the work is represented by Gorard and Selwyn, 1999; Selwyn and Gorard, 1999; Gorard *et al.*, 2000c). It was sent to all of the users of a particular Internet-based

INFORMATION ABOUT YOUR LEARNING

1. How often do you use the online Welsh for learners website?	At least once per week Less than once per week No longer use it
2. Where do you access the Internet from?	Home Work Elsewhere*
If 'elsewhere' please specify	....
3. Are you still in full-time education?	Yes No*
If 'no', how old were you when you left full-time education?	....
4. Which of the following levels best describes your highest qualification?	Level three: 2+ A Levels (or equivalent), GNVQ Advanced, NVQ3, OND, etc. Level two: 5+ GCSEs grade A*–C (or equivalent), 5 O Levels, 5 CSE grade 1, etc. Level one: less than 5 GCSEs grade A*–C (or equivalent)

INFORMATION ABOUT YOURSELF

5. Sex	Male Female
6. Date of birth	....
7. Postcode (or area name)	....
8. Are you currently employed?	Yes No
9. What is your current or usual occupation?	....

Figure 5.1: Draft questionnaire on background to web-based participation

educational course, in an attempt to garner information about their background. It was sent by e-mail (acceptable given the nature of the population), and completed interactively by the recipients (thus reducing transcription). Our primary concern was with widening participation, and we needed to see whether the kind of people using web-based instruction were different in any significant way from those following more traditional courses at the same level. In essence, has technology broken down the barriers faced by those previously excluded from learning in adult life? Or has it reinforced them? We already knew that patterns of participation in traditional adult learning varied by gender, age, location, employment, social class, and prior educational attainment. Therefore, this is what our questions asked about. The temptation to include questions about the nature of their learning experiences and other superficially interesting matters was very strong. We resisted it because we added one final question – 'Would you be willing to be interviewed as part of this project'? It was in the follow-up interviews with a sub-sample that we decided to approach questions about attitudes, learner identities, the nature of barriers, and possible tranformative experiences.

As a result of the responses and follow-up interviews we intend making some modifications even to this simple design. The responses about usual occupation remain hard to classify, and the use of equivalence levels in the question about qualifications was not a great success. Nevertheless, I include this simple instrument to make the point that questionnaires do not have to be complicated to be useful to the researcher (as this one has been). The information we requested includes key predictors of adult learning patterns derived from our previous work. We did not need, in this instance, to ask any more questions. We did need more responses (but that is another story!).

COMMON PROBLEMS IN QUESTIONNAIRE DESIGN

There are many potential pitfalls in the design of a survey instrument, and several have been described in this chapter. Most can be avoided by careful proof-reading followed by a full pilot study. A selection of problems in questionnaire design includes:

- asking the research questions;
- use of leading questions;
- making the instrument too long;
- asking pointless questions;
- use of offensive language.

Asking the Research Questions

Some novices become confused between their research questions which define what they are trying to find out, and the questions they use in an investigation to answer the research questions. Research questions do not generally make good test items. Suppose, as a simple example, you wanted to know whether most teachers believed that boys were more likely to under-achieve at school than girls. You could not use the following item in a questionnaire to a sample of teachers.

Do most teachers believe that boys are more likely to under-achieve than girls?   Yes
(please circle your answer)   No
                                  Don't know

Teachers cannot answer for most teachers, only for themselves. Your job as researcher is to aggregate the answers of many teachers to decide what most of them believe. Even so, you probably cannot simply convert the beginning of the question to 'Do you believe that boys ...?' The question is still too much like the research question and therefore too complex. People may want to know more about what under-achievement is, or in what areas of school life this under-achievement is meant to occur. People may feel resistance to answering either 'Yes' or 'No', sensing that it is too extreme and wanting to assess different parts of school life differently. The proper development of survey items from research questions is a complex, and rewarding, business.

Use of Leading Questions

I have regularly seen introductions to surveys which 'give the game away' by leading the potential respondent to answer in a certain way or share some unnecessary assumptions with the researcher. For example, I recently saw a letter addressed to heads of schools starting: 'I am a student researching the current shortage of teachers ...'. One of the objectives of the research was to establish whether there was a teacher shortage (although the student-researcher clearly believed that there was).

Less common, as it is harder to spot perhaps, is where the lead is in the question (as in the legendary 'when did you stop beating your wife?'). I have paraphrased the following question slightly for anonymity, but the example is a genuine one from a PhD student whose dissertation I was examining:

How important is the quality of music teaching to you when assessing a new school?

1   of some importance
2   of medium importance
3   very important.

This candidate, for whatever reason, could not conceive of someone not caring at all about the quality of music teaching when assessing a school.

Making the Instrument Too Long

All of us tend to make questionnaires too long. I have seldom managed to analyse all the questions in a piece of survey research. Despite planning and piloting, some of the questions simply do not work. Working in a team makes the situation worse as each team member tends to have 'favourite' questions that they wish to retain. All these problems exist and must be faced. What is absurd, however, is any desire for length for its own sake. One of the most ridiculous things I have ever heard concerned a PhD student who was repeatedly criticized during their pilot study for having an insufficiently long questionnaire. The complainants did not point out any key issues that had been omitted, merely claiming that the current length was only suited for a master's project. In their opinion, a government-funded PhD project required a more substantial instrument. While clearly laughable, there is a little of this attitude in many of us. Resist it.

Asking Pointless Questions

Typical problems here involve asking questions we already know the answer to, or asking for information that we can get by other means. One example I have seen in real studies involved questionnaires sent to named pupils who had been selected on the basis of gender. The first question was 'are you a boy or a girl?'. Another involved asking teachers at named schools how many pupils there were in their school, where this information could be more accurately obtained from official statistics (see Chapter 3).

Perhaps the most peculiar example of a pointless question I have come across occurred in a paper by Coldron and Boulton (1991). They asked one group of people for their own views, and for their views of the views of others and then concluded that the 'two' [*sic*] sets of views were related. Even though the researchers were interested in the views of the pupils, only 'parents ... were asked to report their children's reasons for wanting to go to a particular school' (Coldron and Boulton, 1991, p. 175). It is not clear, in this case, why the 11-year-old children were not felt able to speak for themselves. It is, however, hardly surprising that the authors concluded that 'from these figures it appears that children chose mainly on the same basis as their parents', since the two sets of views they were comparing were in fact both from the parents. A similar situation is evident in a study by West *et al.* (1995), in which parents were asked about their child's reasons for choosing a new school, and which found that 83 per cent stated that the child wanted the same school as themselves. The inaccuracy of parents and children's reports about each other has been shown several times (e.g. Pifer and Miller, 1995), and thus the value of findings like the two above are suspect. Even more interestingly, despite the claim by Coldron and Boulton that parents and children used the same reasons, their reported results showed this was not actually so. For example, the most common response for children's reasons (56.9 per cent) was 'because friends were going' to the same school. The most common for parents (31.5 per cent) was the 'nearness of school'. These reasons might be related but they are not the same since friends and nearness also appear separately lower down the respective lists. The paper is therefore doubly interesting in asking pointless questions, and then not even reporting the responses accurately.

Use of Offensive Language
Clearly, no sensible researcher would set out to use deliberately offensive language in a questionnaire, so all the examples I have come across have been unintentional. Sometimes the use of offensive language is the result of a misjudged attempt at informality and therefore approachability. While a questionnaire should not be pompous, or use long technical words inappropriately, it is probably best to stick to a relatively formal style throughout to encourage a serious frame of mind in the respondent. Sometimes the use of offensive language is the result of naïveté or ignorance. Sometimes it is due to cultural or national differences. I have seen a question for teachers in the UK refer to a 'retard' or retarded pupil, and another for students asking whether they were 'low class'. In both cases fashions in terminology had changed and made both questions seem unpleasant in tone. Be careful. Be modern. I have seen questions use analogies and terminology from the drinking of alcoholic beverages in instruments for a general population including Moslems. Why take the risk? Don't turn people away by your use of language.

This chapter has concentrated on the design of a survey instrument. For more on general survey design see Payne (1951), Sudman and Bradburn (1982), Hakim (1992), Oppenheim (1992), Czaja and Blair (1996). See Bernard (2000) for examples of more esoteric survey designs. Chapter 6 continues by describing some simple statistical techniques for analysing the kind of data collected from a survey.

6

Simple non-parametric statistics: minding your table manners

To a large extent, the simple presentation of survey and other findings is dealt with in Chapter 4. More complex and powerful parametric approaches to analysis are dealt with in Chapters 8 and 9. Here we are concerned with going beyond the presentation of data, and its simple arithmetic manipulation, to consider basic patterns within it and differences between sub-groups in our sample.

ANALYSING SURVEY DATA

Suppose that one of the background questions in a survey using a random sample of employees in one factory asked for the sex of the respondent. The results might be presented as in Table 6.1.

Suppose that one of the substantive questions in the same survey asked the respondents whether they had received job-related training in the past two years. The results might be presented as in Table 6.2.

Table 6.1: Frequency by sex in our achieved sample

Gender	Number	Percentage
Male	37	41
Female	54	59
Total	91	100

Table 6.2: Frequency of training in our achieved sample

Frequency of training	Number	Percentage
Training in the past two years	48	53
No training in the past two years	43	47
Total	91	100

We know therefore that our achieved sample contained more women than men, and that slightly more than half reported receiving some job-related training in the past two years. Both of these might be important findings given a good-quality sample of a clearly defined population. In many cases, however, our chief concern as social scientists is to go beyond these simple patterns and answer questions such as 'Are men or women more likely to report being trained?'. In this case we need to consider the two variables simultaneously, and we can present our summary as a cross-tabulation using different rows for one variable, and different columns for the other. The results might be presented as in Table 6.3 (note that tables such as these will be created for you automatically from your datafile by the cross-tabulation function in statistical packages such as SPSS).

Table 6.3: Cross-tabulation of sex by training

Sex	Training	No training	Total
Male	22	15	37
Female	26	28	54
Total	48	43	91

Note that the 'marginal' totals are the same as in the simpler tables above. There are still 91 cases of whom 37 are male and 48 of whom received training, and so on. Table 6.3 also now shows that more than half of the men received training (22/37 or 59 per cent), while fewer than half of the women did (26/54 or 48 per cent). For our sample therefore we can draw safe conclusions about the relative prevalence of training in the two sex categories. The men in our sample are more likely to receive training. In Chapter 2 it was argued that one motive for using probability sampling was that we could then generalize from our sample to the larger population for the study. If the population in this example is the people employed in a certain factory on a certain day, can we generalize from our sample finding about the relationship between sex and training? Put another way, is it likely that men in the *factory* (and not just in the sample) receive more training than women?

In order to answer the question for the population (and not just for the people we asked by selecting them at random from a list of employees), it is very useful to imagine that the answer is 'no' and start our consideration from there. If the answer were actually no,

Table 6.4: The marginal totals of sex by training

Sex	Training	No training	Total
Male			37
Female			54
Total	48	43	91

and men and women were equally likely to receive training, then what would we expect the figures in Table 6.3 to look like? The number of each sex remains as defined in Table 6.1 and the number of people trained remains as defined in Table 6.2. In other words, our table of what we would expect to find starts with the partially completed Table 6.4.

From this outline we can calculate exactly what we expect the numbers in the blank cells to be. We know that 37/91 or 41 per cent of cases are male, and that 48/91 or 53 per cent of cases received training. We would therefore expect 41 per cent *of* 53 per cent of the overall total to be both males and trained. This works out at 22 per cent of 91, or 20 cases as shown in Table 6.5.

Table 6.5: The expected values for trained males

Sex	Training	No training	Total
Male	20		37
Female			54
Total	48	43	91

We can do the same calculation for each cell of the table. For example, as 59 per cent of the cases are female and 53 per cent of the cases received training, we would expect 59 per cent of 53 per cent of the overall total to be females and trained. This works out at 31 per cent of 91, or 28 cases. But then we already knew that this must be so, since there are 48 trained people in our survey of whom 20 are male, so by definition 28 are female. Similarly, 37 cases are male and 20 of these received training so 17 did not. We can now complete the table (Table 6.6). Note that in practice all these calculations would be generated automatically by the computer.

To recap, we obtained the figures in Table 6.3 from our survey (our 'observed' figures) and wanted to know whether the apparent

Table 6.6: The expected values for sex by training

Sex	Training	No training	Total
Male	20	17	37
Female	28	26	54
Total	48	43	91

Table 6.7: Observed and expected values for sex by training

Sex	Training	No training	Total
Male	22 (20)	15 (17)	37
Female	26 (28)	28 (26)	54
Total	48	43	91

difference in training rates for men and women was also likely to be true of the factory as a whole. To work this out, we calculated how many men and women we expect to have been trained assuming that there was actually no difference, and obtained the figures in Table 6.6 (our 'expected' figures). For convenience both sets of figures are repeated in Table 6.7 with the observed figures in each cell followed by the expected figure in brackets.

If there were no difference in the factory between the rates of training for men and women, we would expect 20 of 37 males to be trained but we actually found that 22 of 37 males had been trained. In each cell of Table 6.7 there is a discrepancy of two cases between the observed and expected figures. Is this convincing evidence that men are more likely to be trained than women in this factory? Hardly. In selecting a sample of 91 cases at random it would be easy for us to have inadvertently introduced a bias equivalent to those two cases. We should therefore conclude that we have no evidence of differential training rates for men and women in this factory.

Did you follow that analysis? If not, try reading it again. The argument traced in Tables 6.1 to 6.6 contains just about everything that you need to know about the logic of significance-testing in statistical analysis. If you can follow the logic, and are happy with the conclusion, then you have completed a statistical analysis.

I think that the argument is relatively easy to follow if you try, and is a form of logic that all educational researchers should be able to follow. There is therefore no reason why anyone reading this book should not read and understand statistical evidence of this sort. There is also no reason why anyone should not be able to complete such an analysis for themselves with different figures. Everything that you will learn about statistics is built on this rather simple foundation, and yet nothing in statistics is more complicated than this. Much of what follows is simply the introduction of a technical shorthand for the concepts and techniques used in this introductory argument.

MORE FORMALLY

For example, a concept that has little practical significance for us now that computers handle the calculations is that of 'degrees of freedom'. You will see this term used in books and cited in publications. In the example above the number of degrees of freedom tells you how many of the four main cells you (or rather the computer) would have to complete with an expected value before being able to work the rest out immediately. In the example above, once you have calculated that you expected 20 males to be trained, you could find the other three numbers immediately since they had to add up to the marginal totals. The degrees of freedom for the table is therefore *one*, meaning you only need to calculate any one of the four numbers to see by simple subtraction what the other three must be. Only one cell in the table was free to vary. 'Degrees of freedom' is therefore a posh name for something you already understand.

As another example, consider the concept of a 'null hypothesis'. This is an assumption, merely for convenience, that there is no difference in the population between the two groups you are examining. In the example our null hypothesis was that the training rate for men and women in the factory was the same. We do not say that the null hypothesis is true, merely that it gives us a convenient base against which to judge our actual (observed) findings. We need the null hypothesis of no difference in order to be able to calculate our expected values. It is a matter of arithmetic convenience, no more than that. 'Null hypothesis' is therefore also a posh name for something you already understand.

Our conclusion above was that on the basis of the data collected we had no evidence that the training rates for men and women differed in the population. The rates did differ slightly in the sample we obtained but consideration of the null hypothesis led us to believe that this difference was too small to attach any importance to. What we did therefore was to try and separate, or distinguish between, a real difference in data and one due to random error in the sampling procedure. This is the whole basis of statistical testing. Traditionally we use probability or likelihood to determine the difference between systematic and random events, and this is where the importance of random sampling comes from (see Chapter 2). Because of the nature of random events we can argue that the less likely it is that an event occurred by chance, the more likely it is to reflect a real difference in the population we are examining. We could therefore be more precise in our example than we have been so far. It would be possible to calculate exactly, if the training rates for men and women are the same in the factory, how likely is it that any random sample would find the pattern we did with men appearing to be slightly more likely to be trained. The calculation would be possible, but luckily for us we do not have to bother with it. All such calculations have already been done and are summarized in statistical tables.

We do not even have to bother to consult statistical tables, since a statistical package on a computer (such as SPSS) effectively has these tables in its memory and can tell us the precise probability. In our example the probability of obtaining the results we did (or an even more extreme set of results) if the null hypothesis were true is 0.29 (or 29 per cent). The cross-tabulation function on SPSS has a 'Statistics' option, on which you can check (i.e. tick) a box for a chi-square test. This test will calculate the probability above for you (if interested, see Siegel, 1956 or Clegg, 1990 for a simple introduction to the chi-square distribution used). Apart from the cross-tabulation (i.e. like Table 6.3) the output will look something like Table 6.8.

Now you can begin to see, or remember, why statistics has such a bad press! The important thing when faced with reports like this is not to panic. A lot of this output is easy to understand, and most of

Table 6.8: Results of a chi-square test of significance

	Value	df	Asymp. sig. (2-sided)	Exact sig. (2-sided)	Exact sig. (1-sided)
Pearson chi-square	1.127[b]	1	**0.288**		
Continuity correction[a]	0.719	1	0.396		
Likelihood ratio	1.132	1	0.287		
Fisher's exact test				0.393	0.198
Linear-by-linear association	1.115	1	0.291		
N of valid cases	91				

Notes: [a]Computed only for 2 × 2 table.
[b]0 cells (0.0 per cent) have expected count less than 5. The minimum expected count is 17.48.

the rest of it is irrelevant to us at present. Computer statistical packages are notorious for producing lengthy reports even for relatively simple analyses because, presumably, they are trying to be extra helpful. I tolerate this because they are so helpful. They calculate for me the probability of observing what I observed if the null hypothesis is true, and therefore give me the basis for making a decision about the 'significance' of my findings (more on significance below).

The column headed 'df' we already know about. It tells us how many degrees of freedom there are in Table 6.3. The final row also tells us something we already know. It is the number of cases or individuals in Table 6.3. The five other rows are actually for five different tests of the same thing, which all appear automatically when we asked for chi-square. The one we are concerned with here is the first row labelled 'Pearson chi-square'. For each test the first column gives us the test statistic. It is this which is used by the computer to consult an internal statistical table for conversion into a probability. This statistic has no clear meaning in the real world, and is therefore best ignored (although note that in some areas of social science traditionalists still insist that you quote this value – as a beginner I suggest you humour them). The numbers in the last three columns are all probabilities. The one that concerns us here is the cell reading '0.288' in bold. I have emphasized it here because it is the key number in the report. If this cell contains a large number we would have no reason to disbelieve our null hypothesis, whereas if the number is small we can reject the null hypothesis and assume that males in our population as well as in our sample are more likely to receive training.

The key question is, therefore, how large or small this probability must be before we can decide either way. There is, of course, no clear answer to this. You, as the researcher, make the decision. As with all decisions about research design, sampling and analysis you will need a reason for your decision, and you must publish your decision and your reason with your results. Recall what you are trying to decide here. In our example the question is: if there is really no difference between men and women in terms of training, how likely (or unlikely perhaps) is it that we found the small difference we actually observed? Our answer is that if we selected a sample and ran our survey many many times and there was no difference between men and women in the population, then we would still find a difference as large as, or larger than, we found 29 per cent of the time. This is a very large probability (roughly equivalent to throwing either a three or a four with one die, or picking a playing card of ten or more from a standard pack). Our observed difference is therefore not a safe one, and would be termed 'not significant'.

The most common value used as a cut-off point is 5 per cent (or 0.05). Using this value for the present, our decision simplifies to: if the value in the bold cell is 0.05 or higher, then we retain our null hypothesis and report that we have no evidence of a significant difference in the population. On the other hand, if the bold value is less than 0.05, we reject our null hypothesis, and assume that there *is* a significant difference between men and women in our population. Our significance level, or threshold, is 5 per cent.

If we had decided that our evidence did show a significant difference between the men and women in the factory in terms of their frequency of job-related training, then we would need an alternative to our null hypothesis. The simplest alternative explanation of our results (other than chance that is) is that there *is* a real difference. This may seem a rather laborious way to get to this point, but for the moment pause and check that you are still happy with the argument or logic of statistical testing, perhaps by reviewing the previous section before continuing. The next section introduces further interesting complexities.

SIGNIFICANCE AND SOCIAL SCIENCE

Before continuing with our conversion of the overall logic of statistical testing into a technical vocabulary, we need to consider the most important point of all analyses. In our factory example, we now have a result, and an answer to the question about statistical significance. In my experience, many newcomers to statistics treat this as the end whereas it is only the end of the beginning. The stages of design, sampling, data collection and significance testing are skilled activities but relatively technical ones. Of these stages, significance testing is the easiest to get right, and the quickest to complete. If the design is a good one for the questions being researched, the sample is selected appropriately from a defined population, the method of data collection minimizes observer bias, and the statistics have been used correctly, then we now have a social science finding to be explained. This is not the end. This is why we have been doing all that rigorous work. What does our finding mean? Unfortunately this final stage is far from technical, and not easy to teach as it is heavily dependent on the precise nature of all the preceding stages (but see Huff, 1991 or Thouless, 1974, for illustrations of how not to proceed).

In our example we have two elementary-level explanations. One is that there really is no difference between training rates for men and women. The other is the difference exists but that our research is somehow defective (perhaps by using too small a sample, or having a gender bias in the wording of the questionnaire). If we have any evidence for such defects we should, of course, record and publish it whenever we publish our results. However, the law of parsimony rules here. In the absence of evidence, even with defective research, we err on the side of caution and assume that the social world is as simple as possible (a principle known since the Middle Ages as Ockham's razor). Therefore, given no significant evidence of a difference, we have to assume that there is no difference (the default position in any investigation). At our next level of explanation we need to consider why there is no difference between men and women, or perhaps why other commentators would have expected there to be a difference.

If, on the other hand, we had found a real difference, we would have needed to begin to explain how this difference arose. Is it genetic, or learnt, or a function of management, or motivational, to do with self-confidence, or related to marriage or childbirth? Is it likely to be specific to this industry in this country? Are there variations in the pattern between different age groups, or between occupational groups in the factory? This stage is both creative and exhausting but, as I have already said, this is the point that our research would have been building up to. It provides our motivation for all of the foregoing stages.

A second important point to consider before getting a bit technical again is the meaning of the term significance as used in statistical testing. It is unfortunate that this word has an important meaning in general writing as well, since the two meanings are easily confused. If we find a significant result using a test of significance such as chi-square, we mean that the null hypothesis can be rejected with relative safety. In other words, our difference between the two groups appears not to be a fluke. This does not mean that our finding is, or is not, of any interest or importance to the wider research community. If I took many samples of the table salt and the black pepper sold in a national supermarket chain, analysed their components and found that salt and pepper were significantly different, then this result could be seen as less than exciting. If, on the other hand, I found no significant difference between salt and pepper, and that the supermarkets were selling basically the same product under two headings, then this could be more interesting (worth a newspaper report surely?). Similarly with educational research. Although we tend to get caught up in the flow of significance testing and look forward to a 'positive' result, a negative result can be just as exciting (often more so).

Some examples of my own work illustrated in this book include the findings that different types of schools (fee-paying and comprehensive, for example) are no more or less effective than each other, that boys are not increasingly under-achieving in relation to girls at school, and that the use of targets and performance indicators has not led to the increased polarization of high and low educational outcomes. The reason that these findings are interesting is that many commentators believe the opposite to be true. The findings therefore contradict a moral panic in each area, and are seen by some as counter-intuitive. This makes them interesting. The message here is not that you should seek out controversial findings (or the more common reverse of this, seeking out acceptable or confirmatory findings), but that you should seek findings which are as secure as possible. If this means retaining your null hypothesis of no difference/pattern, then so be it.

ANOTHER WORKED EXAMPLE OF SIGNIFICANCE TESTING

To reinforce the points made so far, and continue our formalization of the logic of testing I include another example of a chi-square test. This one is from real life, or rather it ought to have been! A study by Coldron and Boulton (1991) published in a highly prestigious outlet for research-related findings, made the following claim. They listed the reasons reported by parents for selecting a new school for their child, and then looked at differences in the frequency of responses from sub-groups of parents, such as those in different occupational groups, and those with boys and girls. They stated that for two of the groups of reasons, there were two differences worthy of note between parents of boys and girls. No null hypotheses, or tests of significance were mentioned in the article. As an example of a difference 'worthy of note', they stated that 'the child's own preference of school was mentioned more by parents of boys (15) than of girls (7)' (Coldron and Boulton, 1991, p. 173).

If true, this could be an important finding and it has accordingly passed into the research literature as a 'fact'. The finding has been widely cited by other authors, who like most of us tend to read only the summaries and findings of research reports, while ignoring the methods by which those summaries were reached. The actual finding

Table 6.9: Raw figures from Coldron and Boulton (1991)

Observed	Boys	Girls
Involved in choice	15	7

is that 15 of the parents of boys, but only 7 of the parents of girls in their sample reported taking the views of their child into account when selecting a new school. These figures are summarized in Table 6.9.

We cannot work out from Table 6.9 what we would have expected under our null hypothesis of no difference between the parents of boys and girls, and the authors did not do this or any other form of analysis. Their logic appears to have been that 15 is bigger than 7, so the finding is clear enough. Luckily, they do report their achieved sample size (but not their population, method of selection or response rate be it noted). They had 120 families of boys and 102 of girls. We can therefore construct for the authors a standard cross-tabulation of sex and involvement in choice (see Table 6.10).

Table 6.10: Sex of child and level of involvement

Observed	Boys	Girls	Total
Involved in choice	15	7	22
Not involved	105	95	200
Total	120	102	222

From these figures we can now calculate our expected results under the null hypothesis of no difference between the two groups. The marginal totals are set, and we do not change them. The table of no difference by sex would have 12 of the families of boys involved in choice. This is calculated as in the previous example. The sample includes 120/222 (54 per cent) boys and 22/222 (10 per cent) of the children were involved in choice. Therefore we would expect 54 per cent of 10 per cent of 222 (or 12) cases to be in the top left cell. As the degrees of freedom are one, we can calculate quickly that 108 families of boys would not involve their child in choosing (since $120 - 12 = 108$), and so on. Thus, we have Table 6.11 containing the observed values followed by the expected values in brackets.

Although they have not performed these calculations for their

Table 6.11: Observed and expected values for sex and level of involvement

Involvement	Boys	Girls	Total
Involved in choice	15 (12)	7 (10)	22
Not involved	105 (108)	95 (92)	200
Total	120	102	222

'analysis', what Table 6.11 means is that Coldron and Boulton could have expected to find 108 of the families of boys uninvolved with choice if there was no difference in their population between boys and girls. They actually found 105. Is this difference significant? You would not think so, and the more you learn about the logic of significance testing, the easier it will become to 'predict' the results of tests. In fact, when you get to that stage, statistical tests are not really that much use to you. If there clearly is, or clearly is not, a difference, then a test is not needed. If the difference is unclear, the statistical test will not reduce much uncertainty for you (but this is a more advanced consideration than we need at this point). Returning to the example, creating a datafile that matches the two variables in Table 6.10 allows me to run a chi-square test, again using the SPSS package. I simply select the 'Analysis' menu, a 'Descriptives' sub-menu, a 'Cross-tabulation' sub-menu from that, and check the box for 'Chi-square' under the heading 'Statistics'. A selection of the output is as shown in Table 6.12.

This report confirms that there are 222 cases, and that the 2×2 table has one degree of freedom. More importantly, the chi-square test we are interested in shows a probability of 0.276 that the Coldron and Boulton results arose by chance alone. This suggests that we would be wrong to reject the null hypothesis of no difference between boy and girl families. The logic is the same as in our made-up example of the factory. This re-analysis of existing figures shows

Table 6.12: Chi-square test of sex and level of involvement

	Value	df	Asymp. sig. (2-sided)	Exact sig. (2-sided)	Exact sig. (1-sided)
Pearson chi-square	1.382[a]	1	0.276		
N of valid cases	222				

Note: [a]0 cells (0.0 per cent) have expected count less than 5. The minimum expected count is 10.

that the opposite conclusion should have been drawn to that which is published. Unfortunately this kind of error is common (see Gorard, 1997b, for further problems with this same study, and Gorard, 2000b, for further examples). Of course, we cannot go around re-analysing all of the results we read (and many writers do not give us sufficient detail to do so anyway). We are supposed to rely on peer-review and referees for this, so that the results published in journals are only the best and the most rigorous. Nevertheless, it is instructive to do so occasionally, and the number of times you reach a different conclusion to that published may surprise you. If these published results really are the most rigorous, what must the rest be like? If they are not the most rigorous, then what are they? The most comfortable? The biggest names? The most acceptable to the editors?

Let us finish this section by considering three more technical terms, as used in the two reports from SPSS we have seen. The 'minimum expected count' is, as it sounds, the number in the smallest cell of the expected frequency table (the number of families of girls involved in choice, in this example). The importance of this was described in Chapter 2. In order to draw conclusions we need a good number of expected cases in each cell, otherwise the calculations are too sensitive to the 'movement' of one or two cases between cells. It is important therefore to make your sample as large as possible and consider the number of sub-groups you will use in the analysis when deciding on the scale of your research. Of course, you do not need to have any particular number of cases in each cell for your *observed* frequencies. You might find that all men and no women had received training in the first example, giving you two completely empty cells, but this would not alter your null hypothesis, nor would it lead you to empty cells in your table of expected frequencies (try it out if you can't imagine it). The practical point is that if your minimum *expected* value is less than ten cases approximately, you need to take remedial action (see Siegel, 1956).

The 'alternative hypothesis' is, like the null hypothesis, a technical creation which summarizes the basic situation if the null hypothesis is rejected. In the current example our alternative hypothesis might be that the families of boys and girls involve their children in choice differentially. As discussed above, we would need to go a lot further than this and explain what this means and why it occurs, but at an elementary level this alternative is like an understudy actor waiting to be used if the main actor (the null hypothesis) cannot perform on the night (i.e. if it is rejected). It can be argued that if the null hypothesis is rejected, there are in fact an infinite number of alternatives that could be used instead (for example, by taking a simple explanation and repeatedly adding redundant clauses to it). This is part of the reason why we use parsimony (see above). Parsimony is a general criterion for choosing an appropriate alternative hypothesis, and it eliminates 'silly' explanations with redundant clauses in them. This is also part of the reason why rejecting the null hypothesis does not *prove* an alternative to be right. We may choose an incorrect alternative from the infinite number available, and anyway we would have only rejected the null hypothesis on probability grounds (so we could easily be wrong about that as well).

In our example there appear to be three equally simple alternative hypotheses. If there is a difference, it could be expressed as a general difference (girls and boys will be different), or as a directed difference (girls will score more/less than boys). This is what the report above refers to as 1-sided or 2-sided (or more often one- or two-tailed). A two-tailed test of significance involves checking for an unspecified difference between two groups, such as 'The rates of training will be different for men and women'. A one-tailed test involves checking for a directional difference, such as 'Women are more likely to receive training than men', or its inverse. All three possible explanations are equally simple, but the directional hypotheses are intrinsically more convincing because they set us a more difficult test. If we predict that men and women differ in their frequency of training, we could be right if men do more or if women do more. We are, *a priori*, about twice as likely to find this as to find specifically that men get more training than women (or vice versa). We might therefore wish to adjust our significance level (5 per cent in our first example) accordingly, by decreasing it to 2.5 per cent for two-tailed tests perhaps, or increasing it to 10 per cent for one-tailed directional tests. This is part of the judgement that you, as researcher, must make and explain to your readers.

SUMMARY OF CHI-SQUARE – A SIMPLE TEST OF SIGNIFICANCE

These are the outline steps in carrying out a test of significance, using two groups (e.g. male and female) and a categorical variable (e.g. educated to degree level, or not).

1. State the *null hypothesis* of no difference between the groups (e.g. the same proportion of men and women in the population are educated to degree level).

2. State an alternative hypothesis, either *one-tailed* (e.g. more men in the population are educated to degree level) or *two-tailed* (e.g. a different proportion of men and women in the population are educated to degree level).
3. Decide on a *level of significance*. This is an estimate, based on an assumption of no difference between groups in the population, of the acceptable probability that any apparent difference between groups in the achieved sample is due to chance. For example, using 5 per cent would mean that the researcher is prepared to reject the null hypothesis if the probability of the null hypothesis being true is less than 5 per cent. Using a higher level of significance (e.g. 10 per cent) increases the possibility of incorrectly rejecting the null hypothesis (a *Type I error*), and using a lower level (e.g. 1 per cent) increases the possibility of incorrectly retaining the null hypothesis (a *Type II error*). See Chapter 8 for more on this.
4. Calculate the test statistic (e.g. chi-square) with appropriate *degrees of freedom* (or df). The degrees of freedom represent the number of values in the table of calculation that could be altered (that have the 'freedom' to be different). In a chi-square test, df = (number of rows-1) times (number of columns-1). In Table 6.13, if the sample of 300 cases has 140 males and 100 people with a degree, and any one of the four central cells is known then all others are known as well. If 60 men have a degree, then 40 women have a degree and 80 men do not have. Degrees of freedom are therefore one (two rows and two columns).

Table 6.13: Example of two-by-two cross-tabulation

Sex	Degree	No degree	Total
Male	60	80	140
Female	40	120	160
Total	100	200	300

5. Calculate the probability of the test statistic assuming the null hypothesis. If the result is less than the pre-determined level of significance, then the null hypothesis is rejected and the alternative hypothesis used in its place. If the result is more than or equal to the pre-determined level of significance, the null hypothesis is retained.

It is clear that more men in the sample have degrees. The test of significance is used to help decide whether the results for the sample would also be true for the larger population from which they are drawn. Thus, the population to which the results could generalize must have been described before carrying out the test. 'Significance' is used here to refer to the technical decision about retaining or rejecting the null hypothesis. Statistically significant results can be rather ordinary in social science terms, whereas non-significant results can be surprising (e.g. finding no significant difference in performance between those who had practised a skilled task and those who had not). In carrying out a chi-square test, in practice the actual steps are much simpler than those above. Putting the data in a statistical package and asking for a chi-square test leads to step 5 immediately.

All tests of significance have underlying assumptions which must be met before they can be used. Chi-square is perhaps the most tolerant of the standard tests, and therefore the most widely applicable. It can be used to compare two (or more) categorical variables as long as the expected number of cases in each cell is a reasonable number (at least 10 perhaps). Expected cases are calculated under the null hypothesis. In Table 6.13, if there was no difference between men and women in the population, one would expect around 47 men to have a degree (i.e. 100/300* 140/300) Since df = 1 one would therefore expect 53 women to have degrees etc. Chi-square is calculated from the difference between observed and expected values in each cell (see Table 6.14).

Chi-square can be used for larger tables with more than two categories per variable, but becomes correspondingly harder to interpret. For example, the test may tell you that there is a significant difference within a table of 8 rows and 7 columns but it cannot pinpoint where (see below).

Chi-square is not a very powerful test, where *power* is defined as the ability to find genuine patterns while minimizing Type I errors. Increased power can be attained by increasing the number of cases,

Table 6.14: Expected values for Table 6.13

Sex	Degree	No degree	Total
Male	47	93	140
Female	53	107	160
Total	100	200	300

looking for larger effect sizes, being more precise in the alternative hypothesis by adding a direction of difference, or using a more powerful test (see Chapter 8).

OTHER NON-PARAMETRIC TESTS

This chapter concentrates on the chi-square test for several reasons. My intention is to convey the logic, and some of the technical vocabulary, of significance testing. In the summary steps above you could replace the term chi-square with the name of a different statistic. It would make no practical difference to the overall steps. It is also the case that chi-square is the most general test. It could conceivably be used for any analysis, including checking for reliability in the one-sample case. Siegel (1956) recommends chi-square for all designs involving variables with nominal characteristics.

Nevertheless, there are many other tests (see Kanji, 1999, for example). Which of these should you use and when? The proper answer is, whichever you need whenever it is appropriate. For the novice several textbooks contain charts, tables, or flow diagrams on their inside cover as a prompt to find the section of the book relevant to the test you need, but these also provide a useful reference for identifying which test that is. The charts generally refer to dimensions such as level of measurement (see Chapter 4), the number of sample groups, the relationship between sample groups, and your purpose in using the test (for measuring associations or differences). Table 6.15 provides a simple example for all non-parametric designs (see Chapter 8 for parametric designs, and Reynolds, 1977; Lee *et al.*, 1989 and Gilbert, 1993, for more on the analysis of tables). For any analyses using only nominal variables the chi-square test is appropriate, although this can lead to problems with large tables. For analyses with ordinal variables mixed with nominal variables (e.g. level of qualification by ethic group) more powerful tests (often named after their 'inventors', see Table 6.15) are available that take advantage of the ranked nature of at least one of the variables. In

Table 6.15: Which non-parametric test should you use?

	one-sample	two independent samples	k independent samples
nominal	chi-square	chi-square	chi-square
ordinal	Kolgorov-Smirnov	Mann-Whitney	Kruskal-Wallis

situations where chi-square would be appropriate you can also use Cramer's V as a measure of the actual association between the two categorical variables.

COMMON ERRORS WITH TABLES

This section contains common errors in the construction and presentation of tabular information. I understand their temptations well because I have probably made all of them at some stage. The common errors with tables are:

- making insufficient reference to tables in the text;
- over-description of tables in the text;
- publishing computer printout;
- uncritical use of the omnibus chi-square test;
- *post hoc* recoding of items/collapsing categories;
- violating the assumptions of a test.

Making Insufficient Reference to Tables in the Text
Although it is important that tables are presented in a way that is comprehensible to the reader, it is still necessary to refer to them and explain their significance in the accompanying text. Tables are a way of illustrating or backing up a point made in your argument. If any tables are not relevant to your argument, they should be deleted from the presentation. In the same way, tables should only contain information relevant to that argument and, therefore, often need to be pruned ruthlessly. All analysts are probably guilty of including unwanted information in their tables, and at the same time providing insufficient explanation in the text. A cynic might say that statistics are being displayed in journal articles to help persuade a cursory reader of the validity of the conclusions, but in insufficient detail for the more pedantic reader to attempt to verify them (Gephart, 1988).

An article by Cheung and Lewis (1998) on the expectations by employers of new graduate employers provides several examples of this problem. In what is essentially a long empirical paper of 14 pages they provide only one brief paragraph on the methods they used. Consequently, most of their 'results' have to be taken on trust (not something I like to do too often). There is no description at all of the instrument used to collect their primary data (see Chapter 5 for the possible importance of this). Therefore when the authors present findings, such as the 12 skills rated as 'very important' by employers, we do not know the length of the list from which these 12 were selected. The responses were obtained using a 5-point Likert scale, but no account is taken in the report of four of the possible responses on that scale. Their Tables 2 and 3 show only the percentage of respondents reporting a skill as 'very important'. We have no idea therefore of the distribution of other responses. There may, for example, be skills that all employers rate as 'important' but without being 'very important', and others that a few rate as 'very important' but most rate as 'of no importance'. In the method adopted by Cheung and Lewis, the second of these would be reported and the first would not – a gross distortion of the truth. As with many of the examples used in this book, it would be fascinating to know how this paper was able to 'pass' the peer-review process before acceptance for publishing.

Over-description of Tables in the Text
An alternative but less serious problem arises where the tables are fully explained and described in the text to the extent that the tables themselves are not necessary. This is very common in student dissertations. Consider, for example, Table 6.16.

Table 6.16: Car ownership by sex of respondent

Sex	N	Owns car	%	Doesn't own car	%
Male	56	23	41	33	59
Female	61	37	61	24	39
Total	117	60	51	57	49

I have often seen tables like this presented in dissertations as descriptive treatments of research results. Their purpose may be to describe the findings of a survey and no more complex analysis is presented. In the text, Table 6.16 is described by the student as showing that 41 per cent of males but 61 per cent of females own cars. Assuming that the nature of the sample (size and sex breakdown) has already been described, the use of the table here in addition is ponderous and wasteful. Novices may consider that it has rhetorical appeal, but the last two columns are totally superfluous, and the others may be summarized in a sentence. In many examples, a simple description of frequencies is easier to understand and shorter than a table.

Publishing Computer Printout

Related to the above habit of presenting ponderous tables (and to the use of technical variable names as descriptors, see Chapter 9) is the habit of presenting undigested computer printouts in research reports. As you will have noted, computer packages for data analysis are notoriously profligate in their use of space for reports. A full report even from a simple 2 × 2 chi-square test might look like this (Table 6.17).

This output contains much more detail and information than most readers would want. Decide which part of this report is important to you, and display only that part in your own writing. Do not reproduce the whole, either because you cannot be bothered to work out the key message, or as a flourish to show that you have

Table 6.17: Undigested output from a chi-square test

Case processing summary						

Cases						
	Valid		Missing		Total	
	N	Per cent	N	Per cent	N	Per cent
VAR00001*VAR0002	91	100.0%	0	.0%	91	100.0%

VAR00001*VAR0002 Cross-tabulation

Count

		VAR00002		
		1.00	2.00	Total
VAR00001	1.00	22	15	37
	2.00	26	28	54
Total		48	43	91

Chi-square tests

	Value	df	Asymp. sig. (2-sided)	Exact sig. (2-sided)	Exact sig. (1-sided)
Pearson chi-square	1.127[b]	1	.288		
Continuity correction[a]	.719	1	.396		
Likelihood ratio	1.132	1	.287		
Fisher's exact test				.393	.198
Linear-by-linear association	1.115	1	.291		
N of valid cases	91				

Notes: [a]Computed only for a 2 × 2 table.
[b]0 cells (.0 per cent) have expected count less than 5. The minimum expected count is 17.48.

done the test. Decide for yourself how to structure the report of your findings, how many decimal places to use, and so on.

Uncritical Use of the Omnibus Chi-square Test
In the case of a 2 × 2 table the results of a significant chi-square test are unambiguous. The direction of difference is always clear, since one of the two groups will have the higher value for the test variable. Where the table is larger than this, a significant result shows that there is a pattern/difference in the table but not where it is (as also happens when there are more than two groups for Analysis of Variance, see Chapter 8). Further analysis is needed to characterize the differences in the table. Despite this, I regularly see students who feel that this second stage is too much effort, and that they can see the pattern easily anyway. Their approach is therefore similar to that of finding the outlines of animals in the stars in the night sky, but with the added appeal of a statistically significant omnibus chi-square test. In reality, they are trying to answer hopelessly imprecise or even unthought-of research questions (Rosenthal, 1991). For example, consider the cross-tabulation in Table 6.18.

Table 6.18: Large table analysis

Area of residence	Non-participant	Delayed learner	Transitional learner	Lifelong learner	Still in education	Total
Bridgend	97	43	79	130	20	369
Blaenau Gwent	141	47	81	81	11	361
Neath Port Talbot	101	54	62	142	11	370
Total	339	144	222	353	42	1100

Table 6.18 results from the sample of patterns of adult participation in learning described in Chapter 2. It has eight degrees of freedom, and the probability for the associated chi-square test is reported as 0.000. This means that there is a very small chance indeed that the pattern of learning experiences (columns) is the same in the three geographical areas (rows). We can safely reject the null hypothesis of no difference between the three groups. However, this does not help us identify what the significant difference is. Is it that more people in the area known as Blaenau Gwent (141/361) do not participate in adult education at all? Is it that more people in Neath Port Talbot (142/370) are lifelong learners? Is it that more people in Bridgend (20/369) are still in full-time initial education? There is really only

one way to answer these questions, and that is to consider each pairwise comparison separately in a specially constructed 2 × 2 version of the table. For example the first question could be answered by collapsing Table 6.18 to the following form (Table 6.19).

Table 6.19: Recoding a large table

Location	Non-participant	All other learners	Total
Blaenau Gwent	141	220	361
Bridgend or Neath	198	541	739
Total	339	761	1100

The cells for Bridgend and Neath Port Talbot have been added together, and the cells for all learning experiences except non-participants have been added together. A simpler chi-square test can now be conducted on this 2 × 2 table, and if the result is significant (which it is incidentally) we can attribute it to a difference between areas. A potential problem with this approach is the number of tests that need to be carried out leading to the greater danger of spurious findings. Each test carries a possibility of leading to an error, so conducting more tests mean more chances of error (see Chapter 8 for a discussion of this shotgun approach).

Post-hoc Recoding of Items/Collapsing Categories
Although there are often good reasons why survey items need to be recoded or categories within variables collapsed after the data has been collected (as in the last example), I have a feeling that this approach is over-used. Considering the nature of the analysis during the design stage helps us to reduce the need for such recoding. It should therefore only be necessary when the actual frequencies reported are somewhat skewed or where the preliminary considera-tion of analysis has been deficient. An example of the first sort might be where a questionnaire used the Registrar General's 7-point scale for collecting occupational classifications, but the nature of an achieved sample of 660 random cases was such that 'unskilled manual' and 'semi-skilled manual' occupations were both very rare. In this case, the analyst may wish to collapse these two categories for some forms of analysis requiring robust numbers of cases in each cell of the table (creating one category for 'less-skilled' occupations for example). Providing the compromise is reported, this is a perfectly proper action. An example of the second sort might be where the

same scale was used with a sample of 30 cases. Here, unlike the first example, it would be entirely predictable that some if not all of the seven occupational categories would be very sparsely represented. The 'fault' lies with the analyst for having too many sub-groups for the sample size.

Violating the Assumptions of a Test
All tests of significance are based on underlying assumptions about the research design. If these are violated (i.e. if the test is used even when the assumptions are not true), then the results may be invalid (see Chapter 8 for more on the debate about this). It is therefore important to at least know what these assumptions are. Tests for nominal variables such as chi-square are very tolerant, having the fewest assumptions, making them usable in a wide variety of situations. Two problems that I have seen in beginners' work are as follows. Table 6.20 is an example of a problem already described above. The observed figures in themselves give no cause for concern, appearing to suggest that the rate of failure in a particular test is higher among state-funded students than among fee-paying students. But the expected value for one cell is very small. Since so few students are fee-paying (16) and so few gain a fail grade overall (10), we *expect* only two cases of failure among fee-paying students even if there is no real difference between the types of students (our null hypothesis). In this case any test might not be valid, so we should point out the problem in any publication, and remember to go for a larger sample next time.

Table 6.21 shows a problem I have encountered only once, but

Table 6.20: Small expected count

Students	Pass	Fail	Total
Fee-paying	15 (14)	1 (2)	16
State-funded	60 (61)	9 (8)	69
Total	75	10	85

Table 6.21: Need for mutually exclusive cases

Students	Pass	Fail	Total
Fee-paying	12	12	24
Female	47	17	64
Total	??	??	??

which is typical of a certain type of novice quantitative 'analyst' who feels a need to use a significance test but who does not follow the logic of testing with which this chapter started. If female students could also be fee-paying students, then we cannot complete this cross-tabulation, and we cannot use chi-square. The categories in our cross-tabulation must be mutually exclusive. The example I saw was more complex than this and stemmed from a survey question that asked respondents to 'tick as many answers as apply' (see Chapter 5 for more on the difficulties of such designs).

This chapter has introduced the logic of statistical testing using the most common non-parametric approach. The next chapter considers a range of experimental designs leading to the need for more powerful parametric techniques.

7

Experimental approaches: a return to the gold standard?

WHY USE EXPERIMENTS?

In many ways the experiment is the 'flagship' or gold standard of research designs. The basic advantage of this approach over any other is its convincing claim to be testing for cause and effect, via the manipulation of otherwise identical groups. In addition, some experiments will allow the size of any effect to be measured. The other approaches described so far in this book merely set out to observe an unspecified relationship between two or more variables. It has therefore been argued that only experiments are able to produce secure and uncontested knowledge about the truth of propositions. Educational research has, for too long perhaps, relied on the fancy statistical manipulation of poor datasets, rather than studies that start with a convincing design (FitzGibbon 1996). Experimental designs are flexible, allowing for any number of different groups and variables, and the outcome measures taken can be of any kind, although they are normally coded into numeric form. The design is actually so powerful that it requires smaller numbers of participants as a minimum than would be normal in a survey for example.

As should become clear in this chapter, the experimental method can also be extremely useful to all researchers even if they do not carry out a real experiment. How is this possible? Knowing the format and power of experiments gives us a yardstick against which to measure what we do instead, and even helps us to design what we do better. An obvious example of this occurs in a 'thought experiment', in which we can freely consider how to gain secure and uncontested knowledge about the truth of our propositions without any concern about practical or ethical considerations. This becomes our ideal, and it helps us to recognize the practical limitations of our actual approach. Another example is a natural experiment (see below) where we design an 'experiment' without an intervention, using the same design as a standard experiment but making use of a naturally occurring phenomenon.

EXPERIMENTAL DESIGN

This section outlines the basic experimental design for two groups. In this, the researcher creates two (or more) 'populations' by using different treatments with two samples drawn randomly from a parent population (or by dividing one sample into two at random). Each sample becomes a treatment group. As with all research, the quality and usefulness of the findings depend heavily on the care used in sampling (see Chapter 2). The treatment is known as the 'independent' variable, and the researcher selects a post-treatment test (or measure) known as the 'dependent' variable. Usually one group will receive the treatment and be termed the experimental group and another will not receive the treatment and be termed the control group (see Table 7.1).

The researcher then specifies a null hypothesis (that there will be no difference in the dependent variable between the treatment groups), and an experimental hypothesis (the simplest explanation of any observed difference in the dependent variable between groups). The experimental hypothesis can predict the direction of any observed difference between the groups (a one-tailed hypothesis), or not (a two-tailed hypothesis). Only then does the experimenter obtain the scores on the dependent variable and analyse them (for example, by applying a t-test for the means of independent samples, see Chapter 8). If there is a significant difference between the two groups, it is caused by the treatment.

A one-tailed prediction is intrinsically more convincing and thus permits a higher threshold for the significance level. All predictions, by definition, must be made in advance, else analysing the data is like looking for shapes in the patterns of stars. There are always apparent patterns in data. The experimental design tries to maximize the

Table 7.1: The simple experimental design

	Allocation	Pre-test	Intervention	Post-test
Experimental	random	measurement	treatment	measurement
Control	random	measurement	–	measurement

probability that any pattern uncovered is significant, generalizable and replicable. Merely rejecting the null hypothesis as too improbable to explain a set of observations does not make a poorly crafted experimental hypothesis right. There are, in principle, an infinite number of equally logical explanations for any result. The most useful explanation is therefore that which can be most easily tested by further research. It must be the simplest explanation, usually leading to a further testable prediction.

There are in summary six steps in the basic experiment:

- Formulate a hypothesis (which is confirmatory/disconfirmatory rather than exploratory).
- Randomly assign cases to the intervention or control groups (so that any non-experimental differences are due solely to chance).
- Measure the dependent variable (as a pre-test, but note this step is not always used).
- Introduce the treatment or independent variable.
- Measure the dependent variable again (as a post-test).
- Calculate the significance of the differences between the groups.

A simple example might involve testing the efficacy of a new lesson plan for teaching a particular aspect of mathematics. A large sample is randomly divided into two groups. Both groups sit a test of their understanding of the mathematical concept, giving the researcher a pre-test score. One group is given a lesson (or lessons) on the relevant topic in the usual way. This is the control group. Another group is given a lesson using the new lesson plan. This is the experimental treatment group. Both groups sit a further test of their understanding of the mathematical concept giving the researcher a post-test score. The difference between the pre- and post-test scores for each student yields a gain score. The null hypothesis will be that both groups will show the same average gain score. The alternative hypothesis could be that the treatment group will show a higher average gain score than the control group. These hypotheses can be tested using a t-test for unrelated samples (see Chapter 8). If the null hypothesis is rejected, and if the two groups do not otherwise differ in any systematic way, then the researcher can reasonably claim that the new lesson plan *caused* the improvement gain scores.

CHALLENGES FOR VALIDITY

The logic of an experiment like the example above relies on the only difference between the groups being due to the treatment. Under these conditions, the experiment is said to lead to valid results. There are several threats to this validity in experiments. Some of these are obvious, some less so. An often cited, but still useful, summary of many of these potential threats comes from Campbell and Stanley (1963) and Cook and Campbell (1979). These are conveniently grouped under eight headings, discussed briefly here.

History
Some people taking part in experiments may have other experiences during the course of the study that affect their recorded measurement but which are not under experimental control. An example could be a fire alarm going off during the exposure to one of the treatments (e.g. during the maths lesson for one of the groups above). Thus, an 'infection' or confounding variable enters the system and provides a possible part of the explanation for any observed differences between the experimental groups.

Maturation
By design, the post-treatment measure (or post-test) is taken at some time after the start of the experiment or, put more simply, experiments require the passage of time. It is possible therefore that some of the differences noted stem from confounding factors related to this. These could include ageing (in extreme cases), boredom, and practice effects. Time is important in other ways. If, for example, we are studying the effect of smoking prevention education among 15 year olds, when is the payoff? Are we concerned only with immediate cessation or would we call the treatment a success if it lowered the students' chances of smoking as adults? To consider such long-term outcomes is expensive and not attractive to political sponsors (who usually want quick fixes). A danger for all educational research is therefore a focus on short-term changes, making the studies trivial rather than transformative (Scott and Usher, 1999). Even where the focus is genuinely on the short term, some effects can be significant in size but insignificant in fact because they are so short-lived. Returning to the smoking example, would we call the treatment a success if it lowered the amount of smoking at school for the next day only?

Experimenters need to watch for what has been termed a 'Hawthorne' effect. A study of productivity in a factory (called Hawthorne) in the 1920s tried to boost worker activity by using brighter lighting. The treatment was a success. Factory output increased, but only for a week or so before returning to its previous level. As there was apparently no long-term benefit for the factory owners, the lighting level was reduced to the *status ante*. Surprisingly, this again produced a similar short-term increase in productivity. This suggests that participants in experiments may be sensitive to almost any variation in treatment (either more or less lighting) for a short time. The simple fact of being in an experiment can affect participants' behaviour. If so, this is a huge problem for the validity of almost all experiments and is very difficult to control for in a snapshot design. It can be seen as a particular problem for school-based research, where students might react strongly to any change in routine regardless of its intrinsic pedagogical value.

Testing

The very act of conducting a test or taking a measure can produce a confounding effect. People taking part may come to get used to being tested (showing less nervousness perhaps). Where the design is longitudinal they may wish to appear consistent in their answers when re-tested later, even where their 'genuine' response has changed. A related problem can arise from the demand characteristics of the experimenter who can unwittingly (we hope) indicate to participants their own expectations, or otherwise influence the results in favour of a particular finding. Such effects have been termed 'experimenter effects' and they are some of the most pernicious dangers to validity. In addition, apparently random errors in recording and analysing results have actually been found to favour the experimental hypothesis predominantly (Adair, 1973). If the researcher knows which group is which and what is 'expected' of each group by the experimental hypothesis, then they can give cues to this in their behaviour.

Traditionally, this effect has been illustrated by the history of a horse that could count (Clever Hans). Observers asked Hans a simple sum (such as 3 + 5), and the horse tapped its hoof that number of times (8). This worked whether the observers were believers or sceptics. It was eventually discovered that it only did not work if the observer did not know the answer (i.e. they were 'blind', see below). What appeared to be happening was that the horse was tapping its hoof in response to the question, and after tapping the right number of times it was able to recognize the sense of expectancy, or frisson of excitement, that ran through the observers waiting to see whether it would tap again. The horse presumably learnt that however many times it tapped, if it stopped when that moment came it would then receive praise and a sugar lump. Social science experiments generally involve people both as researchers and as participants. The opportunities for just such an experimenter effect (misconstruing trying to please the experimenter as a real result) are therefore very great. If we add to these problems the other impacts of the person of the researcher (stemming from their clothes, sex, accent, age, etc.) it is clear that the experimenter effect is a key issue for any design (see below).

Instrumentation

'Contamination' can also enter an experimental design through changes in the nature of the measurements taken at different points. Clearly, we would set out to control for (or equalize) the researcher used for each group in the design, and the environment and time of day at which the experiment takes place. However, even where both groups appear to be treated equally, the nature of the instrument used can be a confounding variable. If the instrument used, or the measurement taken, or the characteristics of the experimenter change during the experiment, this could have differential impact on each group. For example, if one group contains more females and another more males and the researcher taking the first measure is male and the researcher taking the second measure is female, then at least some of the difference between the groups could be attributable to the nature of same and different sex interactions. Note that this is so even though both groups had the same researcher on each occasion (i.e. they appeared to be treated equally).

Regression

In most experiments the researcher is not concerned with individuals but with aggregate or overall scores (such as the mean score for each group). When such aggregate scores are near to an extreme value they tend to regress towards the mean over time almost irrespective of the treatment given to each individual, simply because extreme scores have nowhere else to go. In the same way perhaps that the children of very tall people tend to be shorter than their parents, so groups who average zero on a test will tend to improve their score and groups who score 100 per cent will tend towards a lower score. They will regress towards the mean irrespective of other factors. If they show any changes over time, these are the only ones possible, so random fluctuations produce regression. This is a potential problem with designs involving one or more extreme groups.

Selection

As with any design, biased results are obtained via experiments in which the participants have been selected in some way. Whenever a subjective value judgement is made about selection of cases, or where there is a test that participants must 'pass' before joining in, there is a possible source of contamination. This problem is overcome to a large extent by the use of randomization, but note the practical difficulties of achieving this (see Chapter 2).

Mortality
A specific problem arising from the extended nature of some experiments is drop-out among participants, often referred to by the rather grim term 'subject mortality'. Even where a high quality sample is achieved at the start of the experiment, this may become biased by some participants not continuing to the end. As with non-response bias, it is clearly possible that those people less likely to continue with an experiment are systematically different from the rest (perhaps in terms of motivation, leisure time, geographic mobility, and so on).

Diffusion
Perhaps the biggest specific threat to experiments in educational research today comes from potential diffusion of the treatments between groups. In a large-scale study using a field setting it is very difficult to restrict the treatments to each experimental group, and it is therefore all too easy to end up with an 'infected' control group. Imagine the situation where new curriculum materials for Key Stage 2 Geography are being tested out with one experimental group of students and their results compared to a control group using more traditional curriculum material. If any school contains students from both groups it is almost impossible to prevent one child helping another with homework by showing them their 'wonderful' new books. Even where the children are in different schools, this infection is still possible through friendship or family relationships. In my experience of such studies in Singapore the most cross-infection in these circumstances actually comes from the teachers themselves who tend to be collaborative and collegial, and very keen to send their friends photocopies of the super lesson plans that they have just been given by the Ministry of Education. For these teachers, teaching the next lesson is understandably more important than taking part in a national trial. On the other hand, if the experimental groups are isolated from each other, by using students in different countries, for example, then we are introducing greater doubt that the two groups are comparable anyway.

As you can imagine, given these and other potential limitations of experimental evidence, the ideal, the flagship of social science research, is far from realizable for most of us. There will always be some room for doubt about the findings even from a properly conducted experiment. It is important, however, to note two points. First, there are some things we can do with our basic design to counter any possible contamination (see next section). Second, the experiment remains the most completely theorized and understood method in social science. With its familiarity comes our increased awareness of its limitations, but other and newer approaches will have as many and more problems. Worse, other designs will have dangers and limitations that we are not even aware of yet.

CONTROLLING CONTAMINATION

The basic experimental design (see Table 7.1 above) takes care of several possible threats to validity. The random allocation of participants to groups reduces selection bias, so that the only systematic difference between the groups is the treatment, and the control group gives us an estimate of the differences between pre- and post-test regardless of the intervention.

Designs usually get more complex to control for any further threats to internal validity. In psychology in particular some very large, and sometimes rather unwieldy, approaches are used. A 'factorial design' uses one group for each combination of all the independent variables, of which there may be several. So for an experiment involving three two-way independent variables there would be eight conditions plus at least one control group. The effects of these variables would be broken down into the 'main effects' (of each variable in isolation) and the 'interaction effects' (of two or more variables in combination).

As you can imagine, the analysis of such advanced designs becomes accordingly more complex also and is therefore beyond the scope of this book. For despite the fact that psychology undergraduates are routinely taught these designs, they do not always, in my experience, either appreciate or understand them. And they even more rarely use them properly. Factorial designs are anyway sometimes used in situations when they are not necessary (perhaps only because 'we have the technology'). When faced with considerable complexity in the topic of an investigation I feel that a more helpful response is to seek greater simplicity of approach rather than greater sophistication. For example, it is clear that the pre-test phase in an

Table 7.2: The post-test only experimental design

	Allocation	Pre-test	Intervention	Post-test
Group A	random	–	treatment	measurement
Group B	random	–	–	measurement

experiment can sensitize people for their subsequent post-test (an experience/instrumentation effect). So we *could* use at least four groups and alternate both the treatment and whether there is a pre-test or not. A simpler variant with the same advantage is the post-test only design (see Table 7.2). If the sample is large enough it is possible to do away with the pre-test and assume that the randomly allocated groups would have had equivalent mean scores before treatment. As it is even simpler than the basic design we can be even more confident that it is only the intervention which causes any difference between groups.

Since the researcher can have a social impact on the outcomes, this needs to be controlled for in the design, if possible, and made visible in the reporting of results. There are various standard techniques to overcome the experimenter effect, though it is doubtful that all would be available for use in a small-scale student project. To start with, it is important that the participants are 'blind' in that they do not know the precise nature of the experiment until it is complete (see below for a discussion of the ethical considerations relating to this). Ideally, the experimenter should also be 'blind' in not knowing which group any participant belongs to. This double-blind situation is sometimes maintained by means of a placebo (the name deriving from drug trials) in which everyone appears to undergo the same treatment even though some of the treatment is phoney or empty (equivalent to a sugar pill rather than a drug).

Another way of achieving the same end is to automate the experiment and thereby minimize social contact (often not possible of course). Another is to sub-contract the experiment to someone else who does not know the details. You could, for example, offer to conduct an experiment for a colleague in return for them conducting yours. Other ways of minimizing experimenter bias include getting more than one account of any observation, by using several people as observers and looking at the inter-rater reliability of measurements, or by a triangulation of methods wherein the experimental findings are checked against evidence from other sources.

THE SEVEN SAMURAI

So, guard against the possible limitations to your experiment as far as possible. However, problems such as diffusion or the Hawthorne effect are almost impossible to eliminate as possibilities. Therefore consider them, and report them, in your explanations in the same way as I have advised that you do for any other limitations, such as those in your achieved sample.

Although I have not seen the classic film *The Seven Samurai* for many years now, I recall the scene when the Samurai arrive at the village, and begin to arrange for it to be fortified against the bandits. They ask the villagers to build a wall/barrier all around the village, but to leave one large gap. The headsman queries this, and suggests that the fortification should be made continuous. One of the warriors replies that 'every good fort has a defect', and therefore the most important thing is to know where that defect is. If you were attacking the village, you would focus on the gap in the wall, and that is where the defenders (only seven in number remember) will be strongest.

Now I am not suggesting that you leave a gaping hole in your PhD method so that you will know what to discuss in your viva voce examination! Rather, the point is that, like a fort, every good research design has defects. Your job as researcher is both to minimize the defects, and equally importantly to recognize where the remaining defects are. Self-criticism is your best defence against the criticism of others, and using the ideal of an experiment (or at least a fantasy experiment) can help you identify the defects and so make relevant criticisms.

FIELD AND FANTASY TRIALS

The biggest problem in using experiments comes from their chief source of strength – the level of control of the research situation possible in a laboratory. Traditionally experiments, following a natural science model, have been conducted in laboratory conditions. A laboratory allows the experimenter to control extraneous conditions more closely, and so to claim with more conviction that the only difference between the two groups in an experiment is the presence or absence of the treatment variable. This level of control often leads to an unrealistic setting and rather trivial research questions. It has been said that a series of experiments allows us to be more and more certain about less and less. In fact, although it may be desirable in research terms, this level of experimental control is usually absent when confronting research in real-life situations. For example, it is not possible to allocate people randomly to groups in order to investigate war, disease, marriage, employment or imprisonment. Yet these might be seen as some of the most interesting areas for social science research. In addition, it is actually the control of the experiment by the researcher that can lead to self-fulfilment (delusion), or selective bias in observation. There can also be ethical problems in deceiving participants since, even where the treatment is non-harmful, it is usually necessary for the participants to be ignorant of the purpose of the experiment.

For me the laboratory experiment is therefore akin to an ideal. It is how we would like to conduct research to get clear answers about the implications of our actions in education. Therefore, even if you never conduct a true experiment, knowing what it would have been is an important yardstick to help evaluate what you do. Everything that has been said about the problem of internal validity in experiments applies with even greater force to all other designs. If an experimenter, while trying to be neutral, unwittingly conveys demands to participants in fairly meaningless laboratory tasks, imagine the likely effect of an interviewer in personal communication with a interviewee, for example. If an experimenter unwittingly makes favourable mistakes in noting or adding up a simple data collection form, imagine the level of bias possible in interpreting the findings from a focus group discussion. In this way, if we consider the ways in which our actual designs are like a true experiment, it allows us a glimpse of their considerable imperfections and keeps us appropriately humble. It helps with future research synthesis by giving us a common standard against which to compare all studies.

In a sense I am advocating here the use of the 'thought experiment', now widely used in science. Thought, or fantasy, experiments are quick, cheap, and have no ethical problems (since we have no intention of carrying them out). We can think the unthinkable by imagining what a true experiment would be like for our area of investigation, and then compare the actual and ideal designs to help show up the defects in our actual design.

A more common (though currently still far from popular) form of experiment in educational research is the field trial. The most obvious way in which field trials differ from laboratory ones is that they tend to use existing groups as the basis for treatment (Hakim, 1992). These 'quasi-experiments' therefore do not use random selection or allocation to groups but recognize natural clusters in the population (see Chapter 2). It is just about impossible to allocate students to teaching processes (such as schools or classrooms) at random. What is possible is to use existing teaching groups and vary the treatments between them, using statistical procedures to try and iron out any differences in the results due to pre-existing group differences. This approach gives the experiment a lower general level of internal validity but, because the setting is more realistic than a laboratory, the external validity (relevance to real life) is probably greater.

Bernard (2000) draws a useful distinction between a naturalistic field experiment which is most similar to the laboratory set-up since the experimenter intervenes with a treatment, and a natural field experiment in which the researcher merely identifies an existing quasi-experimental situation and monitors it. Selecting 20 classes in different schools across England and Wales, and teaching half of them arithmetic with a calculator and half without, in order to test the impact of calculator use on an eventual test score would be a naturalistic experiment. The researcher has intervened to produce two different treatment groups (and of course the experiment has considerable difficulties in terms of the diffusive effects of calculator use at home). Natural experiments, on the other hand, are going on around us all of the time, when interventions occur as part of the policy process. If one local education authority changes its practice in some way it can be construed as the experimental group, with the remaining authorities as controls, in a natural experiment. In fact, much social science research is of this type – retrospectively trying to explain differences between two (sometimes even just one) groups such as those in Table 7.2 (e.g. Gorard and Taylor, 2001). All these designs are inferior in terms of validity to a true experimental design but much more practical. Knowing how an experiment works is important because it enables us to see how far a natural experiment is from that ideal.

CHALLENGES FOR ETHICS

The biggest challenge facing any increased use of experimental designs in educational research is, however, an ethical and not a technical one. Of course, ethical issues do not apply only to experiments and many of the issues discussed here also apply to other forms of research. While perhaps overplayed in importance by some writers, there will be at least some ethical considerations in any piece of research (see, for example, Walford, 1991). Consider this example. NHS Direct is a telephone helpline set to relieve pressure on other UK National Health Service activities. Callers can ask for help and advice, or reduce their anxiety about minor injuries or repetitive illness, without going to their general practitioner or to hospital out-patients. Research reported by Carter (2000) found serious short-comings in this new service. The evidence for this was collected by making a large number of fake calls to test the consistency, quality and speed of the advice given. In ethical terms, is this OK?

One argument against this study is that it has misused a procedure intended to relieve pressure on an already pressurized and poten-tially life-saving public service. By conducting the research via bogus calls, it is at least possible that individuals have suffered harm as a consequence. One argument for the study would be that realistic (and therefore 'blind') evaluations are an essential part of improving public services, and that the longer-term objective of the study was to produce an amelioration of any shortcomings discovered. If, for the sake of argument, NHS Direct was actually a waste of public funds it would be important to find this out at an early stage and redirect its funding to other approaches. This, in a nutshell, is the major issue facing ethics and research. Researchers will not want to cause damage knowingly, but is it worth them risking possible harm to some individuals for a greater overall gain? As with most decisions I am faced with, I do not have a definite answer to this one. Or rather, my definite answer is 'it depends'.

It depends, of course, on the quality of the research being con-ducted. Most observers would agree with this on reflection, but it is seldom made explicit in any discussion of ethics. It would, for example, be entirely reasonable to come to opposite conclusions about the example above dependent on the quality of the study. If calling the help-line for research purposes runs a risk of replacing other genuine callers, then it has to be considered whether the value of the research is worth that risk. If, for example, the study found that the line was working well, then no more research is needed (and the study has served its evaluative purpose). If it found problems, and as a result these could be ameliorated (although it is clearly not the full responsibility of the researcher if they are not), then the study could claim to be worthwhile. The one outcome that would be of no use to anyone is where the research is of insufficient quality to reach a safe and believable conclusion either way. In this case the risk has been run for no reason and no gain.

Thus, ethically, the first responsibility of all research should be to quality and rigour. If it is decided that the best answer to a specific research question is likely to be obtained via an experimental design, for example, then this is at least part of the justification in ethical terms for its use. In this case, an experiment may be the *most* ethical approach even where it runs a greater risk of endangering participants than another less appropriate design. Pointless research, on the other hand, remains pointless, however 'ethically' it appears to be conducted. Good intentions do not guarantee good outcomes. Such a conclusion may be unpalatable to some readers, but where the research is potentially worthwhile, and the 'danger' (such as the danger of wasting people's time) is small relative to the worth, my conclusion is logically entailed in the considerations above.

Reinforcement for this conclusion comes from a consideration of the nature of funding for educational research. Whether financed by charitable donations or public taxation, research must attempt to justify the use of such public funds by producing high quality results. If the best method to use to generate safe conclusions to a specific question is an experiment (for example), then there should be considerable ethical pressure on the researcher to use an experiment.

The application of experimental designs from clinical research to educational practice does, however, highlight specific ethical issues (Hakuta, 2000). In a simple experiment with two groups, the most common complaint is that the design is discriminatory. If the control group is being denied a treatment in order for researchers to gain greater knowledge, this could be deemed unethical. FitzGibbon (1996) counters that this approach is only unethical if we know which group is to be disadvantaged. In most designs, of course, the whole purpose is to decide which treatment is better (or worse). We need evidence of what works before the denial of what works to one group can be deemed discriminatory. In our current state of relative ignorance about education it is as likely that the treatment will be the inferior approach for some, as that doing nothing to find out what works will damage the chances of others.

On the other hand, is it fair to society (rather than just the control group) to use an intervention without knowing what its impact will be? Would it be reasonable, for example, to try not jailing people sentenced for violent crimes simply to see if this led to less re-offending (De Leon *et al.*, 1995)? Again, the answer would have to be – it depends. What we have to take into account is not simply what is efficient or expedient but what is right or wrong. This judgement depends on values, and values are liable to change over time. In fact, doing the work of research can itself transform our views of what is right and wrong. If an alternative punishment to prison led to less violent crime, who would object (afterwards)?

Is deception of the participants in an experiment OK? Should we   •

always tell the truth? Should we encourage others to behave in ways they may not otherwise (by being violent, for example)? What is the risk to the participants? Can we assure confidentiality? Moral judgements such as these require deliberation of several factors, and there is seldom a clear-cut context-free principle to apply. There are two main contradictory principles in play here: respect for the welfare of participants, and finding the truth. The right to 'know' is an important moral after all, even where the consequences might hurt some individuals. We can never fully ignore the consequences of our study and we need to be tentative in our claims, as even experiments lead to only possible knowledge. Nevertheless, we also need virtues such as honesty to behave as researchers, to publish results even when they are painful or surprising (and the question 'could you be surprised by what you find?' is for me one criterion of demarcation between research and pseudo-research), and the courage to proceed even if this approach is unpopular.

For further discussion of the role of ethical considerations in educational research see Pring (2000). If in doubt whether a method you propose is defensible, check the ethical guidelines for your professional society (BSA, BPS, BERA, etc.). Each society publishes a list of, essentially very similar, 'rules' about honesty, sensitivity, and responsibility in conducting research. Your institution probably also has an ethics board to whom you can apply for informed consent. You should, of course, also check your ideas with your supervisor/ mentor. They should have a clear idea of the norms and standards applied to your field. The most unethical thing I have done was to ask a friend to call a number of fee-paying schools posing as a prospective parent and ask for promotional literature to be mailed to them. My justification is that I wanted not just the literature but notes on the telephone manner, promptness, and so on, of each school. Although I could therefore be accused of wasting the money and time of the school, the situation is not as serious as with the NHS (see above), and I was able to give the schools feedback about their presentation which was generally well received (Gorard, 1997b).

A NEW ERA FOR EDUCATIONAL RESEARCH?

Partly as a response to the debate about the value and relevance of academic educational research, government-appointed bodies in the UK have tried to move some research-funding to practitioner groups. The result has so far been depressing. I would not wish to try and defend the quality of much UK academic educational research (and I have been among its critics, see Hillage *et al.*, 1998), but research by teacher–researchers is likely to be even worse. The Teacher Training Agency (TTA), for example, award small grants to teachers to carry out research 'relevant' to their needs. The research so funded is often actually not research at all, not being aimed at producing knowledge based on the collection of evidence. It often simply describes current practice or uncontrolled attempts to change it (so-called 'action research'). Not all of these studies have produced a report, but those that have omit crucial basic details such as what they had done, or what their evidence was. Their apparent conclusions are mainly repetitions of previously held opinions (there being no sign of the surprise that for me is the hallmark of real discovery), but their 'lack of critical scrutiny also allows the presentation of questionable ideological views about the nature of practice under the banner of scientific research' (Foster, 1999, p. 396). I would not wish to base best-practice on these tiny case studies.

Perhaps the best such study I have seen concerns an 'experiment' on the teaching of mental arithmetic (TTA, 2000). In the school concerned the 1998 Key Stage 1 cohort (54 pupils) were taught mental arithmetic using a new method. A higher proportion gained a Level 3 result than in the 1997 cohort (55 pupils) taught using another method. Thus, the researchers conclude that the new method is better, and the TTA have supported this view by publishing it. Despite being the best study of the first 26 funded (since it presents evidence and a method for example, and has a reasonable number of cases), this is precisely the kind of evidence we do not need or want in education. The findings are simply not safe. The cohorts were different and unmatched, the proportions gaining Level 3 are growing year by year nationally anyway, the two groups sat different test papers, the teachers were not matched for the different cohorts (the more experienced Maths co-ordinator taking the second group), and there is no consideration of either the Hawthorne or experimenter effects.

The danger of the rhetorical power of an experiment may be glimpsed in the way in which a small study by Woolford and McDougall (1998) was built by the UK media into a panacea for boy's under-achievement at school requiring immediate changes in policy (*Western Mail*, 1998; *TES*, 1998). In fact, their 'study' consisted of comparing the end-of-year assessments of two primary classes in the same school, one of which had a male teacher and the other a female teacher. The results of boys in the male class were better than those in the female class, and the researchers conclude therefore that having more male teachers is the answer to the apparent under-achievement of boys. This study has the form of a natural experiment (the two groups were already formed and the treatment was 'accidental'), but has many clear problems. It is a very small study. One of the boy groups was likely to perform better, and *a priori* there is a 50 per cent chance of it being taught by the male teacher. There is no attempt to match the ability of the groups. There are no prior attainment scores (pre-test), no comparison of the skills and experience of the two teachers, the classes were taught in different rooms, and so on. I do not imply that the conclusion is not true, merely that this study provides no evidence for it.

My summary of this chapter would be that experiments can be powerful but they are not 'magic bullets'. Research is not high quality just because it is experimental. If it is high quality *and* experimental then it is probably as good as we are ever going to achieve in educational research.

CONCLUSION

As we have seen, a true experiment with a large representative sample is complex, costly and therefore rare. Laboratory experiments by themselves often answer apparently trivial or feeble questions with very limited samples, so that in educational research quasi-experimental designs such as field trials are more common. These designs may exhibit less rigour, with no control group or else using self-selecting clusters from the population. They therefore require very clear logic in the evaluation of their results, and in the consideration of alternative explanations, to be convincing. Unfortunately this is seldom evident (see the example of TTA-funded research above). The triangulation of different methods can help, so there should be no suggestion that experiments are the only research design of any consequence. However, it is important to remember that all the problems facing experiments apply with equal or even greater force to all other research designs. The experiment is currently the most theoretically-based and considered design available, and it has led to considerable research cumulation in many fields of endeavour of the kind that other, perhaps weaker, designs have yet to achieve. As long as we remind ourselves that the power of experiments comes not just from their design but also from the significance of the problems they are deployed to solve, then the planned growth in experimental studies in education (and public policy more widely) can be seen as valuable and worthy of support.

Good experimental designs testing quite narrowly defined hypotheses (to minimize confounding variables) have considerable power, especially as part of a larger cumulative programme of research via replication, expansion and verification of the findings. Above all, they can help us overcome the equivalent of the potted plant theory which is distressingly common in educational research, policy-making and practice. This theory suggests that if good schools have a potted plant in the foyer then putting a potted plant in the foyer of other, less successful, schools will lead to an improvement in their quality. Sounds ludicrous? I bet that much of the research evidence you have read recently is just as ludicrous in nature, once you think about it carefully. Unless we intervene or rigorously monitor the effect of natural interventions we can never be clear whether our observations of patterns and apparent relationships are real or whether they are superstitions.

The next chapter looks at some the major techniques of data analysis associated with the simple experimental designs discussed here.

Elementary parametric statistics: what do they signify?

Chapter 4 describes methods for analysing results using simple arithmetic techniques, while Chapter 6 introduces the notion of null hypothesis testing for statistical significance using non-parametric techniques. This chapter expands on this theme by describing some simple 'parametric' tests. These are slightly more difficult to use and more likely to be misused than the others because, in general, they make several assumptions about the form and distribution of your data (its parameters, in other words). However, they are worth using for two main reasons. Parametric tests are generally more powerful than non-parametric ones, making them more likely to distinguish between chance occurrences and actual patterns in the data. Using a parametric test is therefore directly equivalent to an increase in your sample size, or in the effect size you are measuring, or to a decrease in the variability of your measurements (see Chapter 2). In addition, there is a wide range of parametric tests and associated statistical models available (some of these are described in Chapter 9).

STATISTICAL POWER AND ERRORS

Before introducing the tests, consider further the general issue of using a statistical test to help make a decision about the significance of your findings. We say that results are 'significant' if we can reject the null hypothesis of no difference between two groups (see Chapter 6). In traditional null hypothesis testing this decision is based on a probability (the significance level). If there is a low probability of the null hypothesis being correct on the basis of what we observe then we reject it. In doing so we *could* be wrong. If we set our significance level high, then we are increasing our chance of obtaining a significant result but also increasing our chance of rejecting the null hypothesis incorrectly (what is unimaginatively called a 'Type I error' in statistics). If we set our significance level lower, then we are decreasing the chance of a Type I error, but we are increasing our chance of retaining our null hypothesis when it is actually incorrect (a 'Type II error' where we are being too stringent). The reason the parametric tests described in this chapter are more powerful is because they are better than tests like chi-square at detecting a pattern or difference in the data without producing a Type I error. They are better at discriminating between patterns and what engineers call 'noise' in the system. This is their analytic power.

A SIMPLE PARAMETRIC TEST

The stages of creating the null and alternative hypotheses, selecting a significance level, calculating a test statistic with the appropriate degrees of freedom, avoiding Type I and II errors, and so on are generally the same for parametric tests as for the simple chi-square test in Chapter 6. There are three key differences. First, the test statistic is different for each test ('t' or 'F', for example, as opposed to chi-square), but since this calculation is handled by a computer it is of little practical importance to us. The associated probability means pretty much the same whatever test we use. Second, the tests are more powerful than non-parametric tests, and so more likely to detect patterns in the data. Third, the tests generally have more important underlying assumptions that have to be met before they can be used.

Perhaps the simplest and most widely used parametric test in social science is the t-test for independent samples. The t-test is used to compare the mean scores of two groups. It is therefore ideal for dealing with the results of a simple experimental design (see Chapter 7) using a treatment group and a control group. Table 8.1 presents some imaginary scores for a simple experiment with 22 subjects (or cases). We can see that there is some difference in the scores between the two groups, since the mean score for the control group is larger. How likely is it that these two groups actually represent sub-samples from the same population such that the experimental treatment to the first group has made no difference to their scores (our null hypothesis of no difference)? Or can we reject this null hypothesis and suggest, on the other hand, that the experimental treatment has made these two sub-samples have different scores? This is what a t-test for independent samples can be used for.

The samples are 'independent' because the individual cases in each group are different people, so that it is possible, as in this example, for

Table 8.1: Scores in a simple experiment

Case	Treatment group	Control group
1	1	1
2	1	2
3	2	2
4	2	3
5	2	3
6	2	4
7	3	4
8	3	4
9	4	5
10	4	5
11	5	–
12	5	–
Mean score per group	2.83	3.30
Standard deviation	1.27	1.34

there to be a different number of cases in each group (12 in the treatment group, and 10 in the control). The degrees of freedom, calculated by the computer package in any case, would be 20 or the sum of the number of cases minus the number of groups. As with the chi-square test, the computer calculates a test statistic from the scores. In this case the statistic is called 't', but as with the chi-square test the precise meaning of this value need not concern the novice researcher. What is of more concern is the associated probability that the two means were actually taken from the same population – or rather that the difference between the means is due only to sampling error. In this example the values might be reported as follows (Table 8.2).

This report shows a probability of 0.411 (or 41 per cent) for the null hypothesis, considerably larger than any level of significance we might conceivably wish to use. Therefore, we have no evidence on the basis of these figures to suggest that our experimental treatment has had any impact on the scores. Although it may be that there actually is an effect but that the sample is too small, the null hypothesis of no effect still remains preferable as being more parsimonious.

Table 8.2: Results of an independent t-test

	t	df	Sig. (2-tailed)
Score (equal variances assumed)	−.839	20	.411

UNDERLYING ASSUMPTIONS

When do we use the t-test? The chi-square test is used with two variables when both are categorical (and nominal). Chapter 9 describes bivariate analyses when both of the variables involved are real numbers. The t-test, and the other tests discussed in this chapter, are used with one nominal/categorical grouping variable and one real number score (either interval or ratio in form). The t-test is used to compare the groups formed by two different values of the nominal variable in terms of their scores on the real number. Thus, the t-test could be used to compare the height of respondents (real number) by their sex (nominal with two categories). Or it could be used with a test score (real) in terms of being either in the experimental or the control group (nominal with two categories). To compare more than two groups see 'Analysis of Variance' on p. 158.

The power of the t-test derives from the known mathematical properties of the t distribution, but this power comes at a price. The calculations involved make several assumptions about the nature of the data used, and the more assumptions a test makes the more likely it is that it is abused. This is one of the best things about the non-parametric approach described in Chapter 6. It is very tolerant of the hiccups in your research design.

One of the assumptions for the use of the t-test (that the metric used for one variable must be at least interval in nature) has already been described. This test is also assumed to be based on two sets of scores which are approximately normally distributed (i.e. they have the standard symmetrical bell-curve pattern when plotted on a graph), and which have approximately equal variances (and standard deviations), or else where the ratio of the two variances is known. As described in Chapter 2 it is also the case that the test assumes that the sample for each group has been selected at random and that each case is independent of every other.

According to traditional statistical theory, where even one of these four assumptions is not valid, the t-test should not be used as it is liable to give biased results. In a sense all decisions based on significance tests carry this proviso: 'if the statistical model used was correct, and the measurement requirement satisfied, then ...' (Siegel, 1956). In practice, all four of the assumptions are commonly flouted, sometimes in combination, and a debate continues about the merits of this approach. I take a fairly middle-of-the-road stance on this issue, but it is up to each researcher when using parametric techniques to face up to these practical problems and resolve them to their own satisfaction. Many statistical users ignore the assumptions underlying the tests they want to use, particularly those concerning the nature and distribution of their data. In itself, this action is not a great problem and many good findings may have come using methods that a purist mathematician might mock (Achen, 1982). It is, however, important to be aware of which assumptions are over-looked, in order to assess the value and applicability of any findings (Berry and Feldman, 1985). This section therefore continues with a general discussion of these 'assumption' issues, which have a bearing on the remainder of this chapter and for the whole of Chapter 9.

The underlying assumption of all statistical testing, which is that samples have been selected at random from a known population, is probably the most commonly flouted. Where care has been exercised in the creation of a high-quality probability-type sample and the sample size for each sub-group is large, then this provides a good defence of the use of non-random sampling. In fact, to a great extent, the use of a large quality sample is the best defence for the violation of any of the following assumptions. If you are intending to use a parametric test, re-read the logic of Chapter 2, use as large a sample as possible, and then don't worry overmuch about this particular assumption.

Perhaps the next most commonly ignored assumption is that concerning the use of real numbers. The types of numbers used in social science research are discussed in Chapter 3. The practice of imagining that ordinal values are actually interval in nature is so widespread that it even has a name. Ignoring the nature of the data in order to be able to use a more powerful parametric test is known as the 'parametric strategy'. It has become almost standard practice in some fields of social science. Aside from the other practical problems that such research often also entails (see below for the problems of indexing attitude scores, for example), I question the use of the strategy on several grounds. It is true that if the assumptions of a test are flouted the result can still be valid, and that Monte Carlo simulations of ordinal data analysed using both parametric and non-parametric techniques give very similar results. Nevertheless. not meeting the assumptions presumably leads to a loss of power in the test used (Siegel, 1956), and therefore defeats the primary purpose of the strategy. If a parametric test is required for its power, the same effect without even a hint of dubious practice can be achieved by simply increasing the size of the sample. It is also true that the range and flexibility of non-parametric techniques have been considerably developed since the parametric strategy became popular. Therefore, if the strategy is pursued not so much for its power as the range of statistical models that are available, then the development of non-parametric approaches such as log-linear modelling or logistic regression should have made the strategy much less attractive.

Despite all these arguments, researchers will presumably continue as they have always done, and treat ordinal values as interval in nature. My advice therefore would be, again, have a good sample. Also, design your data collection instruments so that the respondent/experimenter is clear that the numbers they are recording are supposed to be interval in nature. For example, when using a 5-point Likert scale from 1 (strongly agree) to 5 (strongly disagree) it is hard to argue that the interval or difference in agreement between 'strongly agree' and 'slightly agree' is identical to that between 'slightly agree' and 'neither agree or disagree'. A 3-point scale, on the other hand, is much easier to defend as being equal interval in nature since the only two intervals are between 'agree' and 'neutral' and 'neutral' and 'disagree'. Alternatively, instead of using a written scale at all, you could ask respondents to score or rate their agreement out of a fixed total (which might be seen to imply that the scale of values has equal intervals). There are no right answers. Again, the decision is yours. Be prepared to defend it.

Finally, the assumptions about the distribution and shape of the data are often ignored because they are perhaps the least important, and because their application is not as clear-cut. The key to appreciating this lies in your understanding of the word 'approximately'. What does it mean for a set of figures to be approximately normally distributed, or for two sets to have approximately equal variances? This judgement is another one to be made, and defended, by the researcher. My suggestions for this decision will be familiar to anyone who has read the book through to this point. Do not gloss over the decision. Plot the datasets on a graph (a bar chart of the frequencies is a useful method) and look at the pattern. Does it look like a normal curve? Similarly, calculate the standard deviations (or square root of the variances) for each group. Are they similar, bearing in mind their order of magnitude and that of the scores themselves? If your answer to both questions is 'yes' then you have no problems in using the test, as long as your sample is good and you are prepared to publicize and defend your decision (in a viva voce examination for a PhD student perhaps). Bear in mind the principle above. A large sample cuts a substantial number of the ties from underlying assumptions. A slightly skewed or flattened distribution for 12 cases might not be considered even approximately normal, but the same distribution of 1200 cases probably only needs to look vaguely symmetrical with a cluster of values around the mean and many fewer extreme scores to be considered nearly normal.

A RANGE OF TESTS

The T-test for Related Samples
Another test, also confusingly called a t-test, uses the same theoretical distribution (t) as that above. The t-test for related samples is indeed very similar, with the same assumptions as the t-test for independent (or unrelated or unmatched) samples. The chief advantage of the related t-test is that, correctly used, it is even more powerful in enabling you to reject an untrue null hypothesis. The test is appropriate when each individual in the two groups you wish to compare is related in an important way to one individual in the other group. Since in this design we wish to match each score in one group with a specific score in the other group this means, of course, that the two groups must be the same size.

A typical example of the use of the related samples t-test occurs in an experiment with a pre-test and post-test (see Chapter 7). Here the two 'groups' are actually the same individuals but with two scores, from before and after the experiment respectively. We may wish to find out if their two scores differ, and therefore decide if our experimental treatment has had any effect. Another common situation occurs where the cases in each group are different individuals who have been matched in terms of key characteristics. In an extreme example of this matching, the two groups may each be composed of one of a pair of identical twins.

Other than this 'restriction' about matched individuals the test is the same as that for independent samples. The degrees of freedom are one less than the number of pairs and this, coupled with the use of pairs, affects the calculation of t (by the computer). However, as far as we are concerned, the probability that emerges means the same as in both tests we have met so far. The test estimates the chance that both groups are really from the same population. Has the treatment created a separate population from the one we started with? Consider Table 8.3. The scores in each column are for the same individual in a repeated measures design. The score for each individual in the test which takes place after the experimental treatment is generally higher than their earlier score. Are these differences large enough and consistent enough for us to reject the null hypothesis?

The answer appears in a report of the kind generated by a related

Table 8.3: Scores in a repeated measures design

Case	Pre-test score	Post-test score
1	25	31
2	26	32
3	27	30
4	26	34
5	21	32
6	27	31
7	24	29
8	23	26
9	25	30
10	25	31
Mean score per group	24.90	30.60
Standard deviation	1.85	2.12

Table 8.4: Results of a related t-test

	t	df	Sig. (2-tailed)
Post-test – Pre-test	−7.492	9	.000

samples t-test (Table 8.4). The value of t is reported. Degrees of freedom are one less than the number of people in the study, since both groups are the same size. The associated probability is very low – less than 0.0005 in fact. This means we can safely reject the null hypothesis of no difference, and therefore conclude that the scores for the two groups are significantly different. Whether we can now argue that the difference is attributable to the experimental treatment or whether there are confounding variables depends upon the quality of our experimental design (see Chapter 7). As ever, this is where the fun starts.

One-way Analysis of Variance
If you are interested in looking at the differences between more than two groups, you could look at each of the paired comparisons separately using the appropriate version of the t-test. For example, if you wish to compare groups A, B and C, you can run a t-test for each of A and B, A and C, and B and C. This approach is similar to that described in Chapter 6 using the chi-square test for multiple comparisons. In the same way, however, this approach increases the number

of tests carried out individually and so increases the chances of a Type I error (see below for a discussion of the shotgun approach).

A better solution is provided by a technique from a group known collectively as 'analysis of variance', or sometimes just ANOVA. Here I intend to describe only the simplest version, termed one-way analysis of variance (or just 'one-way'). Apart from the calculation of a value from a different theoretical distribution (called 'F' in all ANOVA), the assumptions for this test are the same as for the independent samples t-test. It provides the flexibility of handling more than two groups at once, while not requiring a series of separate tests. Imagine that we are looking at the mean ages of 1100 respondents living in three different local authorities (Table 8.5). Do we have any evidence that the samples in each group come from populations with differing ages?

Table 8.5: Mean age in three areas

Area of residence	Blaenau Gwent	Bridgend	Neath Port Talbot
Mean age of resident	50.75	51.30	51.76
Standard deviation	13.22	12.97	12.53
Number of cases	361	369	370

The stages of selecting a level of significance, and using a null hypothesis of no difference between the groups, are the same as for other tests. Our computer output might look something like Table 8.6. The probability (labelled 'Sig.') for our null hypothesis is high (57 per cent), and therefore we have no reason to reject it. This is just as well for me since the data are actually from the systematic sample described at the end of Chapter 2, which was intended to be stratified by age. The figures are used here simply as an example of a non-significant ANOVA (and the result tells us nothing about the actual populations of the three areas).

Table 8.6: Results of one-way analysis of variance 1

	Sums of squares	df	Mean square	F	Sig.
Between groups	187.20	2	93.60	.562	.571
Within groups	182859.43	1097	166.69		
Total	183046.63	1099			

Table 8.7: Mean education episodes in three areas

Area of residence	Blaenau Gwent	Bridgend	Neath Port Talbot
Number of episodes	0.26	0.52	0.38
Standard deviation	0.54	0.79	0.72
Number of cases	361	369	370

Table 8.8: Results of one-way analysis of variance 2

	Sums of squares	df	Mean square	F	Sig.
Between groups	12.34	2	6.17	12.883	.000
Within groups	524.98	1096	.479		
Total	537.32	1098			

On the other hand, the data from the same study reported in Tables 8.7 and 8.8 do show a significant difference between the three areas. These represent an analysis of the figures for the same three areas as above, but in relation to the number of episodes of education or training reported by each respondent since leaving school. In the Blaenau Gwent area, for example, the 361 respondents with an average age of 51 reported on average only a quarter of an episode each. Put another way, in this ex-coal-mining valley, no more than one in every four people took part in any further education once reaching school-leaving age. In Bridgend the figure is twice as high. Therefore it is perhaps no surprise to find such a low probability in Table 8.8.

One-way analysis of variance has therefore answered our first question. We can reject the null hypothesis, and conclude that the number of post-compulsory education episodes reported in the three areas shows a significant difference. We can assume, given this, that the difference between Bridgend (with the highest mean score of 0.52) and Blaenau Gwent (with the lowest mean score of 0.26) is also significant. This would be the minimum difference required to produce the overall result in Table 8.8. We are not able at this stage to tell whether the other two possible comparisons also lead to significantly different results. We must therefore conduct a range test to determine which of the six possible differences are significant. This is not difficult since the one-way ANOVA incorporates a choice of different range tests, so that using a computer package the range test you choose will run automatically after a significant result at the

Table 8.9: Tukey's range test

Area of residence	Bridgend	Blaenau Gwent	Neath/Port Talbot
Bridgend	–	.000	.021
Blaenau Gwent	.000	–	.040
Neath/Port Talbot	.021	.040	–

overall level. When you come to try this, do not be confused by the choice of so many range tests. All of them do pretty much the same thing. I tend to use Tukey's Honestly Significant Difference (which I always think sounds a bit like a real ale). For the figures in Table 8.7, the results of Tukey's test are as in Table 8.9.

The figures in Table 8.9 are the probabilities for the null hypotheses of no difference in each two-way comparison as provided by the range test. All of these values would suggest a significant difference between respective pairs at the 5 per cent level, and we could conclude that area of residence is therefore a general predictor, or possibly a determinant, of patterns of post-compulsory education and training. This could be an interesting finding, worthy of further investigation since Blaenau Gwent is the area of South Wales with the highest levels of unemployment and economic inactivity. Bridgend, on the other hand, has attracted a lot of inward investment. Is there, therefore, a relationship between economic activity and patterns of lifelong learning? As with much research, making progress often means finding new questions to answer.

COMMON PROBLEMS IN STATISTICAL TESTING

This section considers a range of problems that can arise in the statistical analysis of results:

- over-reliance on significance tests;
- obsession with indexing;
- the shotgun approach;
- inappropriate level of aggregation.

Over-reliance on Significance Tests

If you think about it carefully, the technique of null hypothesis significance testing (NHST) involves calculating the probability over repeated sampling of observing data as extreme as, or more extreme than, what would be observed if a hypothesis we already believe to be untrue were actually true. What is the point of this? Such a probability could be seen as not very informative, and perhaps even as a hindrance to scientific progress (Harlow *et al.*, 1997). Yet in journals, of psychology especially, there has been a tendency until recently to allow the rather mindless reporting of these probability values as though we the readers should be concerned with them. It is clear that significance testing is essentially a limited technique, and that reporting the probabilities for NHSTs is not very interesting in itself.

Suggested alternatives to reporting NHSTs have been the use of standard confidence intervals for results instead, or the use of more subjective judgements of the worth of results, and even more non-sampled work (an area where the UK psychological, rather than sociological, tradition has been weak). However, there is at present no clear alternative other than the continued use of intelligent judgement. We need to keep in mind the difference between bias (due to the inherent weakness of our design) and random error (due to the vagaries of sampling). Significance tests can only provide us with a probable elimination of random error, since this is what the calculation of confidence intervals in based on. But it is clear that random error is generally only a very small part of the total error in any study (less than 5 per cent has been suggested). So even a 'significant' result is still worth very little in real terms, and will certainly not enable you to generalize safely beyond a poor sample (see Chapter 2). The key issue in research is not about significance but about the quality of the research design.

The importance of this ongoing debate about tests is that it suggests, as I hope this book confirms, that we need to move away from a formulaic approach to research. However, we need to replace empty formulae for reporting results, not with an 'anything goes' philosophy, but with almost anything goes as long as it can be described, justified and replicated. Above all we need to remember that statistical analysis is not our final objective, but the starting point of the more interesting social science that follows.

Obsession with Indexing

In some forms of psychology especially there has been almost an obsession with the use of composite indicators (or indexes). These indexes often appear in attitude questionnaires where the respondent is faced with a battery of questions, all of which are used to assess what is basically the same underlying variable. In essence, the same or very similar questions are asked repeatedly and the answers are used in combination to create an overall attitude score. There may be times when this approach is necessary, and I confess to maybe not appreciating all of the arguments for it, but it is quite clear that indexing has several methodological shortcomings.

First and foremost, the notion that several questions or indicators can be combined to produce a better answer than just one is premised on sampling theory (Anderson and Zelditch, 1968). It assumes that the variability of each indicator is equal to every other and that this variance is due solely to random error. If either assumption is false (and in most actual examples I have seen both are almost certainly false) then one indicator is probably at least as reliable as many. At the very least therefore it is wasteful and time-consuming to ask respondents many questions whose correlation with each other is no greater than the correlation of any one of them with the latent underlying variable you are trying to measure (see Chapter 9 for a full description of correlation). On the other hand, if the correlation between all indicators is very high you have to ask why only one of them would not do anyway, since all of them are so nearly measuring the same thing. Another problem arises in the scoring system (and this is in addition to any doubts about whether the respondents' answers are interval in nature). In a typical index the value of each question is assumed to be the same, and the score for each is totalled and then averaged. I have never seen an argument explaining why, for each test, this is considered appropriate and how we know that the answer to each question is precisely equivalent in importance. I do not recommend that students never use indexes, but that they should have a good reason for doing so, and that they should be careful about the potential flaws and artificialities in the process.

The Shotgun Approach
Making a predictive alternative hypothesis, especially a one-tailed one, deciding on a theoretically suitable level of significance in advance, and then carrying out one test of significance is what the mathematics for each test are based on (originating from an era before computers and hand calculators). However, it is now possible for us to enter a large number of variables into a package like SPSS, run a series of chi-square tests or analyses of variance, pick out those results with probabilities less than a *post-hoc* level of significance, work out alternative hypotheses for only these 'significant' tables and results, and then publicize these hypotheses as our findings. This is what has been termed the 'shotgun' or 'dredging' approach to analysis. The results of such over-use of a test designed for one-off

calculation should be seen as far from convincing (Stevens, 1992), and it is therefore important to report it if this is what you have done.

For example, using a 5 per cent level of significance means that the researcher accepts a 1 in 20 chance of making a Type I error. Probabilities such as these are multiplied (just like the probability of rolling a six with more than one throw of a die). Thus, using the 5 per cent level on two successive tests means that the likelihood of no Type I error occurring on either test drops to $19/20*19/20$ (or 0.9). On ten successive tests the likelihood of no error occurring drops to $19/20^{10}$ (or 0.6). After 100 tests, the probability of at least one error rises to over 99 per cent. Therefore, the more tests you do, the less confident you can be that your result is not a spurious finding emanating from chance alone. Carrying out every combination of one test of bivariate analysis involving as few as 20 variables (and bearing in mind that many student questionnaires have over a hundred variables) means that you will perform 495 tests. The chance of at least one Type I error would therefore be more than 99.999999999 per cent.

There are four key defences to this problem. First of all, even a scatter approach to analysis does not have to be *completely* mindless. You will know that there are relationships between some variables that you are simply not interested in. Exclude these. In addition, you can lower your threshold for significance (to 1 per cent for example), increasing the chance of Type II errors but making your 'significant' results more convincing. You can also often replace multiple bivariate analyses with a more appropriate and one-off multivariate test (see Chapter 9). But above all of these technical solutions, you need to consider your purpose in conducting the analysis. Significance test results can lead to interesting ideas for further investigation, but never to any kind of proof or certainty. Therefore with shotgun results, as with any other, you should treat them as tentative until they can be confirmed by a different methodological approach (triangulation) and until you have worked out a plausible explanation for them. In summary, be a little cavalier in your investigation by all means, but then be more conservative in your explanations. Remember that statistical significance and social science significance are not the same thing at all.

Inappropriate Level of Aggregation
The best-known example of this problem has been termed an 'ecological fallacy' in which data collected at one level of aggregation are used to draw conclusions about phenomena at another level. This

can occur in considering school effects. Suppose we have summary measures of examination outcomes (e.g. pass rate at GCSE) and socio-economic composition (e.g. percentage of pupils from poor families) in a number of schools, we may be able to draw conclusions about the nature of the relationship between these variables. For example, we might conclude that schools with high levels of poverty tend to have lower pass rates. This would be perfectly proper. What we cannot do is draw sensible conclusions about either individuals (lower level of aggregation) or national systems (higher level of aggregation). We would have no reason from this aggregated data to assume that it is the individual pupils from poor families who obtain weaker results (or vice versa).

A clearer, but less well-known, example leads to a kind of 'paradox' (attributed to Simpson, 1951, but probably much earlier). Suppose an authority enrols 2,000 school students of a certain age for an experiment about methods of teaching. Of these, 1,000 are given an experimental treatment involving new methods of teaching and new curriculum materials. The other 1,000 are taught using existing methods and materials. In a post-test 600 of Group A (experimental) pass a test of knowledge in this subject, while 500 of Group B (control) pass. If the design of the experiment is adequate, then this is *prima facie* evidence that the new teaching method leads to better results. Suppose the researcher then considers pass rates in terms of student background characteristics such as sex. The pass rate was higher for female cases (67 per cent) than for male (43 per cent). This, in itself is interesting but when disaggregated by sex and group the results are paradoxical (Table 8.10).

The pass rate for Group A (60 per cent) is higher than for Group B (50 per cent), yet females in Group B (75 per cent) score better than females in Group A (65 per cent) while males in Group B (44 per cent) also score better than males in Group A (40 per cent). This is enough to make you doubt what is going on in the universe. *X Files* or what? I shall leave the reader to ponder this. The message from both examples is that problems can be introduced when changing the

Table 8.10: Pass rates by sex of student and experimental group

Sex/group	A (%)	B (%)	Overall (%)
Female	520/800 (65)	150/200 (75)	670/1000 (67)
Male	80/200 (40)	350/800 (44)	430/1000 (43)
Overall	600/1000 (60)	500/1000 (50)	1100/2000 (55)

level of aggregation of your data. This does not mean you should never do it, but do take care when you do.

This chapter has introduced some common parametric approaches to analysis, which are especially relevant to simple experimental designs. There are a very large number of other tests available to the analyst (see Kanji, 1999 for a description of 100 tests). For more on specific experimental designs and their analysis see Maxwell (1958), Kalton (1966), Edwards (1972), Howell (1989), Everitt and Hay (1992), McIlveen *et al.* (1992), Shaughnessy and Zechmeister (1994), Hinton (1995) and Peers (1996). The next chapter looks at the correlational approach to analysis as an introduction to more complex methods involving more than two variables.

Introducing correlations: progress via regression

This chapter introduces the idea of a correlation, in which two or more variables tend to change values in step with each other. Using this kind of relationship it is possible to predict or explain the value of one variable from the value of the other. This approach is known as regression, and it forms the basis for several more advanced statistical techniques, two of which are discussed here. An understanding of correlation is therefore a useful door into the fascinating world of statistical modelling of social events.

INTRODUCING CORRELATIONS

The relationship between two variables known as a correlation is perhaps easiest understood graphically. Figure 9.1 shows the percentage of the 15-year-old cohort of students in each local education authority in England obtaining five or more GCSE qualifications at grade C or above (the government GCSE benchmark). These scores are plotted against the percentage of children in each area eligible for free schools meals (thus coming from families officially defined as in poverty). The two sets of scores are clearly related, such that areas with high poverty (x-axis) have lower GCSE results overall (y-axis), and areas with less poverty generally have higher GCSE results. This kind of relationship is called a correlation – in this example a negative correlation since the two values are negatively related (i.e. as one increases the other tends to decrease).

Key assumptions of this relationship are that the two variables must be real numbers (see Chapter 4), and they must cross-plot to form an approximately straight line. How close to a straight line this has to be is a matter of judgement, and it is always possible to transform one or more of the scores to try and make the linear fit better. For example, a simple curved relationship can often be altered

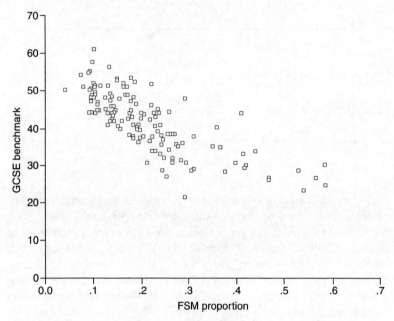

Figure 9.1: Scatterplot for each local authority: GCSE benchmark 1998 against percentage of children eligible for free school meals

to a straight line by converting the scores to logarithms (Figure 9.1 might be improved by doing this, see Gorard, 2000c). Since the analysis of correlations is based on deviations from the best fitting straight line, setting out to use the techniques described here with data exhibiting curvilinear relationships (or worse) is unlikely to be effective. Alternative correlational techniques are available for curved relationships (Norusis, 1994) and for categorical variables (Siegel, 1956).

Where the two variables do appear approximately linearly related it is possible to conduct a significance test for the null hypothesis that they are actually unrelated. The most common of these uses the correlation coefficient known as Pearson's R, with an associated probability for the null hypothesis (see Chapter 6). If this probability is very small (less than 5 per cent, for example), there is clearly some evidence of a correlation, and the null hypothesis can be quite safely rejected. In addition (and unlike the values such as chi-square, t and F introduced so far), the value of R gives us an indication of the nature and strength of the relationship. R has a value between −1 and +1. A value of 0 shows no relationship at all (appearing as random scatter when cross-plotted on a graph). A value of +1 shows a perfect positive correlation between the two variables, meaning that they both increase or decrease in step with each other. A value of −1 shows a perfect negative correlation between the two variables, meaning that as one increases the other decreases in step with it. The scores in Figure 9.1 yield a value of −0.77, showing a fairly strong negative correlation, with an associated probability for the null hypothesis of less than 0.0005 (Table 9.1).

Table 9.1: Correlation between GCSE benchmark and levels of free school meals

		GCSE	FSM
GCSE	Pearson correlation	1.000	−.773**
	Sig.	−	.000
	N	140	140
FSM	Pearson correlation	−.773**	1.000
	Sig.	.000	−
	N	140	140

Note: **Correlation is significant at the 0.01 level (2-tailed)

A computer-based analysis will lead to a report like that in Table 9.1. By this stage of the book you should be aware of the meaning of the terms involved. The report is symmetrical since the same relationship holds between free school meals (FSM) and examination results (GCSE) as between GCSE and FSM. It is, after all, a correlation. The correlation between each variable and itself is 1, by definition. The 'significance' is the probability of the null hypothesis (that there is no correlation) being true. N is the number of observations – in this example, the number of local education authorities (140). The correlation coefficient of −0.773 provides an estimate of the strength of the relationship. The amount of variation in one variable that can be predicted (or explained) by knowing the value for the other is the square of 0.773 (or 60 per cent). Put another way, if you tell me the amount of poverty in the schools in one authority then I can tell you their GCSE results with 60 per cent accuracy. This is the basis of value-added approaches to performance measurement, and of studies of school effectiveness. The approach is called regression, and is the focus of the next section.

To summarize here: Pearson's correlation coefficient (R) is used to measure the common variation in two sets of scores. Whereas a chi-square test compares two categorical variables (Chapter 6), and the t-test compares one interval and one categorical (grouping) variable (Chapter 8), this correlation requires two interval variables. The other main requirement is that the two variables are approximately linearly related (i.e. they cross-plot to form a straight line). It is sometimes possible to transform the variables (e.g. by conversion to logarithms) to make a better line. The probability resulting from the test is used as normal to help decide whether the two variables are related or not (but bear in mind that a non-significant result shows not that they are unrelated, but only that they are not *linearly* related).

The test also provides the researcher with an estimate of the variance common to the two variables. The correlation coefficient is 0 if the two items are completely unrelated, 1 if the two items are 'identical', and -1 if they are the exact opposites. The square of this coefficient shows how much of the variance is common. For example, if two variables have a correlation of 0.5, then 25 per cent of their variance is common (and may measure the same underlying social scientific phenomenon). Correlation is also the basis for regression analysis, where values in one variable are used to 'predict' values in another.

The standard caution given about the interpretation of correlation is that it gives no indication of the real relationship between the two variables (only an experiment can even attempt to uncover this, see Chapter 7). For example, there is a clear correlation over time between the income of the Archbishop of Canterbury, who is head of the Church of England, and the price of marijuana (Huff, 1991). Is this evidence of drug dealing in the Church of England, or are both figures linked to an overall rise in prices (inflation)? There is a clear correlation in Denmark between the number of children in any house and the number of storks nesting in its roof. Is this evidence that the activities of storks are involved in childbirth, or that larger houses tend to have both more roof space and more residents?

A correlation is the start, not the end, of an investigation, and its explanation is likely to involve theoretical considerations, and the triangulation of knowledge from other data sources. Even then, the proposed explanation can only be a tentative one. This basic fact is important to note before we consider more complex designs. There is a danger that novices confuse complexity with rigour, whereas the more complex designs mentioned in this chapter suffer from the same flaws as the simplest correlation (in my experience complexity and rigour are usually negatively 'correlated'). This is true, however extravagantly their results are described.

LINEAR REGRESSION

Simple Regression

Where two variables are linearly related (as they are in Figure 9.1), there is a line of best-fit. This is usually seen as the line that minimizes the mean deviation of all points (note that the issue of whether to include or exclude extreme scores, or 'outliers', is discussed in Chapter 4). Once this line has been calculated, it is possible to use it to read off the values of one variable (the dependent variable) from the values of the other (the independent variable). Any such reading will not be totally accurate unless the correlation is perfect (it will therefore contain a substantial error component). Which of the two variables is termed dependent is a matter for the researcher to decide, and is not derived from the nature of their statistical inter-relationship. In Figure 9.1 it might make more sense to use GCSE as the dependent value as I can see a way in which poverty could affect examination performance, but no way in which the reverse could hold (at least in the short term).

Table 9.2 shows the results of a simple linear regression analysis, based on the scores in Figure 9.1. The dependent variable is the GCSE benchmark for each area, and independent variable is the proportion of children in poverty.

Table 9.2: Regression analysis, predicting GCSE from FSM

Model	Component	B	Std. Error	Beta	t	Sig.
1	Constant	53.01	0.91		58.23	.000
	FSM propn.	−53.32	3.72	−0.773	−14.33	.000

This result leads us to a function, or equation, relating the two variables:

GCSE score = a + b(FSM score) + error component

In this equation, a is the constant (53.01), and b is the coefficient for the FSM score (−53.32). If we ignore the error component (since we know nothing about it, including how large it is), we can estimate the GCSE score for any authority. We can therefore use our equation to predict the scores for authorities not involved in the calculation (such as those in Wales) or to decide which authorities are scoring higher or lower than we expect. For example the proportion of school children eligible for free school meals in Cardiff City in 1998 was 0.23. Our equation suggests that Cardiff City should appear on the line in Figure 9.1 at y = 40.75, since 40.75 is 53.01 − 53.32 (.23). In fact the GCSE benchmark for Cardiff in that year was 43 per cent, slightly higher than expected. The dot for Cardiff would therefore appear just above the line of best fit. However, the level of poverty is not the only factor relating school compositions to school outcomes. There are many other contributory factors, and combining these could make our predictions more accurate. Which leads us onto multiple linear regression.

Multiple Regression
As with any estimate, the one above could probably be improved by considering further variables. It is likely that location, types of school, gender mix, ethnic mix, parental education, and a host of other factors are also related to the GCSE results at a local authority level. A practical problem is that many of these further variables will themselves be inter-related. We cannot therefore simply total the correlations of each variable with the GCSE scores. For example, if the proportion of ethnic minority pupils is negatively correlated with GCSE results, we cannot simply add this correlation to that for poverty. This is so for two main reasons. First, poverty and ethnicity are likely to have some correlation between themselves, so using both together means we end up using their *common* variance twice. The real multiple correlation between ethnicity and poverty, on the one hand, and GCSE score, on the other, is likely to be less than the sum of the two correlations. Second, the real multiple correlation between ethnicity and poverty, on the one hand, and GCSE score, on the other, could be greater than the sum of the two correlations. This would mean that there is an 'interaction' effect between ethnicity and poverty, whereby the one reinforces the impact of the other (Pedhazur, 1982). One technique in common use to overcome both of these problems is multiple linear regression. This takes into account the correlations between multiple independent variables when combining them to predict/explain the variance in the dependent variable.

I used this technique to examine patterns of differential attainment between schools and sectors of schools in the study represented by Gorard (1998b, 1998c, 1998d, 2000d, 2000e). The relationship between poverty and school examination outcomes holds at the school level as well as the local authority. Schools with more than their fair share

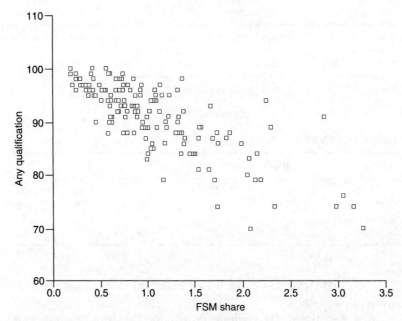

Figure 9.2: Scatterplot for each school: proportion of students attaining any qualification 1999 against school share of students eligible for free school meals

of children from poor families generally have a larger number of children who obtain no qualifications at all at age 16. Figure 9.2 represents scores for every secondary school in Wales in 1999. Schools with few children in poverty (zero on the x-axis) also tend to have few children leaving with no qualification (100 on the y-axis).

A similar relationship exists between qualifications and the proportion of children per school with a statement of special educational need (SEN), and between qualifications and levels of unauthorised absence ('truancy'). Schools in which most children obtain at least one GCSE at grade G or above tend to have fewer SENs and less truancy. These three independent variables were the most powerful predictors of qualification rates at the school level available to me. When all three are used simultaneously in a multiple regression analysis, part of the output appears as in Tables 9.3 and 9.4.

Table 9.3 shows the value of R (0.815), which means the same as it does in simple regression except that it now expresses the multiple correlation between qualifications, on the one hand, and all three independent variables in combination, on the other. The probability is again the same as in a simpler test of significance, and shows the

Table 9.3: Multiple regression analysis

Model	R	R square	Adjusted R square	Std. error of the estimate
3	.815	.665	.656	3.79

Notes: Predictors: Constant, Segregation, Special Needs, Truancy
Prob. .000

Table 9.4: Coefficients for multiple regression analysis

Value	B	Std. error.	Beta	t	Sig.
Constant	100.20	.78		128.69	.000
FSM share	−6.49	.83	−.63	−7.75	.000
Special Needs	−0.38	.12	−.17	−3.10	.002
Truancy	−0.74	.33	−.19	−2.27	.025

likelihood of there being no linear relationship between the two groups of variables.

Table 9.4 shows the coefficients (B) for the resulting multiple regression equation of the form:

Qualification rate
= 100 − 6.49(FSM share) − 0.38(SEN) − 0.74(Truancy)
+ error component

Given the values in Table 9.4, you can therefore calculate (or use the computer to calculate) expected scores for any school, as long as you know its share of free school meals, etc. In part of my study I used an equation based on all of the schools in one sector to predict the scores for schools in another sector. In this way, I showed that once the variation due to poverty and SEN is taken into account, there was no evidence of differential effectiveness of different types or sectors of school. There is therefore, no need for comprehensive schools to look at other types of school as models of improvement.

The underlying assumptions for this analysis are basically the same as for correlation. All values must be real numbers, linearly related to the dependent variable, taken from a random sample, and meeting strict assumptions about the distribution of the error terms (Maxwell, 1977; Achen, 1982; Menard, 1995). In any real research project involving multiple regression, some of the assumptions underlying it are likely to be violated (Berry and Feldman, 1985).

This, in itself, is not fatal to the validity of the work, and even where the regression is flawed it is sometimes only the intercept (the constant 'a' in our first equation) that is affected, and the derived coefficients may still be used with care. As with almost any technique, the best defence against any such problems is a large high quality sample.

Since the technique is so useful, it is frequently used in modelling situations for which it was not intended. Chief among these are the very common situations where some of the independent variables are categorical in nature. Standard regression does not work well with categorical independent variables having more than two values (Hagenaars, 1990), but if a variable (such as sex) has only two possible values, it can be treated as an equal interval variable (since there is only one interval). Further, even variables with more than two categories can be used by converting them to a series of dummy variables. A social class scale with three categories, for example, could be treated as two dummy variables. The first dummy is a yes/no variable representing being in the 'Service' class or not, and the second dummy represents being in the 'Intermediate' class or not. 'Working' class is therefore defined as being not Service and not Intermediate class. Some writers have argued that this treatment is a distortion and not really appropriate, especially now that newer methods have been developed specifically to deal with categorical variables. Since it is assumed in regression that the variables are normally distributed (Lee *et al.*, 1989), and dummy variables cannot have such a distribution (Hagenaars, 1990) simply converting a categorical variable into a set of dummies is not the solution. Dummy variables add to the measurement error (Blalock, 1964). For more on this, and other potential flaws in regression analysis such as omitted variable bias, heteroskedasticity, and multicollinearity, see Maddala (1992) or Norusis (1994).

The remainder of this section raises two less well-known problems in regression as commonly used in educational research – the level of data aggregation, and the order of entering variables into the model. It is generally assumed, although without much evidence, that where we are analysing school outcomes it is better to use data relating to the individual student rather than aggregated figures relating to classes, groups or schools. This is certainly the path followed in standard school effectiveness studies. However, we should all be aware that there is a considerable error component in the allocation of school outcomes. Whatever the system of moderation used, public examinations are inaccurate, so much so that they are estimated to be accurate only to within a grade or two (Nuttall, 1987; Gorard *et al.*, 1999d). In a large aggregate analysis (e.g. at school level), we can assume that these errors are largely cancelled out, but this is not so when the analysis focuses on individuals.

For any study, the regression model explaining the greatest variance in the dependent variable (e.g. exam score) will use all available independent variables. This is the model you get if you simply enter all of the variables at once. However, it is possible to create simpler models containing fewer variables but still explaining a large proportion of the variance. These models are easier to use and understand, and so more practical. It may be that ethnicity and first language, as variables, are measuring much the same thing in terms of school outcomes. The same may be true of social class and indicators of poverty. In such cases, we are better off picking the best single indicator from a group of related measures, and using only that one. We could pick the best indicator on theoretical grounds, or in terms of availability. Both of these approaches are fine. However, the most common ground for selection of variables is the proportion of variance that they explain. If language and ethnicity are related and language is a better predictor of examination scores, then we might omit ethnicity from our analysis.

It is extremely convenient for us that software packages like SPSS will select variables and add them to the model in the order of the variance that they explain ('Stepwise'), and in several other ways as well ('Forward', 'Backward'). However, it is important that we are the ones to take the decision to use one of these methods (not the computer software), and that we can express a reason for doing so. The order in which variables are entered into an analysis can have an impact on how significant they appear to be (as explained in Chapter 4, our findings often depend on our method of analysis). Therefore, different solutions are, in certain circumstances, derivable from the same data using the same variables, by simply processing them in a different order (and this problem applies to the order of processing the different levels in a 'multi-level' regression model, as well as the order of processing the variables at each level).

LOGISTIC REGRESSION

Linear regression is both inelegant to use with categorical independent variables, and impossible to use with a categorical dependent variable (Achen, 1982). However, a range of regression-type techniques are available which can deal with both situations while still coping with real-number independent variables, and with the added advantage that the variables need not be linearly related. A simple binomial (two-category) 'logistic regression' is briefly described here as an example of the type (see Allison, 1984; Mare and Winship, 1985; Main and Shelly, 1990; Whitfield and Bourlakis, 1991, for descriptions of others, such as probit and logit log-linear models). Note that there are now also procedures for multinomial regression (where the dependent variable has more than two categories).

Logistic regression uses predictor variables (of any sort) to compute a score on an underlying latent variable. If this score is above a specified critical value the dependent variable is set to one category, otherwise it is set to the other. In other words, the procedure is used to 'predict' which of two categories each individual case will manifest, and in doing so creates a model based on the predictor variables. How this works, how variables are selected for inclusion, and how to understand the resulting coefficients are all beyond the scope of this book. For further details see (Gambetta, 1987; Greenhalgh and Stewart, 1987; Gilbert, 1993; Norusis, 1994; Lehtonen and Pahkinen, 1995; Gorard *et al.*, 1997). The example here is taken from Gorard *et al.* (1999b), using the sample described at the end of Chapter 2.

One of the things I was trying to explain was the changing nature of extended initial education. Over the past 50 years, UK compulsory schooling has been extended from age 14 to age 16, and staying-on rates for further and higher education have increased considerably. Using a sample of 1,100 households representing nearly 4,000 people aged 16–65, logistic regression was able to predict/explain whether these people had stayed on after compulsory schooling with 80 per cent success. This result is much better than could be achieved by chance, since only around 50 per cent of the cases had stayed on. In order to achieve this prediction the model used a number of predictor variables, of which the most important were personal characteristics, such as sex, which were known when each individual was born. This leads to the quite depressing thought that we can predict with nearly 80 per cent success who is going to stay on at school or not from birth (despite the historical changes over 50 years). I do not mean this statement to sound determinist, merely to make the point that in the period in question family and social background was a key influence in educational careers.

The regression analysis calculates a coefficient for each predictor. For real variables these coefficients are similar to those in linear regression. Thus, my model gives a coefficient of 0.96 for age in years.

The probability that an individual stayed on at school is one, multiplied by 0.96 for every year of their age (as older people in the sample are much less likely to have stayed on). For categorical variables, a coefficient is calculated for each category compared to another one. Thus, my model gives a coefficient of 2.15 for male cases in comparison to female. This means that men are over twice as likely as women to have stayed on at school.

When the sample is divided into two equal-sized age cohorts, some of these coefficients remain the same for both groups (age is an example). Some coefficients, however, change dramatically in their impact over the 50 years represented by this study. Among the older cohort men are actually over three times as likely as women to have stayed on at school, but in the younger cohort men and women are equally likely to have stayed on. Conversely, in the younger cohort those who have not moved (i.e. whose families have always lived in the area where they were born) are nearly one third as likely to stay on as those who have been geographically mobile. In the older cohort, geographical mobility does not make a significant difference. Over time, factors such as social class, parental education, ethnicity and first language have become less important as predictors of post-compulsory participation. This is, presumably, good news. These factors have been replaced in the regression model by early childhood experiences, which are therefore becoming increasingly key determinants of later patterns of education. Whether this is good news or not is still far from clear.

COMMON PROBLEMS WITH MULTIVARIATE ANALYSIS

Because multivariate analysis is rather complex, and often rather specialist as well, it is possible for readers to be easily misled about the nature and value of findings so derived. There may be a tendency for readers to assume that anything so 'clever' must be OK, but the reality is, of course, that there are errors in multivariate analyses just as in any other. In fact, due to the relative complexity of the techniques and the lack of independent peer-reviewers with sufficient technical knowledge, errors are probably more common in the published results of multivariate techniques than in those from any other. Here are just two examples of potential problems.

Superfluity of Technical Information
This is probably the biggest catch-all problem area in statistical educational research today. Readers are given both too much and

too little information about the methods used in multivariate analyses. This has become a commonplace in school effectiveness work,
especially that using multi-level modelling. The nature of the techniques used means that there are very few people outside what has
become a kind of cult or club who can follow this kind of work, and it
sometimes seems that writers work to keep it that way. A clear
example is the tradition of using technical variable names to report
findings. It is now standard practice to present findings in terms of
brief acronymic names rather than descriptions. At the next level of
absurdity writers then try to explain the meaning of their variable
names. Why? Why not just use the description? I do not care what the
variables were called.

For example, in their main chapter about the relationship between
school choice and school performance – the empirical guts of their
book – Lauder *et al.* (1999) present these less than fascinating facts: 'in
the Year 11 School Certificate Study we included a Level 1 variable
called FAMSTR which was not included in the Year 10 skills study'
(p. 116), and 'at Level 1 the variable name was MAPTITUDE' (p. 117).
In fact, their Table 7.1, which looks at first sight like a set of results, is
actually just a summary of their variable names. Why should I want
to know this? I would not report a t-test and point out that when
entering some numbers into SPSS I referred to them as 'X' or
'VAR00001'. This is not what my readers would need to know.

The reason I refer to this technical mumbo jumbo as a 'superfluity'
is that it is usually presented instead of, rather than in addition to,
information that I do actually need. Lauder *et al.* (1999) present the
chief results in their Table 7.4 which contains only variable names
and associated alpha levels. We are not told what the units of
measurement are for each variable, so when shown the coefficients
from their regression analysis we can have no idea what these values
mean. The coefficients by themselves are useless information for us,
and like the variable names therefore simply become rhetorical noise.
Again, they do not report for their multi-level (actually 2-level) model
the order in which the variance for each level is calculated. Are both
levels calculated at once, or did the researchers start with an
individual level analysis and move to a school level, or vice versa?
For each level, were all the appropriate variables entered at once into
the model or were they selected somehow, and if so how? The order
of entering variables into the model can make a big difference to the
conclusions drawn. I need to know these things before I can give any
credence to their claims. But, to repeat, I do not need to know what
they chose as variable names when entering data into a computer.

Error Propagation

Statistical analysis by computer involves very many calculations of which most of us are usually only dimly aware, and one of the dangers of this is that we cannot therefore make a reliable estimate of the 'propagation' of our measurement errors. It is a standard assumption in social science that any measurements we make are in error. I do not mean completely wrong, but not totally accurate. This has implications for school effectiveness research of the kind which attempts to partition (or subtract) the variance in school outcomes due to socio-economic background and prior attainment of the students. If, for example, it is possible to explain around 90 per cent of the variance in these terms, this means that only 10 per cent is left to be explained by school effects. It is this 10 per cent that most research and improvement measures focus on. However, the total variance has an unknown (in size) error component. So at least part of that 10 per cent variance which appears to be due to schools and teachers is actually due to error. The fact that the size of this residual variance decreases with the size of the sample, sometimes to zero (see Gorard, 2000c), suggests that the 10 per cent may be almost entirely composed of error.

We introduce small errors into our results by restricting our working to a certain number of decimal places or significant figures. We simply do our best to take accurate readings, and include an error component in our subsequent modelling of society to represent these general flaws. To a large extent we then behave as though the error component in our analysis remains constant, so that if we start with figures at a certain level of accuracy, we will end up with results at approximately the same level of accuracy. In some cases this belief may be appropriate but in others, it is not so.

If we assume that all our measurements are slightly in error (and with most educational measures this is a safe assumption), then adding two figures also involves adding their error components. The error components may partly cancel each other out, or they may increase each other. More formally, imagine two numbers whose true value is A and B, for which our measurements a and b are only approximations such that:

$a = (A + Ea)$
$b = (B + Eb)$, where Ea is the error in our measurement of A, and Eb the error in B

If we add our estimates of A and B we actually reach the sum a+b (equal to A+B+Ea+Eb). This is unlikely to be a major problem since the proportion (Ea+Eb)/(A+B) is probably not much larger than either Ea/A or Eb/B (i.e. the proportionate errors with which we started). Since we do not know whether Ea and Eb are positive or negative, the same result occurs when we subtract A and B. If we multiply a by b we obtain (A + Ea). (B + Eb) which equals A.B + B.Ea + A.Eb + Ea.Eb (and similarly for division). The error term B.Ea could be large if B is very large. In this way the original error in our measurements could propagate with every calculation we make, being added to and multiplied in turn. Unless we track this propagation it is therefore possible for our answer effectively to 'cancel out' the estimates we started with, and so contain a much larger proportion of error component than we started with. Consider the simultaneous equations:

$$200 = 100y + 100z$$
$$201 = 101y + 100z$$

Their solution is that y = 1 and z = 1.

If the sum (i.e. 201) in the second equation is a measurement and it is incorrect by less than half a per cent, then the true value could have been 200, making the equations:

$$200 = 100y + 100z$$
$$200 = 101y + 100z$$

The solution now is that y = 0 and z = 2. This is a totally different solution 'caused' by a small proportionate error in one term. If y and z represent different components of an effective school, then our policy for school improvement would be completely different depending on whether we had this error of half a per cent in one score. In the first solution, y and z have equal impact. In the second, y is irrelevant.

For some problems the introduction of an error component makes a very large difference, and for some problems the error makes *all* the difference. Yet all statistical models used in educational research contain significant error terms.

This chapter has considered a range of multivariate approaches to analysis and modelling which emerge from the concept of correlations. There are many other statistical techniques available, for multiple analyses of variance or covariance (Hinton, 1995), or to explore the complexity of systems via simulation techniques (Gilbert and Troitzsch, 1999), or building on multiple regression by examining datasets in hierarchical layers via multi-level modelling (Plewis,

1997), or cluster analysis to examine the relationships between cases rather than between variables (Everitt, 1980), or multi-dimensional scaling where the 'distance' between variables is plotted on a multi-dimensional map according to their inter-correlations (Kruskal and Wish, 1978). There is also the heavily over-used, in my opinion, set of techniques known as factor analysis (Child, 1970; Comrey, 1973; Marradi, 1981; Cureton and D'Agostino, 1983; Kline, 1994; Gorard, 1997b).

No short book can possibly hope to look at all of these techniques for 'quantitative' data gathering and analysis. What I have tried to do here is summarize some of the most fruitful basic approaches in educational research, and suggest some general principles for all research. I hope you have found it of some help, both as a novice researcher yourself, and as a consumer of the research of others.

Glossary of selected terms

achievement gap   The measure of differences in attainment between groups (such as boys and girls) used by the Equal Opportunities Commission is called an achievement gap. It is identical to the segregation index (S) for a 2 × 2 table. An achievement gap between girls and boys would be calculated as the score (number attaining a certain examination level) for girls minus the score for boys all divided by the sum of the scores for boys and girls. If the total number of girls and boys taking the examination is not even, an entry gap is subtracted from the achievement gap. The entry gap is the number of girls taking the examination minus the number of boys taking the examination, all divided by the total number taking the examination. More formally: $A = (gb - bp)/gp + bp) - (ge - be)/(ge + be)$.

ANOVA   This is simply an abbreviation of Analysis of Variance. This is a test of differences between groups in terms of an interval measure. One-way analysis is used to test one dependent variable in terms of one independent variable (examination scores by social class for example). Factorial ANOVA deals with many independent variables. MANOVA deals with multiple dependent variables.

bias   Any research design contains at least two sources of error – the random variation due to sampling, and systematic bias. Bias may arise from a variety of sources including non-response and design error. Traditional statistical analysis can evaluate the random error, but leaves the bias untouched which is a shame since the bias is likely to be much larger in impact. Bias needs to be overcome directly by the common sense of the researcher, for example by dealing with non-response and curing design flaws. There is no magic bullet.

box and whisker plot   Also known as a boxplot. A diagram used by some analysts to express the distribution of a set of values. A line (whisker) is drawn from the smallest to largest values which are not outliers, and a box is drawn in the middle of the line covering the median and the middle 50 per cent of the values.

Cronbach's alpha   This is a measure of reliability. It assesses the extent to which a group of questions are asking for the same basic underlying information. A value of zero means the questions are all completely different, and 1 means that they are effectively identical. Precisely what use this is remains unclear. A high value for alpha implies that a questionnaire is wasting the respondents' time by repeating the same question, yet a high value is what most textbooks tell readers to look for.

degrees of freedom   This represents the number of scores that are free to vary in any analysis. When analysing data we tend to use summary information such as the total of all scores. The degrees of freedom are the number of scores we need to know before we can calculate the rest. If the total of two numbers is 37 and we know that one number is 20, then we can calculate that the other must be 17, so the degrees of freedom would be one. This value is used to help estimate the impact of random variation in null hypothesis significance testing.

finite population correction   Where your sample is large in comparison to the size of the population (typically more than 5 per cent), you can apply a correction when calculating the required size of your sample for any given level of confidence using the standard error. This allows you to use a smaller sample.

Flesch index of readability   Grammar checkers on many popular word-processors will produce an estimated reading level for a piece of text. One such measure is the Flesch index between 0 'very difficult' and 100 'very easy'. The measure can also be converted into school grade or reading age scores.

interval measure   This is a score or value based on a real number. Technically it means that each value on the scale of measurement is an equal interval from the next value (the difference between 15 and 16 degrees centigrade is the same as between 115 and 116 degrees). In reality very few social science measures are interval without also being ratio in nature.

Likert-type scale   This is used to try and assess attitudes and related concepts (multidimensional underlying variables). Respondents are asked to read a statement or question and then rate their response on a scale of agreement (agree/disagree) or quality (good/bad). The scales usually have five or seven points, sometimes three or an even number. While clearly ordinal in nature, these scales are often treated as equal interval and used with parametric techniques.

Mann-Whitney test   This is a null hypothesis significance test for differences between two or more groups. This difference is measured in terms of an ordinal measure. As such, Mann-Whitney does much the same thing as a t-test or one-way analysis of variance but for ordinal, rather than interval values.

mean   This is the most popular form of average, giving the reader an idea of the central or most representative value of a set of measurements. It is the sum of a set of measurements divided by the number of measurements, and can only be used with data of interval or ratio level.

median   This is a form of average, giving the reader an idea of the central or most representative value of a set of measurements. If the measurements are placed in order of size, the median is the value in the middle (with an equal number of values higher and lower than it). It can only be used with data of ordinal, interval or ratio level.

minimum expected count   In a tables of scores the expected values for each cell are calculated assuming that each category (row and column) is proportionately represented. If the minimum (smallest) expected value is below a reasonable number (10 perhaps), then standard analytical techniques are appropriate.

mode   This is a form of average, giving the reader an idea of the central or most representative value of a set of measurements. If the measurements are grouped into frequencies, the mode is the most frequently occurring value. It can be used with data at any level of measurement (even nominal).

nominal measure   This is a score or value from a scale which is not based on real numbers and in which the order is a matter of convention only. Examples would include binary variables such as male/female, and categorical variables such as industrial classifications.

normal curve   This is a bell-shaped symmetrical frequency distribution that underlies many social and psychological phenomena (such as population height or scores on an IQ test); 50 per cent of the area under the curve is above and below the mean respectively, 68 per cent is within one standard deviation of the mean.

one-tailed test   This is a calculation based on a prediction that two samples (or sub-groups within your achieved sample) will differ significantly in terms of their scores, making clear before collecting data which set of scores will be the larger. This is a stronger prediction, and therefore intrinsically more convincing if confirmed, than in a two-tailed test.

ordinal measure   This is a score or value from a scale in which an order is clear, but which is not based on real numbers. A common example would be a Likert-type scale.

outlier   This is a score in your results which is clearly outside the range of normal frequencies. It may be the result of an error in recording or transcription, or it may simply be a fluke result. A few such scores can have a disproportionate impact on your analysis (producing a mean score very different to the median, for example). Whatever you do about outliers, they must be handled with care and transparency.

parsimony   This is a principle used to decide between competing explanations. The most parsimonious would be the simplest explanation. Technically this means the one that makes the fewest assumptions for which we have no direct evidence. The practical advantage of parsimony is that simple explanations are easier to test, thus encouraging cumulative social scientific progress. Not using this principle would allow a researcher to produce an untestable explanation for their results (akin to a superstition).

Pearson's chi-square   This is a statistic calculated to test for differences in frequencies between categories. Named 'Pearson' after its developer, and chi-square for the Greek symbol 'χ'.

population   This is the group (usually of individuals) to whom you wish your research results to generalize (be relevant to). Any, and only, individuals with a chance of being selected for your sample form the population you are researching.

ratio measure   This is a score or value based on a real number, with equal intervals on the scale of measurement and a real value of zero. Technically this means that all points on the scale are in direct ratio to each other, so that 40 centimetres is exactly twice as much as 20. Note that for interval and other measures this is not so, since 40 degrees is not twice as hot as 20 degrees.

reliability This is an assessment of the extent to which a question, instrument or measure gives safe results (e.g. that it gives the same result on different occasions). See Cronbach's alpha.

standard deviation This is the square root of the variance. It is a summary of the average difference between each score in your set of results and the overall mean. It therefore provides a measure of how spread out (how variable) your results are.

standard error This is the standard deviation of the distribution of sample statistics. Using the mean as an example, the standard error of the mean is a summary of the average difference between any sample mean and the overall mean of all means taken from equivalent samples. It therefore provides a measure of how closely your achieved mean matches the best estimate of the population mean.

stem and leaf plot This is similar to a histogram. Scores are divided into intervals (between 30 and 39, for example), and the diagram has a row for each interval. The length of the row represents the number of cases with scores in that interval (how many scores in the 30s, etc.). Each row is labelled with the 'stem' (the common or leading digits) of all scores in that interval (3 for scores 30–39), and the actual entries in each row are the 'leaves' denoted by the remaining digits for each score. Thus the scores 31, 31, 31 and 32 would be represented as: 3 * 1112.

two-tailed test This is a calculation based on a prediction that two samples (or sub-groups within your achieved sample) will differ significantly in terms of their scores, but without a prediction of which set of scores will be larger. This is a weaker prediction, and therefore intrinsically less convincing if confirmed, than a one-tailed test.

weight This is a value used to correct for deficiency in the sample. If a particular sub-group is disproportionately represented in the achieved sample (too many males, for example), then the scores for this group can be multiplied by a weight to achieve a more balanced result (e.g. in which the scores for females are given due prominence).

Useful Addresses

Central Statistical Office,
Cardiff Road,
Newport
NP9 1XG

Economic and Social Research Council Data Archive,
University of Essex,
Colchester
CO4 3SQ

National On-Line Manpower System,
Unit 1L,
Mountjoy Research Centre,
Durham
DH1 3SW

SPSS UK Ltd,
1st Floor St Andrews House,
West Street,
Woking,
Surrey
GU21 1EB

WEBSITES

dfee@prologistics.co.uk
http://tramss.data-archive.ac.uk/
http://www.dfee.gov.uk/index.htm
http://www.mimas.ac.uk/
http://www.teach-tta.gov.uk/itt/funding/alloc.htm
www.dfee.gov.uk/datasphere

References

Achen, C. (1982) *Interpreting and Using Regression*, London: Sage.

Adair, J. (1973) *The Human Subject*, Boston: Little, Brown and Co.

Allison, P. (1984) *Event History Analysis: Regression for Longitudinal Event Data*, London: Sage.

Anderson, T. and Zelditch, M. (1968) *A Basic Course in Statistics, with Sociological Applications*, London: Holt, Rinehart and Winston.

Babbie, E. and Halley, F. (1995) *Adventures in Social Research: Data Analysis using SPSS for Windows*, Thousand Oaks, CA: Pine Forge Press.

Banks, M., Bates, I., Breakwell, G., Bynner, J. and Emler, N. (1992) *Careers and Identities*, Milton Keynes: Open University Press.

Basic Skills Agency (1997) *Literacy and Numeracy Skills in Wales*, London: The Basic Skills Agency.

Beinart, S. and Smith, P. (1998) *National Adult Learning Survey 1997*, Sudbury: DfEE Publications.

Bernard, H. R. (2000) *Social Research Methods: Qualitative and Quantitative Approaches*, London: Sage.

Berry, W. and Feldman, S. (1985) *Multiple Regression in Practice*, London: Sage.

Blalock, H. (1964) *Causal Inferences in Nonexperimental Research*, Chapel Hill, NC: University of North Carolina Press.

Bridges, D. (1999) 'Educational research: pursuit of truth or flight into fancy?', *British Educational Research Journal*, 25, 5, 597–616.

Brown, A. and Dowling, P. (1998) *Doing Research/Reading Research: A Mode of Interrogation for Education*, London: Falmer.

Bryman, A. and Cramer, D. (1990) *Quantitative Data Analysis with SPSS for Windows*, London: Routledge.

Bulmer, M. (1980) 'Why don't sociologists make more use of official statistics?', *Sociology*, 14, 4, 505–23.

Campbell, D. and Stanley, J. (1963) *Experimental and Quasi-experimental Designs for Research*, Boston: Houghton Mifflin.

Carter, H. (2000) 'NHS helpline offers bad advice, survey claims', *The Guardian*, 8 August, p. 2.

CERI (1997) *Education Policy Analysis 1997*, Paris: OECD.

CERI (1998) *Education at a Glance: OECD Indicators*, Paris: OECD.

Cheung, C. and Lewis, D. (1998) 'Expectations of employers of High School leavers in Hong Kong', *Journal of Vocational Education and Training*, 50, 1, 97–111.

Child, D. (1970) *The Essentials of Factor Analysis*, London: Holt, Rinehart and Winston.

Clegg, F. (1990) *Simple Statistics: A Course Book for the Social Sciences*, Cambridge: Cambridge University Press.

Cohen, L. and Manion, L. (2000) *Research Methods in Education*, London: Routledge.

Coldron, J. and Boulton, P. (1991) ' "Happiness" as a criterion of parents' choice of school', *Journal of Education Policy*, 6, 2, 169–78.

Comrey, A. (1973) *A First Course on Factor Analysis*, London: Academic Press.

Cook, T. and Campbell, D. (1979) *Quasi-experimentation: Design and Analysis Issues for Field Settings*, Chicago: Rand McNally.

Cooper, H. (1998) *Synthesizing Research: A Guide for Literature Reviews*, London: Sage.

Crouchley, R. (1987) *Longitudinal Data Analysis. Surrey Conferences on Sociological Theory and Method 4*, Aldershot: Avebury.

Cureton, E. and D'Agostino, R. (1983) *Factor Analysis: An Applied Approach*, London: Lawrence Erlbaum.

Czaja, R. and Blair, J. (1996) *Designing Surveys: A Guide to Decisions and Procedures*, Thousand Oaks, CA: Pine Forge Press.

Dale, A., Arber, S. and Proctor, M. (1988) *Doing Secondary Analysis*, London: Unwin.

David, M., West, A. and Ribbens, J. (1994) *Mother's Intuition? Choosing Secondary Schools*, East Sussex: Falmer Press.

Davies, R. (1994) 'From cross-sectional to longitudinal analysis', in Dale, A. and Davies, R. (eds) *Analyzing Social and Political Change: A Casebook of Methods*, London: Sage.

De Leon, G., Inciardi, J. and Martin, S. (1995) 'Residential drug abuse treatment research: are conventional control designs appropriate for assessing treatment effectiveness?', *Journal of Psychoactive Drugs*, 27, 85–91.

Deloitte Haskins and Sells (1989) *Training in Britain: A Study of Funding, Activity and Attitudes. Employers' Attitudes*, London: HMSO.

Dennison, W. (1995) 'Researching the competitive edge: detractors and attractors in school marketing', paper presented at ESRC/CEPAM Invitation Seminar, Milton Keynes, July.

DfEE (1994a) *Statistics of Education: Public Examinations GCSE and GCE in England 1994*, London: HMSO.

DfEE (1994b) *Statistics of Education: Schools in England 1994*, London: HMSO.

Dolton, P., Makepeace, G. and Treble, J. (1994) 'Measuring the effects of training in the Youth Cohort Study', in McNabb, R. and Whitfield, K. (eds) *The Market for Training*, Aldershot: Avebury, p. 195.

Education and Training Statistics (1997) *Welsh Training and Education Survey 1995/96*, Cardiff: Welsh Office.

Edwards, A. (1972) *Experimental Design in Psychological Research*, New York: Holt, Rinehart and Winston.

ETAG (1999) *An Education and Training Action Plan for Wales*, Cardiff: National Assembly for Wales.

Eurostat (1995) *Education across the European Union: Statistics and Indicators*, Brussels: Statistical Office of the European Communities.

Eurostat (1998) *Social Portrait of Europe, September 1998*, Brussels: Statistical Office of the European Communities.

Everitt, B. (1980) *Cluster Analysis*, London: Heinemann.

Everitt, B. and Hay, D. (1992) *Talking about Statistics: A Psychologist's Guide to Design and Analysis*, London: Edward Arnold.

Fairbairn, G. and Winch, C. (1996) *Reading, Writing and Reasoning: A Guide for Students*, Buckingham: Open University Press.

Farrall, S., Bannister, J., Ditton, J. and Gilchrist, E. (1997) 'Open and closed questions', *Social Research Update*, 17, 1–4.

FEU (1993) *Paying their Way: The Experiences of Adult Learners in Vocational Education and Training in FE Colleges*, London: Further Education Unit.

Fielding, J. and Gilbert, N. (2000) *Understanding Social Statistics*, London: Sage.

Firestone, W. (1987) 'Meaning in method: the rhetoric of quantitative and qualitative research', *Educational Researcher*, 16, 7, 16.

FitzGibbon, C. (1996) *Monitoring Education: Indicators, Quality and Effectiveness*, London: Cassell.

Foster, P. (1999) ' "Never mind the quality, feel the impact": a methodological assessment of teacher research sponsored by the Teacher Training Agency', *British Journal of Educational Studies*, 47, 4, 380–98.

Frankfort-Nachmias, C. and Nachmias, D. (1996) *Research Methods in the Social Sciences*, London: Arnold.

Frazer, E. (1995) 'What's new in the philosophy of science?', *Oxford Review of Education*, 21, 3, 267–79.

Furlong, J. (1996) 'Do teachers need higher education?', in Furlong, J. and Smith, R. (eds) *The Role of Higher Education in Initial Teacher Education*, London: Kogan Page.

Future Skills Wales (1998) *Technical Report*, London: MORI.

Gambetta, D. (1987) *Were They Pushed or Did They Jump? Individual Decision Mechanisms in Education*, London: Cambridge University Press.

Gephart, R. (1988) *Ethnostatistics: Qualitative Foundations for Quantitative Research*, London: Sage.

Gershuny, J. and Marsh, C. (1994) 'Unemployment in work histories', in Gallie, D., Marsh, C. and Vogler, C. (eds) *Social Change and the Experience of Unemployment*, Oxford: Oxford University Press.

Ghouri, N. (1999) 'Football approach risks an own goal', *Times Educational Supplement*, 4 June, p. 9.

Giacquinta, J. and Shaw, F. (2000) 'Judging non-returner induced sample bias from the study of early and late returners: a useful approach?', presentation at AERA Conference, New Orleans, April 2000.

Gilbert, N. (1993) *Analysing Tabular Data: Loglinear and Logistic Models for Social Researchers*, London: UCL Press.

Gilbert, N. (1997) *Researching Social Life*, London: Sage.

Gilbert, N. and Troitzsch, K. (1999) *Simulation for the Social Scientist*, Buckingham: Open University Press.

Gillborn, D. and Youdell, D. (2000) *Rationing Education: Policy, Practice, Reform and Equality*, Buckingham: Open University Press.

Gillham, B. (2000a) *The Research Interview*, London: Continuum.

Gillham, B. (2000b) *Developing a Questionnaire*, London: Continuum.

Glass, G., McGraw, B. and Smith, M. (1981) *Meta-analysis in Social Research*, London: Sage.

Gleeson, D., Glover, D., Gough, G., Johnson, M. and Pye, D. (1996) 'Reflections on youth training: towards a new model of training experience?', *British Educational Research Journal*, 22, 5, 597–613.

Glenn, N. (1977) *Cohort Analysis*, London: Sage.

Goldstein, H., Huiqi, P., Rath, T. and Hill, N. (2000) *The Use of Value-added Information in Judging School Performance*, London: Institute of Education.

Gorard, S. (1996) 'Three steps to "heaven": the family and school choice', *Educational Review*, 48, 3, 237–52.

Gorard, S. (1997a) 'A choice of methods: the methodology of choice', *Research in Education*, 57, 45–56.

Gorard, S. (1997b) *School Choice in an Established Market*, Aldershot: Ashgate.

Gorard, S. (1997c) *The Region of Study: Patterns of Participation in Adult Education and Training*, Working paper 1, Cardiff: School of Education.

Gorard, S. (1998a) *The Middle Way*, BERA Internet Conference, www.scre.ac.uk/bera/debate/index.html (accessed 28 December 2000).

Gorard, S. (1998b) 'Four errors ... and a conspiracy? The effectiveness of schools in Wales', *Oxford Review of Education*, 24, 4, 459–72.

Gorard, S. (1998c) 'Schooled to fail? Revisiting the Welsh school-effect', *Journal of Education Policy*, 13, 1, 115–24.

Gorard, S. (1998d) 'In defence of local comprehensive schools in South Wales', *Forum*, 40, 2, 58–9.

Gorard, S. (1999a) 'Keeping a sense of proportion: the "politician's error" in analysing school outcomes', *British Journal of Educational Studies*, 47, 3, 235–46.

Gorard, S. (1999b) 'Examining the paradox of achievement gaps', *Social Research Update*, 26, 1–4.

Gorard, S. (1999c) 'Well. That about wraps it up for school choice research: a state of the art review', *School Leadership and Management*, 19, 1, 25–47.

Gorard, S. (2000a) 'One of us cannot be wrong: the paradox of achievement gaps', *British Journal of Sociology of Education*, 21, 3, 391–400.

Gorard, S. (2000b) 'Questioning the crisis account: a review of evidence for increasing polarisation in schools', *Educational Research*, 42, 3, 309–21.

Gorard, S. (2000c) *Education and Social Justice*, Cardiff: University of Wales Press.

Gorard, S. (2000d) 'A reexamination of the effectiveness of school in Wales', in Daugherty, R., Phillips, R. and Rees, G. (eds) *Education Policy in Wales: Explorations in Devolved Governance*, Cardiff: University of Wales Press.

Gorard, S. (2000e) '"Underachievement" is still an ugly word: reconsidering the relative effectiveness of schools in England and Wales', *Journal of Education Policy*, 15, 5, 559–73.

Gorard, S., Fevre, R. and Rees, G. (1999a) 'The apparent decline of informal learning', *Oxford Review of Education*, 25, 4, 437–54.

Gorard, S. and Fitz, J. (1998a) 'Under starter's orders: the established market, the Cardiff study and the Smithfield project', *International Studies in Sociology of Education*, 8, 3, 299–314.

Gorard, S. and Fitz, J. (1998b) 'The more things change ... the missing impact of marketisation', *British Journal of Sociology of Education*, 19, 3, 365–76.

Gorard, S. and Fitz, J. (2000) 'Investigating the determinants of segregation between schools', *Research Papers in Education*, 15, 2, 115–32.

Gorard, S., Rees, G. and Fevre, R. (1999b) 'Two dimensions of time: the changing social context of lifelong learning', *Studies in the Education of Adults*, 31, 1, 35–48.

Gorard, S., Rees, G. and Fevre, R. (1999c) 'Patterns of participation in lifelong learning: do families make a difference?', *British Educational Research Journal*, 25, 4, 517–32.

Gorard, S., Rees, G., Fevre, R., and Furlong, J. (1998a) 'Learning trajectories: travelling towards a learning society?', *International Journal of Lifelong Education*, 17, 6, 400–10.

Gorard, S., Rees, G., Fevre, R. and Furlong, J. (1998b) 'The two components of a new Learning Society', *Journal of Vocational Education and Training*, 50, 1, 5–19.

Gorard, S., Rees, G., Furlong, J. and Fevre, R. (1997) *Outline Methodology of the Study: Patterns of Participation in Adult Education and Training*. Working paper 2, Cardiff: School of Education.

Gorard, S., Rees, G. and Jephcote, M. (1998c) 'The role of contour lines in school improvement', *Research Intelligence*, 66, 30–1.

Gorard, S., Rees, G. and Salisbury, J. (2000a) 'The differential attainment of boys and girls at school: investigating the patterns and their determinants', *British Educational Research Journal*, 26, 5.

Gorard, S., Rees, G. and Selwyn, N. (1999d) *Lifetime Learning Targets in Wales: A Research Summary*, Cardiff: National Assembly for Wales.

Gorard, S., Rees, G. and Selwyn, N. (2000b) 'Meeting targets?', *Adults Learning*, April, 18–20.

Gorard, S., Salisbury, J. and Rees, G. (1999e) 'Reappraising the apparent underachievement of boys at school', *Gender and Education*, 11, 4, 441–54.

Gorard, S., Salisbury, J., Rees, G. and Fitz, J. (1999f) *The Comparative Performance of Boys and Girls at School in Wales*, Cardiff: Qualifications, Curriculum and Assessment Authority for Wales.

Gorard, S. and Selwyn, N. (1999) 'Switching on the Learning Society? Questioning the role of technology in widening participation in lifelong learning', *Journal of Education Policy*, 14, 5, 523–34.

Gorard, S., Selwyn, N. and Williams, S. (2000c) 'Could try harder!: Problems facing technological solutions to non-participation in adult learning', *British Educational Research Journal*, 26, 4.

Gorard, S. and Taylor, C. (2000) *A Comparison of Segregation Indices Used for Assessing the Socio-economic Composition of Schools. Measuring Markets: The Case of the ERA 1988*, Working Paper 37, Cardiff: Cardiff University School of Social Sciences.

Gorard, S. and Taylor, C. (2001) *Market Forces and Standards in Education: A Preliminary Consideration. Measuring Markets: The Case of the ERA 1988*, Working Paper 38, Cardiff: Cardiff University School of Social Sciences.

Greenhalgh, C. and Stewart, M. (1987) 'The effects and determinants of training', *Oxford Bulletin of Economics and Statistics*, 49, 2, 171–90.

Hagenaars, J. (1990) *Categorical Longitudinal Data: Log-linear, Panel, Trend and Cohort Analysis*, London: Sage.

Hakim, C. (1982) *Secondary Analysis in Social Research: A Guide to Data Sources and Methods with Examples*, London: Allen and Unwin.

Hakim, C. (1992) *Research Design: Strategies and Choices in the Design of Social Research*, London: Routledge.

Hakuta, K. (2000) 'Perspectives on the state of education research in the US', presentation at AERA Conference, New Orleans, April.

Hammersley, M. (1995) *The Politics of Social Research*, London: Sage.

Hand, A., Gambles, J. and Cooper, E. (1994) *Individual Commitment to Learning. Individuals' Decision-making about Lifetime Learning*, London: Employment Department.

Hargreaves, D. (1997) 'In defence of research for evidence-based teaching: a rejoinder to Martyn Hammersley', *British Educational Research Journal*, 23, 4, 405–19.

Harlow, L., Mulaik, S. and Steiger, J. (1997) *What if There Were No Significance Tests?*, Mawah, NJ: Lawrence Erlbaum.

Henry, G. (1990) *Practical Sampling*, London: Sage.

Hillage, J., Pearson, R., Anderson, A. and Tamkin, P. (1998) *Excellence on Research in Schools*, Sudbury: DfEE.

Hinton, P. (1995) *Statistics Explained: A Guide for Social Science Students*, London: Routledge.

Howell, D. (1989) *Fundamental Statistics for the Behavioural Sciences*, Boston: PWS-Kent.

Huff, D. (1991) *How to Lie with Statistics*, Harmondsworth: Penguin.

Kalton, G. (1966) *Introduction to Statistical Ideas for Social Scientists*, London: Chapman and Hall.

Kanji, G. (1999) *100 Statistical Tests*, London: Sage.

Kim, J. and Mueller, C. (1978a) *Introduction to Factor Analysis: What It Is and How To Do It*, London: Sage.

Kim, J. and Mueller, C. (1978b) *Factor Analysis: Statistical Methods and Practical Issues*, London: Sage.

Kline, P. (1994) *An Easy Guide to Factor Analysis*, London: Routledge.

Kruskal, J. and Wish, M. (1978) *Multidimensional Scaling*, London: Sage.

Lauder, H., Hughes, D., Watson, S., Waslander, S., Thrupp, M., Strathdee, R., Simiyu, I., Dupuis, A., McGlinn, J. and Hamlin, J. (1999) *Trading in Futures: Why Markets in Education Don't Work*, Buckingham: Open University Press.

Lee, E., Forthofer, R. and Lorimor, R. (1989) *Analyzing Complex Survey Data*, London: Sage.

Lehtonen, R. and Pahkinen, E. (1995) *Practical Methods for Design and Analysis of Complex Surveys*, Chichester: John Wiley and Sons.

Lynn, J. and Jay, A. (1986) *Yes, Prime Minister*, London: BBC Publications.

Maddala, G. (1992) *Introduction to Econometrics*, New York: Macmillan.

Mahoney, J. (2000) 'Strategies of causal inference in small-N analysis', *Sociological Methods and Research*, 28, 4, 387–424.

Main, B. and Shelly, M. (1990) 'The effectiveness of the Youth Training Scheme as a manpower policy', *Economica*, 57, 495–514.

Mare, R. and Winship, C. (1985) 'School enrollment, military enlistment, and the transition to work: implications for the age pattern of employment', in Heckman, J. and Singer, B. (eds) *Longitudinal Analysis of Labor Market Data*, London: Cambridge University Press.

Marradi, A. (1981) 'Factor analysis as an aid in the formation and refinement of empirically useful concepts', in Jackson, D. and Borgatta, E. (eds) *Factor Analysis and Measurement*, London: Sage.

Martin, J. and Roberts, C. (1984) *The Women and Employment Survey: A Lifetime Perspective*, London: HMSO.

Massey, D. and Denton, N. (1988) 'The dimensions of residential segregation', *Social Forces*, 67, 373–93.

Matthews, R. (2000) 'How to spot an Olympic cheat with a calculator', *Sunday Telegraph*, 24 September, p. 13.

Maxwell, A. (1958) *Experimental Design in Psychology and the Medical Sciences*, London: Methuen.

Maxwell, A. (1977) *Multivariate Analysis in Behavioural Research*, New York: Chapman and Hall.

May, T. (1997) *Social Research: Issues, Methods and Process*, Buckingham: Open University Press.

McIlveen, R., Higgins, L., Wadeley, A. and Humphreys, P. (1992) *BPS Manual of Psychology Practicals: Experiment, Observation and Correlation*, Leicester: British Psychological Society.

McNabb, R. and Whitfield, K. (1994) *The Market for Training*, Aldershot: Avebury.

Menard, S. (1995) *Applied Logistic Regression Analysis*, London: Sage.

Millett, A. (1997) 'Speech to TTA Research Conference', 5 December. 1997, London, TTA.

Mitchell, P. (1994) 'The impact of educational technology: a radical reappraisal of research methods', *Alt-J*, 5, 1, 48–54.

Mortimore, P. (2000) 'Does educational research matter?', *British Educational Research Journal*, 26, 1, 5–24.

NACETT (1995) *Report on Progress Towards the National Targets*, London: National Advisory Council for Education and Training.

National Educational Research Policy and Priorities Board (1999) *Investing in Learning: A Policy Statement with Recommendations on Research in Education*, Washington, DC: NERPP.

National Educational Research Policy and Priorities Board (2000) *Second Policy Statement with Recommendations on Research in Education*, Washington, DC: NERPP.

National Research Council (1999) *Improving Student Learning: A Strategic Plan for Educational Research and its Utilization*, Washington, DC: National Academy Press.

Noden, P. (2000) 'Rediscovering the impact of marketisation: dimensions of social segregation in England's secondary schools', *British Journal of Sociology of Education*, 21, 3, 371–90.

Norusis, M. (1994) *SPSS for Windows: Base System User's Guide*, Chicago: SPSS Inc.

Nuttall, D. (1987) 'The validity of assessments', *European Journal of Psychology of Education*, 11, 2, 109–18.

OECD (1993) *OECD Education Statistics 1985–1992*, Paris: OECD.

OECD (2000) *Education at a Glance: OECD Indicators: Education and Skills*, Paris: OECD.

Oppenheim, A. (1992) *Questionnaire Design, Interviewing and Attitude Measurement*, London: Continuum.

Park, A. (1994) *Individual Commitment to Lifelong Learning: Individuals' Attitudes. Report on the Quantitative Survey*, London: Employment Department.

Park, A. and Tremlett, N. (1995) *Individual Commitment to Learning: Comparative Findings from the Surveys of Individuals', Employers' and Providers' Attitudes*, London: Employment Department.

Payne, S. (1951) *The Art of Asking Questions*, Princeton. NJ: Princeton University Press.

Pedhazur, E. (1982) *Multiple Regression in Behavioural Research*, London: Holt, Rinehart and Winston.

Peers, I. (1996) *Statistical Analysis for Education and Psychology Researchers*, London: Falmer Press.

Peters, S. (1998) 'Finding information on the World Wide Web', *Social Research Update*, 20.

Pettigrew, A., Hendry, C. and Sparrow, P. (1989) *Training in Britain. A Study of Funding, Activity and Attitudes. Employers' Perspectives on Human Resources*, London: HMSO.

Pifer, L. and Miller, J. (1995) 'The accuracy of student and parent reports about each other', presentation at AERA Conference, San Francisco.

Pike, C. and Forrester, M. (1997) 'The influence of number-sense on children's ability to estimate measures', *Educational Psychology*, 17, 4, 483–99.

Plewis, I. (1990) 'Longitudinal multilevel models', in Dale, A. and Davies, R. (eds) *Analyzing Social and Political Change: A Casebook of Methods*, London: Sage.

Plewis, I. (1997) *Statistics in Education*, London: Arnold.

Popkewitz, T. (1984) *Paradigm and Ideology in Educational Research*, London: Falmer.

Preece, R. (1994) *Starting Research: An Introduction to Academic Research and Dissertation Writing*, London: Continuum.

Pring, R. (2000) *Philosophy of Educational Research*, London: Continuum.

Reay, D. and Lucey, H. (2000) 'Children, school choice and social differences', *Educational Studies*, 26, 1, 83–100.

Resnick, L. (2000) 'Strengthening the capacity of the research system: a report of the National Academy of Education', presentation at AERA Conference, New Orleans, April.

Reynolds, D. (1990) 'The great Welsh education debate', *History of Education*, 19, 3, 251–7.

Reynolds, H. (1977) *Analysis of Nominal Data*, London: Sage.

Rose, D. (1996) 'Official social classifications in the UK', *Social Research Update*, 9, 1–6.

Rose, D. and Sullivan, O. (1993) *Introducing Data Analysis for Social Scientists*, Buckingham: Open University Press.

Rosenthal, R. (1991) *Meta-analytic Procedures for Social Science Research*, London: Sage.

SCELI (1991) *Social Change and Economic Life Initiative Surveys 1986–1987*, Colchester: ESRC Data Archive.

Scott, D. and Usher, R. (1999) *Researching Education: Data, Methods and Theory in Educational Enquiry*, London: Cassell.

Selwyn, N. and Gorard, S. (1999) 'Can technology really widen participation in lifelong learning?', *Adults Learning*, 10, 6, 27–9.

Selwyn, N. and Robson, K. (1998) 'Using e-mail as a research tool', *Social Research Update*, 21, 1–4.

Shaughnessy, J. and Zechmeister, E. (1994) *Research Methods in Psychology*, New York: McGraw-Hill.

Siegel, S. (1956) *Nonparametric Statistics*, Tokyo: McGraw-Hill.

Simpson, E. (1951) 'The interpretation of interaction in contingency tables', *Journal of the Royal Statistical Society*, Series B, 13, 238–51.

Solomon, R. and Winch, C. (1994) *Calculating and Computing for Social Science and Arts Students*, Buckingham: Open University Press.

Stevens, J. (1992) *Applied Multivariate Statistics for the Social Sciences*, London: Lawrence Erlbaum.

Sudman, S. and Bradburn, N. (1982) *Asking Questions*, San Francisco: Jossey-Bass.

Swadener, M. and Hannafin, M. (1987) 'Gender similarities and differences in sixth graders' attitudes toward computers', *Educational Technology*, January, 37–42.

Taylor, S. and Spencer, L. (1994) *Individual Commitment to Lifelong Learning: Individuals' Attitudes. Report on the Qualitative Phase*, London: Employment Department.

TES (1998) 'Man's class helps boys', *Times Educational Supplement*, 6 February, p. 21.

Thouless, R. (1974) *Straight and Crooked Thinking*, London: Pan.

Tooley, J. and Darby, D. (1998) *Educational Research: A Critique*, London: OFSTED.

TTA (2000) *The Teacher Research Grant Scheme: Summaries from the Second Year of the Scheme*, London: Teacher Training Agency.

Wales in Figures (1999) Cardiff: National Assembly for Wales.

Walford, G. (1991) *Doing Educational Research*, London: Routledge.

Walford, G. (2001) *Doing Qualitative Educational Research*, London: Continuum.

Waslander, S. and Thrupp, M. (1997) 'Choice, competition, and segregation: an empirical analysis of a New Zealand secondary school market, 1990–93', in Halsey, A., Lauder, H., Brown, P. and Wells, A. (eds) *Education, Culture, Economy, and Society*, Oxford: Oxford University Press.

Welsh Office (1994) *1992 Welsh Social Survey: Report on Education and Training*, Cardiff: Welsh Office.

Welsh Office (1995a) *Statistics of Education and Training in Wales: Schools No. 3*, Cardiff: HMSO.

Welsh Office (1995b) *1994/95 Welsh Training and Education Survey*, Cardiff: Welsh Office.

Welsh Office (1996) *1996 Welsh Employers Survey*, Cardiff: Welsh Office.

Welsh Office (1999) *Progress Towards Meeting the Targets in the 'BEST' White Paper*, Cardiff: Welsh Office Statistical Brief SDB 76/99.

West, A., David, M., Hailes, J. and Ribbens, J. (1995) 'Parents and the process of choosing secondary schools: implications for schools', *Educational Management and Administration*, 23, 1, 28–38.

Western Mail (1998) 'Boys need more male teachers', *The Western Mail*, 5 February, p. 1.

White, P. and Gorard, S. (1999) 'Ethnicity, attainment and progress: a cautionary note regarding percentages and percentage points', *Research in Education*, 62, 66–9.

Whitfield, K. and Bourlakis, C. (1991) 'An empirical analysis of YTS, employment and earnings', *Journal of Economic Studies*, 18, 1, 42–56.

Woodhead, C. (1998) 'Academia gone to seed', *New Statesman*, 26 March, 51–2.

Woolford, H. and McDougall, S. (1998) 'The teacher as role model', presentation to British Psychological Society (mimeo, Department of Psychology, Swansea).

Index